UNDERSTANDING NEURAL NETWORKS
AND FUZZY LOGIC

T0205698

IEEE PRESS Understanding Science & Technology Series

The IEEE PRESS Understanding Series treats important topics in science and technology in a simple and easy-to-understand manner. Designed expressly for the nonspecialist engineer, scientist, or technician, as well as the technologically curious, each volume stresses practical information over mathematical theorems and complicated derivations.

Books in the Series

Deutsch, S., *Understanding the Nervous System: An Engineering Perspective*

Evans, B., *Understanding Digital TV: The Route to HDTV*

Hecht, J., *Understanding Lasers: An Entry-Level Guide*, Second Edition

Kamm, L., *Understanding Electro-Mechanical Engineering: An Introduction to Mechatronics*

Kartalopoulos, S. V., *Understanding Neural Networks and Fuzzy Logic: Basic Concepts and Applications*

Nellist, J. G., *Understanding Telecommunications and Lightwave Systems: An Entry-Level Guide*, Second Edition

Sigfried, S., *Understanding Object-Oriented Software Engineering*

Ideas for future topics and authorship inquiries are welcome. Please write to the IEEE PRESS Understanding Series.

UNDERSTANDING NEURAL NETWORKS AND FUZZY LOGIC

Basic Concepts and Applications

Stamatios V. Kartalopoulos, Ph.D.
AT&T Bell Laboratories

IEEE Neural Networks Council, *Sponsor*

The Institute of Electrical and Electronics Engineers, Inc., New York

IEEE Press
445 Hoes Lane, P.O. Box 1331
Piscataway, NJ 08855-1331

John B. Anderson, *Editor in Chief*
Dudley R. Kay, *Director of Book Publishing*
Carrie Briggs, *Administrative Assistant*
Lisa S. Mizrahi, *Review and Publicity Coordinator*

IEEE Neural Networks Council, *Sponsor*
Richard Saeks, NNC Liaison to IEEE PRESS

Technical Reviewers
Dr. Mo-Yuen Chow, *North Carolina State University*
Dr. Murray Eden, *National Institutes of Health*
Dr. Roger Hoyt, *IBM Almaden Research Center*
Dr. Phillip Laplante, *Burlington County College*

This book may be purchased at a discount from the publisher when
ordered in bulk quantities. For more information contact:

IEEE PRESS Marketing
Attn: Special Sales
P.O. Box 1331/445 Hoes Lane
Piscataway, NJ 08855-1331
Fax: (732) 981-9334

Copyright © 1996 AT&T.

10 9 8 7 6 5 4 3

ISBN 0-7803-1128-0
IEEE Order Number: PP5591

Library of Congress Cataloging-in-Publication Data

Kartalopoulos, Stamatios V.
  Understanding neural networks and fuzzy logic : basic concepts and
applications / Stamatios V. Kartalopoulos ; IEEE Neural Networks Council, sponsor.
      p.   cm.—(IEEE Press understanding science & technology series)
  Includes bibliographical references and index.
  ISBN 0-7803-1128-0 (alk. paper)
  1. Neural networks (Computer science)   2. Fuzzy systems.   I. IEEE
Neural Networks Council.   II. Title.   III. Series.
QA76.87.K38 1996
006.3—dc20   95-378
                                                                           CIP

To Anita, Bill, and Stephanie

CONTENTS

PREFACE

The workings of the brain have fascinated me since childhood. I had observed with interest that whenever a question was asked in the classroom many different answers were given. Every classmate was thinking and perceiving the same question from an entirely different viewpoint and thus an answer was given according to their own particular perspective. This diversity in perspective is so profound. It adds even more dimension to world around us. We (humans) have a depth of visualization so powerful that we can close our eyes and . . . imagine. Imagination is timeless, boundless, unlimited and it happens right there in a few cubic centimeters of soft matter, the brain. Close your eyes and you can "see" faces you have not seen for years or "smell" summer fragrances in the middle of the winter; or "travel" through space, crossing distant galaxies with an incomprehensible speed that defies all laws of physics. Close your eyes and you can create ideas that never before existed. Someone "saw" a wheel for the first time and made a cart; another heard the first music before music was sung. Someone for the first time "saw" the benefit of the volcanic fire and used it to warm houses, to cook, to extract metals from rocks, and to make tools and weapons. And this inventiveness continues to this day. We "saw" the invisible forces of matter, controlled them, and produced electricity, we made radios and computers and we escaped into space. So, is it surprising that for many years this mind-boggling power of the brain has been the subject of research?

I have been compiling information about the biology of the brain and sifting through articles and studies on neural research for quite a few years now. As a physicist and an engineer, I wanted to understand the mechanics and innerworkings of the brain. As soon as I had an organized set of notes that I thought had pedagogical value, I decided to give a tutorial in neural networks at the Globecom '91 communications conference. To the best of my knowledge, such a tutorial had not been presented previously at any communications conference and I thought this would be a good chance to find out how much interest there is in this area. We expected a relatively small audience. To our surprise, we had an overwhelming attendance—a full house. The feedback I received at the end of the tutorial was very enthusiastic. I therefore enhanced my tutorial notes, simplified certain math-intensive sections, and included fuzzy logic and fuzzy neural networks. I also organized conference sessions on neural networks and fuzzy logic. Although participation was small at first, it has steadily increased. The interest from the communications community alone has so increased that, in 1993, a conference was organized on neural networks in communications. I presented my tutorial a few more times and, every time, the audience suggested that I should publish my notes as a book.

The intention of this book is to provide an introduction to the subject of neural networks, fuzzy logic, and fuzzy neural networks; to provide, in a coherent and methodical manner, the concepts of neural networks and fuzzy logic with easy to understand examples that describe a number of applications in a nonmathematical way; to address a need of the scientific community that other books in neural networks and in fuzzy logic do not address; and to provide a linkage between neural networks and fuzzy logic. The majority of books I have seen on this subject require a level of expertise to understand the material. Some, however, are invaluable tools for the connoiseur. The material and depth of this book was prepared for those who want an introduction to neural networks and fuzzy logic but need more than a tutorial. For a more advanced textbook, IEEE PRESS, as well as other publishers, has a number of them available by catalog. I wish you happy and easy reading.

ACKNOWLEDGMENTS

Throughout history, few achievements of note have been the production of individual effort but, instead, have been accomplished through the efforts of many. Unfortunately, the many have been rarely recognized. Consider these contributions: of the anonymous scribes to the walls of the pyramids; of the stone cutters, polishers, and scribes to the creation of the Rosetta stone; and of the writers, illuminators, parchment makers and book binders to the manufacture of illuminated manuscripts. Durer's woodcuts are famous but surely they are the product of many laborers and not the achievement of just one, albeit gifted, individual. Therefore, to avoid repeating this regrettable habit of history, I wish to express my gratitude to all those that helped make this book a reality.

I would first like to acknowledge Dudley Kay, Director of Book Publishing at IEEE PRESS, who provided the stimulus and encouragement for transforming a tutorial manuscript into a volume in the IEEE PRESS Understanding Science & Technology Series. I would also like to thank the IEEE PRESS staff for their many contributions; in particular, Lisa Mizrahi for her enthusiasm and ability in obtaining constructive book reviews and Debbie Graffox for handling the production of this book. Deserved thanks also go to the reviewers who provided the valuable criticism that improved the scope and readability of the book, both those listed on the copyright page and those who prefer anonymity, and to the professionals at Beehive Production Services, Roaring Mountain Editorial Services, the Asterisk Group, Inc., and Techsetters, Inc., for their valued assistance.

I also thank my anonymous colleagues at AT&T who reviewed and approved the text, enabling me to publish my manuscript with IEEE PRESS. Finally, I would like to thank my family for the infinite patience and understanding they've demonstrated in allowing me to allocate family time to the writing of this book.

INTRODUCTION

A NEW BREED OF PROCESSOR: THE BRAIN

A new kind of arithmetic, called **Boolean logic**, was developed in the 19th century. The product of propositional logic, Boolean logic was based on binary rather than decimal arithmetic. Most people thought it useless, so it remained in obscurity for decades. However, Boolean logic was rediscovered and, along with integrated circuitry, brought to light the microprocessor and the modern computer.

The modern computer, based on binary arithmetic in conjunction with sophisticated programming, has changed the way we do business and exchange information. In many ways, it has changed our lifestyles and thinking. It is a primary tool in science especially in the development of intelligent machines, applications such as information processing (data, video, speech, etc.), intelligent communications networks, and control applications, from sophisticated research instruments to dishwashers. Despite the outstanding performance of today's computer, there is an increasing demand for higher speed, larger storage capacity, greater machine intelligence, and "ingenuity." Computer power keeps increasing while its size, as well as cost, keeps decreasing. In the computer industry, the pressure is on to have a "next generation" approximately every six to twelve months, with still lower cost and greater performance.

Advance in microelectronics continually shrink the size of the transistor, so that increasingly more circuitry (measured by many millions of transistors) is integrated into less silicon space. At the beginning of the 1970s the number of transistors integrated was around a few thousand, whereas in the beginning of the 1990s it was several million. In 1980, the largest random access memory circuit was 64,000 bits; by the end of the decade it was 1 million bits and before the end of this decade it is expected to be 64 million bits. Moreover, transistor power consumption keeps decreasing, making it possible to use smaller, longer-lasting batteries (necessary for portable computers and communicators), thereby increasing the switching speed of the transistor and its performance. Presently, microprocessors with speeds above 100 MHz are supplied by several vendors and, at this rate of evolution, it won't be long before we have speeds of several hundred megahertz.

It is estimated that today's top-performance processor, with 100–150 million instructions per second (MIPS), will be the lower performer in just a few years. One of the metrics for evaluating the performance of a processor is the SPECint92 (for System Performance Evaluation Corporation integer calculations). Based on this metric, today's top performers have in excess of 100 SPECint92; before the end of the century they are expected to have more than 1000 SPECint92 (see Figure 1). As soon as greater speed is achieved, new applications emerge that demand even more.

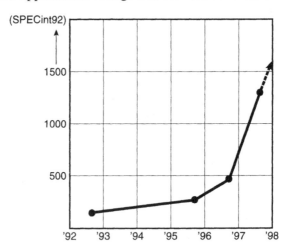

Figure 1 Expected processor performance increase.

With this gargantuan appetite for more computing power at lower cost, can current computer architecture satisfy us? Can present technology evolve at this rate ad infinitum? When will its limitations be reached?

Current technology is at an exponential rate of performance/cost increase, which in nature means, first, a rapid increase in exponential form and then, before an uncontrollable state is reached, saturation, i.e., no further increase. Thus, being in the exponential phase, advances in technology should start slowing down at the start of the next millenium and should soon reach a plateau beyond which no significant performance/cost improvements can be achieved with the same processor architecture. Therefore, researchers are looking into new, more efficient, processor architectures. For example, the simple "pipeline" architecture of microprocessors used in personal computers has been replaced by the CISC (complex instruction set computer), which, in turn, is being replaced by the RISC (reduced instruction set computer) architecture, which itself will be soon replaced by superscalar and multiprocessor computer architectures. Each new architecture is the next optimum and, once all possible architectures have been explored, sooner or later a plateau of performance-to-cost will be reached, beyond which significant optimization cannot be achieved.

This forecasted plateau by no means implies the death of the microprocessor. The next century will demand high-performance processors coupled with sophisticated computing algorithms and techniques, such as genetic algorithms and evolutionary programming, and myriads of sophisticated applications will be seen. Therefore, the scientific community is searching not only the next generation of computing but also for the next **breed of processing machines**—small machines many times faster and more potent than those yet developed that can rapidly process massive amounts of data and that will figuratively learn, listen, and "think." But to create this "brainlike machine," revolutionary theories, technology, and architectures, such as the following, are required:

- Theories that explain what intelligence is, how it processes imprecise information, and stores, recalls, associates, correlates, infers, and extracts precise values

- Technology that, with a relatively small amount of circuitry, can process vast amounts of imprecise information in a very short time and provide precise results

- Architectures that encompass the new theories and technologies

THE ENGINEERING OF THE BRAIN

Biologists have studied **biological neural networks** for many years. The human brain is such a network. Discovering how the brain works has been an ongoing effort that started more than 2000 years ago with Aristotle and Heraclitus and has continued with the work of Ramon y Cajal, Colgi, Hebb, and others. The better we understand the brain, the better we can emulate it and build artificial "thinking machines" and "repair" biological damage that leads to brain disorders.

As information about the functions of the brain was accumulated, a new technology emerged and the quest for an **artificial neural network** started. The brain processes information superquickly and superaccurately. It can be trained to recognize patterns and to identify incomplete patterns. Moreover, the trained network performs even if certain neurons fail. For example, even in a noisy football stadium with many thousands of people, we can still recognize a friend from afar or distinguish voices from the pandemonic noise. This ability of the brain (signal processing) to recognize information, literally buried in noise, and retrieve it correctly is one of the amazing processes that we wish could be duplicated by machine. Hence, if we manage to build a machine—an artificial neural network—that emulates the human brain, even at only 0.1% of its performance, we still have an extraordinary information processing and controlling machine. These training and learning features make neural networks suitable for applications in signal processing (image, speech, or data), control (robotics, power systems, communications systems, intelligent automotive vehicles), and many other fields.

Artificial neural networks made a rapid transition from the cognitive and neurobiology field to engineering with the pioneering work of McCullough and Pitts, Rosenblatt, Widrow, Kohonen, Grossberg and Carpenter, Hopfield, Werbos, Anderson, and many others, who developed paradigms that are still applied today. Engineers from all disciplines (such as hardware, software, systems, and materials) are working on artificial neural networks.

A WORLD OF FUZZY THINKING

Parallel to the development of neural network theory, **fuzzy theory** or **fuzzy logic** emerged, with the pioneering work of Lotfi Zadeh, and immediately drew the attention of those technologists who had a special interest in artificial neural networks.

What is fuzzy theory? Why is the term *fuzzy* used? "Fuzziness" is found in our decisions, in our thinking, in the way we process information, and, particularly, in our language; statements can be unclear or subject to different interpretation. Phrases like "see you later," "a little more," or "I don't feel very well" are fuzzy expressions. The fuzziness stems from the different interpretations or perceptions we give to "later," "a little more," and "very well." For example, "later" for fast-phenomena engineers may be on the order of nanoseconds, but for paleontologists it may be on the order of thousands of years. The order of magnitude is relative; therefore, if *some* fuzzy units are used, one should look at it within its context and find a point of reference and a measuring unit.

Occasionaly, fuzzy statements indicate relative units and subunits that do not indicate absolute units. Consider this example: "Runner A is fast," "runner B is faster than A," and "runner C is slower than B." We make two observations: Fuzzy statements may establish *taxonomy* (B is faster than A, and C is slower than B) or *ambiguity* (it is not clear if A is faster than C) and there is no measure of the speed of A, B, or C. The statement "George is very tall" is fuzzy because there is no reference measurement. On a basketball team with an average height of 6 ft 2 in, "very tall" most likely means taller than 6 ft 2 in. To the average person, "very tall" often means taller than 5 ft 8 in, often but not necessarily 6 ft 2 in.

Fuzziness is often confused with probability. A statement is probabilistic if it expresses a likelihood or degree of certainty or if it is the outcome of clearly defined but randomly occurring events. For example, the statement "There is a 50/50 chance that I'll be there" is purely probabilistic. Probability itself can have some degree of fuzziness. In the statement "Most likely I'll be there," all odds have been mentally weighed and some degree of certainty or probability has been expressed. On the other hand, the statement "I may be there" expresses complete uncertainty, undecidability, and, hence, fuzziness.

CRISP VERSUS FUZZY LOGICS

You are probably familiar with logic that has well-defined decision levels or thresholds (binary, multivalue). *Boolean* or *binary logic* is based on two *crisp extremes*—yes–no or 1–0. Yes or no is an answer beyond doubt. *Trivalent logic* is a logic of three definite answers, such as empty–half full–full or 0–0.5–1. The binary numbers 1 or 0, or 1, 0.5, 0 in trivalent logic represent normalized thresholds. Similarly, the *multivalue logic* has many well-defined threshold levels.

Fuzzy logic, however, has *unclear* thresholds. For example, if we take the trivalent logic and *fuzzify* it (i.e., change the crisp thresholds to obscure ones), then the values of the thresholds can be stated as a range of values. The crispness of the numbers 0, 0.5, and 1 may be replaced by "from 0 to about 0.4," "from about 0.2 to about 0.8," and "from about 0.6 to 1," respectively. For example, if you look at three distinct dots through a well-focused camera lens, you will see the dots with crisp perimeters. If the image is out of focus, however, the dots become unclear and "fuzzy," perhaps overlapping each other. This action is termed *fuzzification* and in fuzzy control systems is routinely done.

Fuzzy logic has been applied to military intelligence machines, the stock market, and even dishwashers. In communications, it has been used on the systems level and in signal processing. On the systems level, fuzzy logic applications determine the best parameter values for call switching, call routing, system reconfiguration, and so on. In signal processing, fuzzy logic applications determine the degree of the fuzzified received signal (distortions due to environmental variations, electrical interferences, medium mismatches, and other) and then "defuzzify" the signal. In a nutshell, fuzzy logic is a powerful tool for the intelligent retrieval of nonstatistical, ill-defined information in static, sequential, and real-time applications.

FUZZY AND NEURAL NETWORKS

Artificial neural networks and fuzzy logic work together, artificial neural networks classify and learn rules for fuzzy logic and fuzzy logic infers from unclear neural network parameters. The latter is a network with fast learning capabilities that produces intelligent, crisp output from fuzzy input and/or from fuzzy parameters and avoids time-consuming arithmetic manipulation.

Incorporating fuzzy principles in a neural network gives more user flexibility and a more robust system. Fuzziness in this case means more flexibility in the definition of the system; boundaries may be described more generally, not crisply; inputs may be described more vaguely, yet better control may be obtained. The network itself may be fuzzy, not well defined, and able to reconfigure itself for best performance. The power of such machines may be illustrated with the following "gedanken" examples.

Visualize a machine that has learned to analyze scenery, animals, other machines, and other items. A user describes a vague scene in terms of features such as "something like a tree, about here" and "something like an animal with four legs and a long tail and so tall, there," and so on. Then the machine draws a three-dimensional landscape with a tree and a dog nearby (and perhaps a mountain in the background, with a lake). Then the user may instruct the machine to make corrections to this scene, again in vague language, and the machine immediately projects a three-dimensional scene, very similar to the one the user had in mind. As all that is done, a train with a whistling sound may be crossing the scene (if the parameters are set right) and nearby a frightened bird flies away.

Imagine a machine that is instructed to design a new three-dimensional machine, based on some approximate specifications. Our gedanken machine designs a model from the vague specifications, simulates the created machine, makes corrections on the model, and, if the corrected one performs as expected, manufactures the first prototype—all in just a few minutes!

WHERE ARE FUZZY NEURAL NETWORKS HEADING?

Fuzzy logic follows the same path as Boolean and multiple value logic. Initially, binary logic started as a linguistic set of statements, such as if $A = B$, and if $B = C$, then is $A = C$? Then mathematical notation translated the linguistic statements into equations and theories were developed that are taught today. These theories have been applied successfully in the development of many logical applications.

Fuzzy logic also started as a linguistic set of statements. For example, if A is taller than B, B is shorter than C, what is A with respect to C? A number of mathematical theories can be found in the literature. Thus, we may make a reasonable extrapolation and deduce that fuzzy logic will prove itself as binary logic did. The fusion of fuzzy logic and neural networks combines the best of each. Fuzzy concepts fused with "thinking" promise superior technology. These claims are validated by various integrated circuits, fuzzy controllers for general applicability, and applications for automobile engine control, robot control, cameras (film and video), appliances, and the military. In addition to hardware solutions, numerous "fuzzy algorithmic solutions" have been applied in communications, signal processing (speech, image), and other areas. The number of companies banking on fuzzy logic is growing rapidly. Many significant American, European, and Asian-Pasific companies have announced products or are exploring and advancing fuzzy logic for potential applicability in their own products (see Chapter 6 for examples). In the near future we will see applications that encompass algorithmic fuzzy logic, fuzzy neural networks, and combinations of fuzzy and/or neural networks with high-performance microprocessors.

OBJECTIVES

The objectives of this text are simple and crisp: to provide a simplified yet comprehensive description of the concepts and potential applications of neural networks and fuzzy logic, to give an insight into fuzzy neural networks, and to demonstrate their applicability through examples.

Chapter 1 is an overview of biological neural networks. Specifically, I briefly describe the physiology of the neuron and neural networks. The intent is to sketch out the amazing microcosm of live neurons, including their function and organization. Chapter 2 describes concepts of artificial neural networks, most of which come from the biological and behavioral sciences. Chapter 3 provides a tutorial of the most popular paradigms and a brief description of several others. The first part of Chapter 4 provides a tutorial of fuzzy logic set forth by basic examples, and the second part is a more advanced treatment of temporal fuzzy logic, yet all are simplified to the greatest degree possible. Chapter 5 describes how fuzzy logic and neural networks are combined to build a fuzzy neural network, and Chapter 6 describes applications with neural networks, fuzzy logic, and fuzzy neural networks.

The material is organized so that it will serve both the reader who wants a simple introduction to the subject and the reader who is at an undergraduate level. To achieve this, we have followed four rules:

- The reader is not a biologist or a mathematician.

- The language has been simplified to eliminate unecessary jargon yet retain necessary terminology.

- Mathematical description has been reduced to basics and those sections that involve extensive mathematics have been segregated in a description and math section. Thus, the reader may skip the math section at the first reading without any loss of understanding.

- Mathematical notation has been simplified. In a few cases, for simplicity, vectorial notation is used. Simple numerical examples demonstrate the math applicability and clarify any difficulties.

UNDERSTANDING NEURAL NETWORKS
AND FUZZY LOGIC

1

BIOLOGICAL NEURAL NETWORKS

1.1 Neuron Physiology

The **neuron** (Greek: nerve cell) is the fundamental unit of the nervous system, particularly the brain [1, 2, 3]. Considering its microscopic size, it is an amazingly complex biochemical and electrical signal processing factory. From a classical viewpoint, the neuron is a simple processing unit that receives and combines signals from many other neurons through filamentary input paths, the **dendrites** (Greek: treelings) (Figure 1-1).

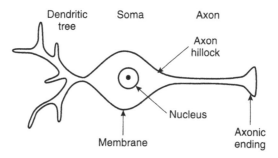

Figure 1-1 Representation of a neuron.

Dendrites are bunched into highly complex "dendritic trees," which have an enormous total surface area. Dendritic trees are connected with the main body of the nerve cell, the **soma** (Greek: body). The soma has a pyramidal or cylindrical shape. The outer boundary of the cell is the **membrane**. The interior of the cell is filled with the **intracellular fluid**, and outside the cell is the **extracellular fluid**. The neuron's membrane and the substances inside and outside the neuron play an important role in its operation and survival. When excited above a certain level, the **threshold**, the neuron *fires*; that is, it transmits an electrical signal, the **action potential**, along a single path called the **axon**.* The axon meets the soma at the **axon hillock**. The axon ends in a tree of filamentary paths called the **axonic endings** that are connected with dendrites of other neurons. The connection (or junction) between a neuron's axon and another neuron's dendrite is called a **synapse** (Greek: contact). A synapse consists of the **presynaptic terminal**, the **cleft** or the synaptic junction, and the **postsynaptic terminal** (Figure 1-2).

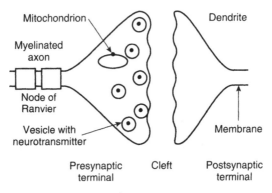

Figure 1-2 Synapse in detail.

A single neuron may have 1000 to 10,000 synapses and may be connected with some 1000 neurons. Not all synapses are excited at the same time, however. Because a received sensory pattern via the synapses probably excites a relatively small percentage of sites, an almost endless number of patterns can be presented at the neuron without saturating the neuron's capacity. When the action potential reaches the axonic ending, *chemical messengers*, known as **neurotransmitters**, are released. The neurotransmitters are stored in tiny spherical structures called **vesicles** (see Figure 1-2) and are responsible for the effective communication of information between neurons.

When a neurotransmitter is released, it drifts across the synaptic junction or cleft and initiates the **depolarization** of the postsynaptic membrane; in other words, the ion distribution at the surface of the membrane changes, and thus the voltage across the membrane of the receiving neuron, the **postsynaptic potential**, changes. The stronger the junction, the

---

* In some neurons, a *collateral axon* may grow from the main axon.

more neurotransmitter reaches the postsynaptic membrane. Known neurotransmitters include synapsin 1, synaptophysin, calelectrin, mediatophore,
and synuclein. Depending on the type of neurotransmitter, the postsynaptic
potential is either **excitatory** (more positive) or **inhibitory** (more negative).

Decoding at the synapse is accomplished by **temporal** summation
(Figure 1-3) and **spatial** summation [4]. In temporal summation each
potential of an impulse (consider signals in the form of a train of impulses)
adds to the sum of the potentials of the previous impulses. The total sum
is the result of impulses and their amplitude. Spatial summation reflects
the integration of excitations or inhibitions by all neurons at the target neuron. The total potential charge from temporal and spatial (**spatiotemporal**)
summations is encoded as a nerve impulse transmitted to other cells. The
impulses received by the synapses of a neuron are further integrated over
a short time as the charge is stored in the cell membrane. This membrane
acts first as a capacitor and later as an internal second messenger when
complex biochemical mechanisms take place.

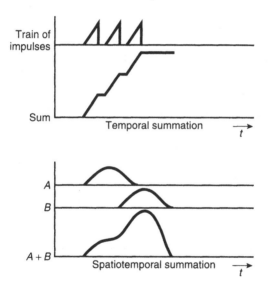

Figure 1-3 Temporal and spatiotemporal
summation.

All integrated signals are combined at the soma, and if the amplitude of
the combined signal reaches the threshold of the neuron, a "firing" process
is activated and an output signal is produced. This signal, either a single
pulse or a sequence of pulses at a particular rate, is transmitted along the
cell's axon to the axonic endings.

1.1.1 The Soma

The *soma* operates like a highly complex biological, chemical, and electrical plant. The membrane of the cell encloses the cytoplasm. Looking under a microscope, one recognizes the nucleus, the Golgi apparatus, the vacuole, the endoplasmic reticulum with ribosomes, the mitochondria, and the centrosome. The endoplasmic reticulum with ribosomes forms a series of canals and is the chemical plant of the cell. Enzymes in this structure convert glucose to glycogen, which is stored in the canals. When energy is needed, the glycogen is converted back to glucose, thereby releasing energy. The mitochondria are the power plants of the cell. When oxygen and nutrients enter this organelle, an enzyme causes a chemical reaction to manufacture adenosine triphosphate (ATP) from adenosine diphosphate (ADP). Upon formation, ATP [5] is used for synthesizing chemical compounds, such as DNA, in the cell's **ribosomes**. It is also believed that ATP is responsible for, or contributes to, the action potential. When ATP is used, it converts to ADP, which returns to mitochondria for reactivation to ATP by the use of oxygen. The product of the reaction, carbon dioxide (CO_2), diffuses out of the cell, finds its way into the blood vessels, and is eliminated by the lungs. The detailed chemistry in the mitochondria is described by the Krebs cycle and can be found in biochemistry and physiology textbooks.

For the study of the action potential, it is important to understand the electrical charge distribution around the membrane—that is, the ionic concentrations and the potentials inside and outside the cell. The electrical charge distribution in the squid cell,* for example, is listed in Table 1-1. In comparing the ionic concentration of potassium and sodium, notice that there is a strong imbalance between the exterior and interior of the cell. The interior is rich in potassium, whereas the exterior is rich in sodium. The potential difference, due to ionic concentration imbalance at either side of the membrane, is expressed in terms of the internal and external ionic concentration (N_{in}, N_{ext}), the ionic charge, q, and absolute temperature, T:

$$V_t = \frac{kT}{q} \frac{N_{in}}{N_{ext}}, \qquad (1.1)$$

where k is Boltzmann's constant, 1.38×10^{-23} joules/K, and $q = 6.09 \times 10^{-19}$ coulombs.

---

* Squid cells have been extensively used in experiments because of their relatively large cell size.

Table 1-1. Electrical Charge Distribution in the Squid Cell

Ion Type	Ionic Concentration Inside Cell (mM/L)	Ionic Concentration Outside Cell (mM/L)	Reversal Potential (mV)
Potassium	155	4	−92
Sodium	12	145	+55
Chloride	5	105	−65

1.1.2   Cell Membrane Structure

The skin of the nerve cell is the **membrane**. The basic building blocks of the nerve membrane are long **phospholipid** molecules. At one end of a phospholipid molecule is a **hydrophobic** (Greek: water repellent) hydrocarbon chain; at the other end is a **hydrophilic** (Greek: water friendly) **polar head group**. Similarly, the long molecule of common soap has a hydrophobic end and a hydrophilic end. Because of this structure of the soap molecule, oil-based substances can be removed with soap and water during wash. Now, consider many phospholipid molecules such that they form a two-dimensional matrix layer with the hydrocarbon (hydrophobic) chains all at the same surface. The membrane consists of two such layers. The layers are placed atop each other with the hydrocarbon surfaces face to face. Thus, this bilayer membrane has the (hydrophilic) polar head-groups at both surfaces. Proteins are also in the membrane structure (Figure 1-4).

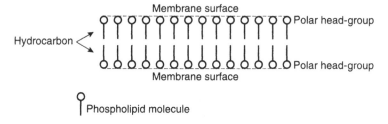

Figure 1-4 Membrane structure cross section.

1.1.3   Proteins: The Cell's Signature

Proteins are essential components of a cell [6]. They are long polymers composed of some 20 types of **amino acids** that form chains of about 300 in a specific sequence. Hence, the potential number of different proteins is enormous. Each sequence constitutes a specific code that characterizes a protein and distinguishes it from any other. This code is referred to as a **gene**. Genes contain the amino acid deoxyribonucleic acid (DNA). In the 1950s, Crick and Watson proved that DNA consists of two long spiral strands of polymerized sugar forming a double helix. The two strands are held together between a pyrine and a pyrimidine base by hydrogen bonds. These bonds project inward from two chains containing alternate links of deoxyribose and phosphate. Thus, the two strands are interlocked. Proteins are arranged in a definite configuration, believed to be different for every organism, that determines that cell's functionality. Think of it as the *signature* of the cell. This signature determines every physiological and mental* characteristic of the cell.

When a protein is formed, certain amino acid links are weaker than others, thus deforming (or forming) the protein geometry. Protein geometry plays an important role in the recognition process. Proteins of a certain geometry recognize other proteins with matching geometry and combine to give enzymes with interesting properties. Thus, *the shape of a protein constitutes the protein's program to perform a particular function.* Certain proteins are not programmed. Fortunately, this lack of programmability of proteins may be an advantage in gene engineering whereby links may be manipulated to produce *artificially programmed* proteins that perform a desired function. This concept is used in biocomputing research (see Section 1.1.11).

Protein is continuously manufactured by the cell for its growth, function, and maintenance. The protein factory of the cell is the endoplasmic reticulum with ribosomes. The DNA molecule forms various types of ribonucleic acid (RNA), such as messenger RNA (mRNA) and soluble or transfer RNA (tRNA); each has a different role. For instance, the mRNA carries the genetic code to the endoplasmic reticulum, and the soluble RNA finds the proper amino acids and brings them to this site. Each form of tRNA is a specific carrier for each of the 20 known amino acids. Arginine, for example, is transported by the tRNA specialized to transport arginine; leucine is transported by the specific tRNA for leucine, and so on. Once an amino acid is delivered, the tRNA goes back for more. As each type of amino acid is delivered at the site, a remarkable creation begins. The ribosomes move along the mRNA, *read* the code, and, according to this code, synthesize from the received amino acids a polypeptide chain [7]. From this chain a "cloning process" takes place whereby exact replicas of the protein molecules are produced. Thus, we may conclude that genes

---

* Here the word *mental* should be considered within the framework of this text, without any intention of raising philosophical or religious eyebrows.

constitute the permanent memory of the cell, which is carried from parent to children cells. This process is a submicroscopic, highly complex, and precisely timed biochemical factory, the details of which are beyond our present understanding. How does the RNA know what to do, when to do it, and how? Where is the knowledge of processing and formation stored? Is it a probabilistic or accidental phenomenon, or is there something beyond our understanding? Obviously, this process cannot be random or accidental because it is reproducible, predictable, and under nature's control.

1.1.4   Membrane Proteins

Proteins manufactured in the soma are either free to move within the cell by diffusion or are firmly embedded in the lipid layers of the membrane. Proteins embedded in the membrane are called **intrinsic**. Intrinsic proteins are not uniformly distributed over the membrane surface. Membrane proteins are essential for many aspects of neuron functions and are classified as **pump, channel, receptor, enzyme,** and **structural** proteins.

Pump proteins move particular ions from one side of the membrane to the other, thus altering the ion concentrations. The pumps are highly important in the functioning and survival of the cell; see Section 1.1.6 for more detail.

Channel proteins provide pathways through which specific ions can diffuse at command, thus helping to cancel the ion buildup of the pumps. The opening of the sodium channel is from 0.4 to 0.6 nm. Channels open at different times, stay open for different time intervals, and allow different types of ions (sodium, potassium, or calcium) to pass. Two fundamental properties of channels are selectivity and gating. The channels are selective to sodium or potassium. When these channels open, sodium or potassium diffuses through them. Some selective channels may pass seven sodium ions for every 100 potassium ions. Some channels are nonselective; they allow about 85 sodium ions for every 100 potassium. These channels are known as *acetylcholine activated channels*. Water (H_2O) in the channel also seems to be important in ion selection. Potassium channels contain less water and have a smaller opening than sodium channels. The density of channels in the membrane is reported to be from zero to 10,000 per square micrometer.

The gating mechanism of a channel may be voltage activated (i.e., it opens and closes in response to a voltage difference across the membrane) or chemically activated (i.e., it opens and closes in the presence of certain neurotransmitters). Chemically activated channels are named after the chemical that activates them: the GABA-activated channel, for instance, is so named because it activates gamma-aminobutyric acid (GABA). Axons have mostly electrically activated channels, whereas the postsynaptic membrane has mostly chemically activated channels.

Receptor proteins provide selective binding sites to neurotransmitters. **Enzymes** are placed in or at the membrane to facilitate chemical reactions at the membrane surface. The enzyme adenylate cyclase is an important protein that regulates the intracellular substance cyclic adenosine monophosphate.

Structural proteins are responsible for maintaining the cellular structure and interconnecting cells.

Moreover, other proteins at the membrane carry different essential nervous-system functions, many of which are not yet well understood. It is believed that some proteins may have more than one function in the neuron.

1.1.5   Membrane Strength

Despite the complex structure of the neuron's membrane, it is only 5 to 50 angstroms (50 to 500 nm) thick. One would think that such a thin membrane would be highly unstable and would collapse easily, yet it is so stable that it can withstand electrical fields across it that can easily exceed 100 mV to 100 kV/cm without damage. Interestingly, this voltage difference is in the neighborhood of the breakdown voltage of the SiO_2 layer in metal oxide semiconductor (MOS) transistors. This remarkable stability of the membrane is attributed to the extremely strong binding forces created by the interaction of the aqueous solution with charges in the hydrophilic polar head-group of the lipid molecules at either side of the membrane.

1.1.6   The Sodium Pump: A Pump of Life?

According to nature's laws, when an ionic concentration difference is formed, an electric field that causes diffusion in a direction that balances out the ionic concentration difference is created. Despite nature, a substantial ionic concentration difference and an electric field across the cell membrane are well sustained. This irregularity puzzled scientists who tried to explain this nature-defying mechanism. The only logical explanation is the presence of a mechanism at the membrane that counteracts nature's diffusion process.

Imagine a pumping mechanism embedded in the cell membrane that keeps sodium ions outside and potassium ions inside the cell [8]. If this mechanism pumps sodium out faster than nature diffuses sodium into the cell, then a sodium imbalance is created; in other words, the mechanism is direction-selective ion pumping. Direction-selective pumps explain how a nonequilibrium condition—and, hence, the electrical potential difference across the membrane, known as the **resting potential**—is sustained. Such a pump should not be thought of as a single device in the cell's membrane but, instead, as many submicroscopic ion-pumping mechanisms embedded in and distributed over the molecular structure of the membrane. It has been found, however, that pump distribution in the cell's membrane is not uniform. Most neurons have approximately 100 to 200 sodium pumps per square micrometer of membrane surface; some parts of the cell membrane have 10 times more than that, others have less.

The sodium-potassium adenosine triphosphate pump or, briefly, the **sodium pump**, consists of intrinsic proteins. It is slightly larger than the membrane thickness and has a molecular weight of 275,000 daltons. Each sodium pump expends the energy stored in the phosphate bond of the ATP to exchange three sodium ions from inside the cell for two potassium ions from outside the cell. The rate at which this ion exchange takes place depends on the needs and conditions of the cell. It has been calculated that at a maximum rate, each pump can transport 200 sodium ions and 130 potassium ions per second.

1.1.7   Cell Resting Potential

One can simulate the membrane with an equivalent circuit in terms of the conductance (or resistance) of the membrane for each ion and the potential difference each ion generates across the membrane. From simple circuit analysis at equilibrium with V_0 for the resting potential we obtain

$$I = 0 = (V_K - V_0)G_K + (V_{Na} - V_0)G_{Na} + (V_{Cl} - V_0)G_{Cl}, \quad (1.2)$$

where G_K, G_{Na}, G_{Cl} are the conductances $(1/R)$ of the membrane for potassium (K), sodium (Na), and chloride (Cl), respectively, and V_K, V_{Na}, and V_{Cl} are the potential differences across the membrane due to K, Na, and Cl, respectively. The chloride current is comparatively small and can be neglected, and the membrane conductance for potassium is about 20 times larger than the sodium conductance. Thus, the resting potential V_0 is approximately

$$V_0 = \frac{V_K G_K + V_{Na} G_{Na}}{G_K + G_{Na}} \approx V_K + \frac{V_{Na}}{21}. \quad (1.3)$$

The cell rests at a negative potential because its membrane is selectively permeable to potassium. This resting potential, depending on conditions and the type of cell, is about -65 to -85 mV.

1.1.8   Action Potential: Cell Firing

In living organisms the electrical activity of a neuron is triggered by many mechanisms. For example, light triggers photoreceptors in the eye, mechanical deflection of hair triggers cells in the ear, chemical substances affect the responsivity of synapses or the ionic concentration inside and outside the cell, and voltage affects the firing process of the cell and the axon.

When the permeability of the membrane is locally disturbed by signals at one or more synapses, the pumping process at this location is disturbed. If the applied potential is more positive than the resting potential, in other words, if the applied signal is **excitatory**, then it *depolarizes* the membrane and the pumps stop functioning for the duration of the depolarization. Then, naturally, sodium rushes in through the sodium channels and potassium rushes out through the potassium channels of the depolarized part of the membrane in an attempt to balance the ionic concentration difference. Thus, the ionic concentrations across the membrane at the location of disturbance change and the potential difference collapses because it is not able to sustain the ionic concentration difference across the membrane at that location. If the "collapse" of potential is intense enough (i.e., if it exceeds certain characteristics that determine the cell's threshold), then the neighboring areas of the membrane are influenced and the depolarization starts traveling along the membrane; in other words, a wave of depolarization sweeps along the membrane that eventually reaches the axon hillock. At that point the depolarization wave, or the **action potential**, propagates along the axon down to the axonic endings (see Section 1.1.9).

If, on the other hand, the applied potential is more negative—that is, the disturbance is **inhibitory**—then the membrane is *hyperpolarized*. Hyperpolarization and depolarization may take place at the same time at two or more neighboring parts of a cell membrane. Obviously, hyperpolarization influencies depolarization of a membrane, and vice versa. Thus, it is believed that the resultant action potential is the algebraic sum of both hyperpolarization and depolarization activities provided that the net sum exceeds the threshold characteristics of the cell; the latter forms the basis of modeling artificial neurons.

1.1.9   The Axon: A Transmission Line

The axon is the neuron's transmission line. It transfers the excitation signal, or action potential, from the hillock down to the axonic endings. The axon exhibits certain fundamental differences in structure and properties from the dendrites. In the classical simplistic neuron, the axon is thought of as a tube filled with **axoplasm**, which is rich in potassium and poor in sodium. In addition, the axon consists of many microfilaments (thin fibers) called **neurofibrils** or **neurofilaments**. The branches of the dendrites cluster closer to the main body of the cell while the axon is longer and thinner than the dendritic branch, and it branches out at the end of the axon fiber. The membrane of the axon is specialized. At the terminal of the axon, the membrane is structured to release neurotransmitters, whereas the membrane of the dendrites is structured to receive neurotransmitters. The proteins in the axonic membrane are electrically activated, the proteins at the postsynaptic membrane are mostly chemically activated, and the soma membrane contains many kinds of proteins. The electrical resistance of the nerve's cytoplasm is so high (1000–10,000 ohms/cm) that it would dissipate the energy of the electrical signal, the action potential, within a few millimeters of travel. Thus, another paradox is presented: How can the axon sustain data transmission in the form of action potential over relatively long distances without severe signal attenuation?

The axon's structure is ingenious. It is equipped with a regeneration mechanism that restores the attenuated pulses as they propagate, a familiar practice to transmission systems engineers. The regeneration mechanism, depending on the type of neuron and species, may be continuous or repeated at fixed intervals, similar to the repeaters in transmission lines of communication systems. For example, in the squid's neuron the amplification mechanism is continuous along the axon (Figure 1-5a), whereas in higher animals it is repeated at fixed intervals (Figure 1-5b). In the latter case, the axon is covered with an insulating material called **myelin**. Myelin reduces membrane capacitance, thus increasing signal propagation speed, and amplifies signal strength. Amplification occurs as follows. Every few millimeters the continuous sheath of myelin is interrupted, forming gaps known as **nodes of Ranvier**. The gaps act as *repeaters* or regeneration sites where the signal is periodically restored. This amplification is so successful that myelinated axons can carry signals up to 1 m in length.

When depolarization exceeds the threshold of the cell, a nerve impulse starts at the origin of the axon, the axon hillock, and the voltage difference across the axon membrane is locally lowered. Immediately ahead of the electrically altered region, channels in the membrane open and let sodium ions pour into the axon. Then the voltage across this membrane region is lowered, which causes more sodium channels to open just a little farther ahead. Thus, once the depolarization process of the axonic membrane is triggered, it becomes self-stimulated and continues until it reaches the axonic endings. The axonic membrane does not stay depolarized for long. As soon as the depolarization impulse is gone, in a matter of milliseconds the sodium channels close, known as **sodium inactivation**, and the pump mechanism restores the nonequilibrium state of the ion concentration of the membrane, starting from the origin of the axon. Thus, if an electrical probe is placed in the axon, one could detect a signal in the shape of a pulse propagating down the axon (Figure 1-5). For the squid axon, which is about 600 μm, the speed of the action potential is about 20 m/s (or approximately 70 km/h).

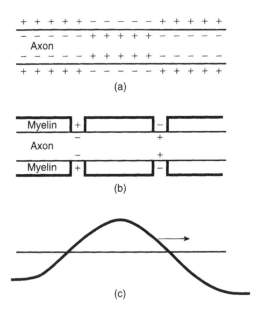

(a)

(b)

(c)

Figure 1-5 (a) Charge distribution in unmyelinated axon. (b) Charge distribution in myelinated axon. (c) Action potential.

1.1.10   The Synapse

The synapse is where two neurons connect. It consists of the flattened-tip, buttonlike terminal of an axonic ending, or **presynaptic terminal**, and the receptor part of another neuron, or **postsynaptic terminal**. The presynaptic and postsynaptic terminals are separated by the **synaptic cleft**, which is about 200 nm thin. Within the presynaptic terminal are **mitochondria** and **vesicles**. The mitochondria produce chemical **neurotransmitters** and the vesicles store them (Figure 1-6). About 50 neurotransmitters have been identified so far.

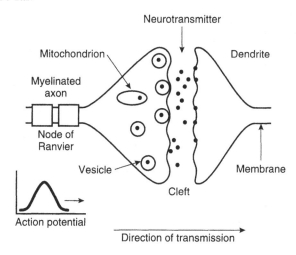

Figure 1-6 Synapsis in action.

The cleft is filled with extracellular material containing, for example, calcium ions. Calcium is extremely important for transmitting signals between neurons. When an action potential arrives at the presynaptic terminal, the electrical impulse opens voltage-activated calcium channels in the membrane. Through these channels calcium ions flow from the extracellular environment into the presynaptic terminal. The calcium ions attract the vesicles close to the presynaptic membrane and, in a synchronized manner, aid the fusion of the vesicles to the membrane. The vesicles then break up and "spray" the cleft space with the neurotransmitter. This fusion of vesicles and subsequent neurotransmitter release is called **exocytosis**. The time span of the calcium ions' inrush is quite brief and, once the ions accomplish their job, they are neutralized by an as yet indeterminate mechanism, so that the ion concentration in the presynaptic terminal returns to normal. The almost empty vesicles are reclaimed and quickly refilled with a new neurotransmitter. Every vesicle is filled with about 10,000 molecules of the same neurotransmitter. Some neurons may have only one type of neurotransmitter, whereas others, such as those in the brain, may have more than one.

When the cleft is sprayed with the neurotransmitter, postsynaptic membrane channels are chemically activated (i.e., they open) and pass the neurotransmitter inside. These channels may be either sodium or chloride. At the other end of the channels, inside the neuron, is a concentration of receptor proteins that react with the incoming neurotransmitter. The reaction product may lower or raise the potential difference across the membrane, depending on which receptor matches with the received neurotransmitter and how well they match. It has been experimentally verified that, although the neurotransmitter may be the same (acetylcholine, serotonin, dopamine, GABA, histamine, etc.), depending on the type of synapse, the excitation, referred to as **neuronal modulation**, may be inhibitory or excitatory. For example, the intrinsic rhythm of the human heart is the result of neuronal modulation. Two types of neurons—*cholinergic* and *nonadrenergic*—are responsible for the heart's fast or slow beat. Cholinergic neurons connect to the vagus nerve and exhibit an inhibitory action when activated; nonadrenergic neurons, on the other hand, connect to the accelerator nerve and when activated exhibit an excitatory action. Either neuron type is activated by acetylcholine (ACh).

Another facet to the synapse's complexity is its **plasticity** [9]—its tendency to change its synaptic efficacy as a result of synaptic activity, strength, and frequency. Action potentials not only encode information; they also have metabolic aftereffects that alter network parameters over time.

Thus, each neuron is a sophisticated computer that continuously integrates up to 1000 synaptic inputs that do not add up in a simple linear manner.

1.1.11   The Synapse: A Biocomputer

Currently in computing research, a substantial effort to understand how nature computes is under way. The thinking here is entirely different from familiar binary computation. In pattern recognition, nature matches complete patterns in one simple step; in contrast, binary computers compare patterns bit by bit, which is an enormous expenditure of computing power and time. This thinking is based on the fact that proteins have characteristic shapes. When a neurotransmitter meets a receptor with the correct complementary shape, they form a specific messenger molecule (e.g., cyclic adenosine monophosphate, cAMP) similar to matching puzzle pieces.[*] This molecule is recognized by another readout enzyme that, in turn, triggers the membrane's depolarization process.

---

[*] The cAMP messenger may also trigger events in the cytoskeleton, a network of microtubules and microfilaments (see Section 1.1.9).

Based on this operation of the synapse, a new technology has developed, **biocomputation** or **molecular computation**. Researchers in molecular engineering and computer architecture are looking for proteins and biocomputing structures to perform complicated computations in simple steps. (Other disciplines involved include gene and protein engineering, membrane engineering, polymer chemistry, and biochemistry.) This effort, though embryonic, has produced biosensors [10, 11, 12] that act as dedicated biocomputers to sense substances and their physical properties quickly and in minuscule quantities (glucose, oxygen, protein, etc.). For example, a fiber-optic biosensor is used to detect parts per billion of warfare agents, explosives, pathogens, and toxic materials [13] in a hazardous environment. In addition to biosensors, other molecular materials have been considered, such as rhodopsin—a purple, light-sensitive pigment in the eye responsible for vision (see Section 1.4)—as a fast optical switch in biochips and in processing synthetic aperture radar (SAR) signals [14].

1.1.12 Types of Synapses

One neuron can make many contacts with other neurons, thus forming a complicated network. The axonic endings of a neuron may contact another neuron to form a simple **excitatory** dendritic contact, an **inhibitory** dendritic contact, a direct contact with the trunk of a dendritic tree, a contact with the soma of a neuron, or even a contact with the axon itself. Moreover, some synapses—enabling synapses, modulating synapses, and inactive synapses—are more complicated (Figure 1-7). Some neurons feed back directly to themselves or indirectly via a third or fourth neuron. This diversity in synapse type is believed to control the operation and firing mechanism of the neuron; the function of each type, however, is not clearly understood in many neural networks.

1.1.13 The Developing Neuron: Forming Networks

How does an embryonic neuron (i.e., a neuron under development) know which neurons to contact so that a specific neural network can be formed? Developmental neuron research is addressing this question, and some evidence is available. In an embryonic neuron its axon is not fully developed and contacts with other neurons have not been fully formed. As the axon grows, however, the neuron recognizes the correct pathway using an ingenious mechanism that I call the **electrochemical seeking radar** (ECSR) to contact the target neuron. A radar transmits an electromagnetic wave,

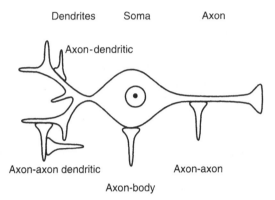

Figure 1-7 Types of synapses.

pauses briefly, receives the reflections of the transmitted wave, and analyzes the reflected signal, from which it identifies the location, movement pattern, and shape of the reflecting object. The *electrochemical seeking radar* is a strong hypothesis supported by scientific evidence as follows: A growing neuron seeks another neuron, the target neuron, by detecting specific cues left by it, similar to cues left in a trail and recognized by a hunting dog. In experiments with embryonic neuron growth in vitro, the addition of minute amounts of the cue, known as the **nerve-growth factor** (NGF) [15], everywhere in the culture resulted in a complete disorientation of the neuron's development and its growth in every possible direction (since the cues were present everywhere in the culture), resulting in a dense network of nerve fibers.

Moreover, it has been established that, during growth, the growing neuron fires periodically [16], and each firing is followed by a brief period of silence. Based on the ECSR hypothesis, the seeking neuron transmits a burst of a periodic signal, and the target neuron reacts to the received signal by releasing molecular cues. The latter cues are sensed by the growing neuron, decoded and recognized, and the neuron grows its axon a little toward it. This cycle repeats itself until the growing neuron eventually reaches its target neuron and makes one or more contacts with it. Thus, the growing neuron recognizes the correct target neuron from myriad other neurons with remarkable precision. From all the contacts made, those in which subsequent action potentials frequently appear increase their synaptic efficacy, whereas those in which the action potential is less frequent lose their strength. The ECSR hypothesis, however, has not yet been validated; the author encourages researchers to pursue this hypothesis.

1.1.14   Neuronal Specialization

All neurons are not the same, nor do they perform the same function. There are many categories of neurons with unique and highly specialized functions. Research has shown that some neurons have simple functions such as contracting or releasing a muscle, while other neurons control the excitatory or inhibitory behavior of other neurons. These neurons are known as **command cells**. It has been found that there are dual-action command neurons in a variety of animals. Command neurons may also remember a complete sequence of commands. Another type of neuron is the **neuroendocrine cell**. This neuron releases chemical substances called **hormones** in the bloodstream to be carried to remote sites. Such neurons form clusters called **bagcells**. Other types of neurons are specialized receptors (photonic, deflection, pressure, chemical, etc.). From an engineering point of view, the operation of some specialized neurons may be compared to a *communications network*, in which the bloodstream serves as the information highway with packets of information flowing in it. A protocol exists whereby a source receives acknowledgment that a chemical has reached its target via direct or indirect feedback mechanisms, causing the source to stop sending the chemical. In the next chapter some examples of biological neuronal networks with highly specialized neurons will be described. The purpose is to provide future direction and to support the argument that artificial neural networks could learn from the neuronal diversity in nature.

1.1.15   The Cell's Biological Memory

It is believed that a pattern is formed and stored when a group of events is associated in time (a belief shared by Aristotle). Patterns evoke other patterns. For instance, a friend's face can be linked with an event that took place at a different time. Thus, patterns are stored and linked with already stored ones. This type of memory is called **associative**. Experimental evidence [17] shows that the formation of memory involves molecular changes at the dendritic trees of neurons. Evidence suggests that each neuron can store thousands of patterns in the dendritic trees. The actual biochemical mechanism of storing and retrieving new information, however, has not been fully explored or understood.

There is no doubt that genes are memory banks of the cell that are preprogrammed permanently. But we don't know how, when, or with what these memory banks were programmed. It may be reasonable to assume that, in addition, there are "unprogrammed" genes that can store new patterns on a more temporary basis because these patterns are induced to the cell by the synapses; this would explain the short-term memory, as opposed to the long-term or permanent memory, of a neural network [18]. If this assumption is true, then new patterns may be stored and may stay for some finite time, the length of which depends on how often the pattern appears or is evoked (i.e., refreshed) and on the type of compounds in its environment. If a pattern becomes inactive for some time, it may fade out. The assumption is based on evidence of molecular modification in the synaptic area [19]. When a phosphate group attaches to a protein, the protein's function is altered; this process is known as **phosphorilation**. Due to a recently discovered family of genes called **immediate early genes** (IEG), the protein may be activated rapidly by brief bursts of action potentials.

1.1.16 Weighting Factor

Recall that when a signal appears at a synapse, a charge is generated at the postsynaptic site. The magnitude of this charge depends on the strength of the incoming signal, which is weighted by a factor associated with this input. The **weighting factor** may not be constant over a long time. Ordinarily, potassium-ion flow is responsible for keeping the charge on a cell membrane well below the threshold potential. Moreover, the reduction of the potassium-ion flow is responsible for changing the weighting factors of electrical signals that can last for many days.

1.1.17 Factors Affecting Potassium-Ion Flow

Experiments have shown that a protein in the cytoplasm of rabbits and snails, kinasse (PKC), is calcium sensitive. When stimuli appear within a short period at the synapses, they cause changes in the calcium-ion concentration and in the diacylglycerol, another messenger. The PKC then moves from the cell cytoplasm to the cell membrane where it reduces the potassium-ion flow and thus alters the neuron's properties. In addition, another calcium-activated protein, CAM kinasse II, may also help reduce potassium-ion flow at the membrane.

1.1.18 Firing, in a Nutshell

In conclusion, when the potassium-ion flow decreases at the membrane, particular input signals trigger impulses more readily. When the stimuli are intense enough so that the potential difference across the membrane exceeds the threshold level, the sodium pump starts collapsing across the membrane and the potential difference moves toward the axon, where it propagates toward the axonic endings. Thus, the cell has fired. Since some of the synaptic inputs are contributing to and some are inhibiting the firing, and since the stimuli occur not simultaneously but within a time window, it is easy to think of a situation where the cell fires and then, shortly thereafter, the inhibitory stimuli appear for a short period and briefly reverse the firing process. If the contributing stimuli are still persistent, the action potential may result in some kind of temporary oscillation. In a neuronal system the inhibitory inputs may also come from other neurons. The firing of neurons thus activated reflects the distribution within each neuron and within each neuronal system of those sites that have conditioned excitability.

1.2 Neuronal Diversity

In the real world of neural networks, the neurons do not all perform exactly the same function or in exactly the same way (see Section 1.1.14). In fact, the functions of sensory neurons (compare optical and auditory sensors) and neural networks (compare visual and auditory neural networks) are quite diverse. This diversity adds to the complexity of the neural network. Whereas all neurons contain the same set of genes, individual neurons activate only a small subset of them; selective gene activation has been found in different neurons. Nevertheless, all neural networks exhibit certain properties, namely:

1. Many parallel connections exist between many neurons.
2. Many of the parallel connections provide feedback mechanisms to other neurons and to themselves.
3. Some neurons may excite other neurons while inhibiting the operation of still others.
4. Some parts of the network may be prewired, whereas other parts may be evolving or under development.
5. The output is not necessarily yes–no or (10), that is, of a binary nature.
6. Neural networks are asynchronous in operation.
7. Neural networks have a gross and slow synchronizing mechanism, as slow as the heartbeat, that supports their vital functions.

8. Neural networks execute a program that is fully distributed and not sequentially executed.

9. Neural networks do not have a central processor, but processing is distributed.

Biological neural networks are characterized by a hierarchical architecture. Lower-level networks preprocess raw information and pass their outcome to higher levels for higher-level processing.

The incredible functionality and the ability to process vast amounts of information have puzzled many from antiquity to modern times. Plato (427–347 B.C.), Aristotle (384–322 B.C.), Ramon y Cajal, Colgi, others in the nineteenth century, and many thousands in the twentieth century have searched for an answer. The following fundamental questions are often asked:

• How is the human neural network, the brain, designed?

• How does the brain process information?

• With what "algorithms" and "arithmetic" does the brain "calculate"?

• How can the brain imagine?

• How can the brain invent?

• What is "thought"?

• What are "feelings"?

From extensive research in biology, biochemistry, brain anatomy, behavioral and cognitive sciences, psychology, and other fields, we know that biological neural networks have the ability to learn from new information, to classify, store, recall, cross-reference, interpolate and extrapolate, to adapt network parameters, and to perform network maintenance. Research continues on all fronts.

Under certain circumstances, memories are brought back so strongly that we can almost "feel"; these *virtual senses* become mental reality for a short time. A few years ago during an operation on a human brain, part of the brain was electrically stimulated. After recovery, the patient told the doctors that during the operation he vividly remembered some pleasant events from the past; in fact, he almost relived these events. The doctors attributed this experience to the stimulation of the brain, which brought back memories so intensively that pleasure centers may have been activated, thus emulating the feeling of reality.

In summary, during the learning phases (i.e., input via senses), patterns are formed, stored, and associated (and experience is gained). Memories are linked and associated ("associative memories"). When a pattern is invoked, it triggers (recalls) other patterns, which then trigger others, so that a cascade of memories (recalled patterns) occurs.

1.3 Specifications of the Brain

Researchers estimate that there are 100 billion neurons in the human cerebral cortex. Each neuron may have as many as 1000 dendrites and, hence, 100,000 billion synapses (Table 1-2). Since each neuron can fire about 100 times per second, the brain can thus possibly execute 10,000 trillion synaptic activities per second. This number is even more impressive when we

Table 1-2. Data Sheet of Human Cortical Tissue (numbers are approximate)

Number of neurons	100 billion
Number of synapses/neuron	1000
Total number of synapses	100,000 billion
Operations/s/neuron	100
Total number of operations	10,000 trillion/s
Neuronal density	$40,000/\text{mm}^3$
Human brain volume	300 cm^3
Human brain weight	1.5 kg
Dendritic length of a neuron	1 cm
Duration of action potential	3 ms
Firing length of an axon	10 cm
Velocity of axon potential	3000 cm/s (108 km/h)
Resting potential across membrane	65 to -85 mV
Resistance of neuron's cytoplasm	1 k to 10 kΩ
Sodium pump size	6 to 8 nm
Sodium pump density	$200/\mu\text{m}^2$
Membrane thickness	5 to 50 Å
Membrane's breakdown voltage	10,000 V/cm
SiO_2 breakdown voltage	10,000 V/cm
Power dissipation per neuron	25×10^{-10} W
Power dissipation per binary act	3×10^{-3} erg

realize that the human brain weighs about 3 lb and occupies about 300 cm^3 (about a third of a liter). If we formed a 1-mm-thick layer with the brain, its dimensions would be about 0.6 m by 0.5 m. A fast supercomputer like the Cray C90 with 16 processors can execute at peak theoretical speed about 16 gigaflops (i.e., about 10^9 floating-point operations per second) and the Thinking Machines CM-2, with 16,384 processors, has a peak theoretical speed of 35 gigaflops [20, 21], not even close to the biological computer, the brain. Does this mean that there is no hope to emulate certain functions with an artificial neural computer? On the contrary, with the evolution of technology, certain human functions, such as vision (scene recognition and interpretation), speech (recognition and generation), logical interpretation of situations, and motion control, can possibly be emulated in the near future. Many are either deployed or in experimental stages. This belief is based on many factors: modern technology and materials that lend themselves to integration on the same substrate of optical and electronic components with switching characteristics on the order of terahertz [22] (1000 billion), materials and transistor structures with integration of more than several million transistors per square centimeter, integrated amplifiers with excellent characteristics, circuitry that consumes extremely low power, and materials such as amorphous crystals with new compound crystalline structures and molecular processors integrated on films (**biochips**) that may revolutionize the electronics and computer industry in the future.

1.4   The Eye's Neural Network

The eye is the visual window of the brain. It is an optical instrument marvel and an amazing bioelectrochemical computer. Light enters the eye and focuses on the **retina** [23, 24, 25] (Figure 1-8), and an amazing process then begins. The optical structure of the eye is similar to a fully automatic camera that has a lens focusing on a photographic film. The camera's lens, diaphragm, and film directly correspond to the eye's lens, iris, and retina.

1.4.1   Retina Structure

The retina consists of a dense matrix of photoreceptors of which there are two distinct types, according to their shape: **rods** and **cones**. From electron microphotographs, we can see that the rods are tubular and larger than the cones. The function of the rods and cones is highly specialized in

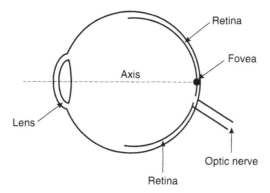

Figure 1-8 Simplified cross section of the eye.

responsiveness and sensitivity. Rods are about 100 times more sensitive to light than cones, but cones are about four times faster in response to light than rods. Rod cells form black-and-white images in dim light, and cones mediate color vision [26, 27]. Rods are activated by very few **photons** and thus mediate vision in dim light; cones sense color, are richer in spatial and temporal detail, and need many photons to be activated. Consequently, cones mediate color vision in ordinary light. As a result, we can see colors better in daylight than in dim light.

There is a high concentration of cones in the **fovea**, that part of the retina on the visual axis of the lens, and it is thus the area of highest resolution. The fovea, only 1.5 mm in diameter, contains about 2000 cones. Away from the fovea the concentration of cones decreases and the concentration of rods increases. The most sensitive light receptors are 20 degrees from the fovea. The total of rods and cones is estimated to be 130 million, about six percent of which are cones.

Photoreceptors (rods or cones) convert light to electrical signals. These signals are preprocessed by other retinal neurons that extract high-level information from the image on the retina. This information is transmitted to the brain by the **optic nerve** for further processing.

1.4.2   Rods and Cones

Conversion from light energy to electrochemical energy in the photo-receptors is a highly complex, perplexing process. Rods are narrow tubes that consist of an orderly pile of approximately 2000 microminiature disks placed flat, one on top of the other (Figure 1-9). This pile is covered by a separate surface membrane. The disks and outer membrane are made

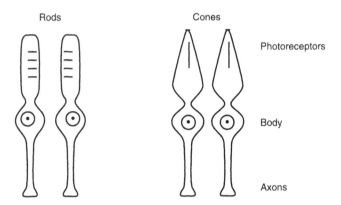

Rods   Cones

Photoreceptors

Body

Axons

Figure 1-9 Rods and cones.

of the same type of bilayer membrane; the outer membrane, however, has a different protein consistency and response to the reception of light than does the disk membrane. The disk membrane contains most of the protein molecules that absorb light and initiate the excitation response. The outer membrane responds to a chemical signal with an electrical one.

In cones, the membrane consists of one continuous and elaborately folded sheet that serves as both the photosensitive membrane, similar to the disks of a rod, and the surface membrane. The human retina has three kinds of cones. Each contains a pigment that absorbs strongly in the short (blue), middle (green), or long (red) wavelength of the visible spectrum. This difference in color absorption of the three cone pigments provides the basis for color vision. Color television capitalizes on this fact, and the sensation of many colors is created by synthesis of these three fundamental colors.

1.4.3 From Photons to Electrons: A Photochemical Chain Reaction

Proteins are key ingredients for the response of rods and cones. In the absence of light, there is high concentration of cyclic guanosine monophosphate (cGMP), a chemical transmitter that binds to the pores of the surface membrane and keeps them open, allowing sodium to enter. To maintain the ionic equilibrium, the membrane continually pumps the sodium ions out. Rods contain the reddish protein **rhodopsin**[*] in disks that absorb photons singly and contribute to the initial response of a chain of events that un-

---

[*] Rhodopsin turns the retina or salt ponds purple. It may play a key role in tomorrow's biochips and biocomputers (see Section 1.1.11).

derlies vision. Rhodopsin has two components, **11-*cis*-retinal** and **opsin**. An organic molecule derived from vitamin A, 11-*cis*-retinal, (11-*cis*) is isomerized when light falls on it (i.e., it changes shape but retains the same number of atoms). Opsin is a protein that can act as an enzyme in the presence of the isomerized 11-*cis*. When light falls on a rod, it is absorbed by its rhodopsin in a disk, and the 11-*cis* is isomerized. The isomerized 11-*cis* triggers the enzymatic activity of the opsin. Then the active opsin catalytically activates many molecules of the protein **transducin** [28]. The activated transducin molecules in turn activate the enzyme **phosphodiesterase**, which cleaves cGMP by inserting a water molecule into it. This process is known as **hydrolysis**. Each enzyme molecule can cleave several thousand cGMPs, which now are not capable of keeping the membrane pores open. Thus, many pores close and the concentration of cGMP drops, reducing the permeability of the membrane and thus the influx of sodium. This causes the negative polarization of the cell interior to increase—the cell is **hyperpolarized**—and the generated action potential to travel down to the axonic endings. Thus, this chemical reaction behaves like a **chemical photomultiplier**. Subsequent to this a restoration process begins: the cGMP is restored and attached to the membrane pores, which reopen, and the transducin and rhodopsin are deactivated so that the cycle may repeat.

Each rod contains about 100 million rhodopsin molecules. One photon is capable of activating one rhodopsin molecule, which eventually triggers an action potential. Obviously, the more photons absorbed, the stronger the action potential. Because of their photomultiplier effect, rods are so sensitive to light that under normal conditions the human eye can see a lighted candle at a distance of 27 km [29]. The light energy reaching the photoreceptors is integrated in the first 0.1 s and not thereafter [30]. That is, a light stimulus lasting 0.01 s has the same effect with a stimulus that lasts 0.0001 s but is 100 times stronger. On the other hand, if it has the same strength, then the faster stimulus will be noticed less. This temporal response of the rods and cones explains how magicians can deceive the human eye by acting fast, how we can see the movement of a clock's second hand but not its hour hand, and how we perceive continuous motion in cinematography and television.

1.4.4   Organization and Communication of the Retina Neural Network

The complex structure of the retina consists of cells arranged in layers of differently specialized neurons with numerous interconnections between them. The eye's rods and cones convert photonic signals into electrochemical ones, as described earlier. Other neurons in the retina are the **bipolar**, the **horizontal**, the **amacrine**, and the **ganglions** (Figure 1-10).

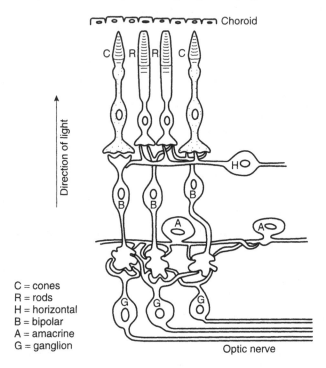

C = cones
R = rods
H = horizontal
B = bipolar
A = amacrine
G = ganglion

Figure 1-10 Neurons in the retina.

Rods and cones synapse with bipolar neurons, which in turn synapse with ganglion neurons. The axons of the ganglions form the **optic nerve**. Although there are 120 million rods and 7 million cones, there are only 1 million ganglions and optic-nerve fibers. In the central fovea region there is a one-to-one connection between cones, bipolars, and ganglions, whereas in other regions of the retina many rods and cones synapse with one bipolar. The one-to-one connection explains the superb resolution of the fine features of a scene.

Horizontal neurons connect rods and cones with bipolars. They are inhibitory in function and provide feedback from one receptor to another, adjusting their response so that the retina can deal with the dynamic range of light intensities that far exceed the dynamic range of individual neurons. Remarkably, vision responds to both sunlight and starlight, a range of 10 billion.

The ganglion neurons have special functions. They are "wired" with other neurons such that different ganglions convey different elemental features from a scene. Direction-selective ganglions transmit a maximum signal when movement is in a preferred direction, no signal when movement is opposite to the preferred direction, and a weak signal if the direction is in between.

Amacrine neurons are inhibitory, connect bipolars with ganglions, and regulate ganglion behavior with transient response to stimulation by light. When light strikes photoreceptors, the amacrine cells fire a burst of action potential, but they cease firing under continued light stimulation. In certain species amacrine-to-amacrine chains contribute to the more complex data processing operations in the retina. The four best-known amacrine neurons are **cholinergic** or **acetylcholine** (their name comes from their chemical neurotransmitter), **AII, dopaminergic**, and **indoleamine accumulating**.

Cholinergic neurons are numerous, and their branching dendrites form an almost uninterrupted mesh, particularly in the peripheral retina. They excite certain ganglions, among them the direction-selective ones. AII amacrine neurons are small, their dendrites are sparser but numerous, and they cover the entire surface of the retina. They connect rod-activated bipolars with ganglions to function under both bright- and dim-light conditions, and they transmit a transient response to ganglions, sharpening their response to light changes. The flow of information here is from rod to bipolar to AII to ganglion. Dopaminergic neurons are very sparse, with longer dendrites that form a loose mesh. These neurons synapse only with other amacrine neurons. Although their exact function is not known, it is possible that they calculate the average activity of other amacrine neurons over the entire retina, thus making second-order adjustments to transient light and light intensity responses. Indoleamine-accumulating neurons are part of the dense plexus lining the inner part of the inner synaptic layer. These neurons make a characteristic synapse, called a **reciprocal** synapse, from dendrite to dendrite, that allows for information flow from one amacrine to another in either direction. Their function is not well understood.

1.4.5   Image Preprocessing in the Retina

Let us recapture the information processing that takes place in retinal neurons. When the photoreceptors are excited, their information is transmitted to one or more bipolars and to horizontal neurons. The horizontals receive signals from a group of photoreceptors and, depending on received signal strength and their functionality, make adjustments to the responsivity of the bipolars. The bipolars receive signals from one or more photoreceptors and from the horizontal neurons. When all conditions are satisfied, based on their functionality, they transmit their signal to one or more ganglions and to the amacrine neurons. The ganglions receive signals from one or more bipolars and from the amacrine neurons, and if all conditions are met, they transmit their electrical signal down their axons, which make up the optic nerve (Figure 1-11).

Thus, an amazing preprocessing of the image takes place right at the retina level where "prewired" neural networks recognize bits of information, or elemental features, and generate signals. The results of this "preprocessed picture" are then transmitted via the optic nerve to the inner brain where they are further processed [31, 32].

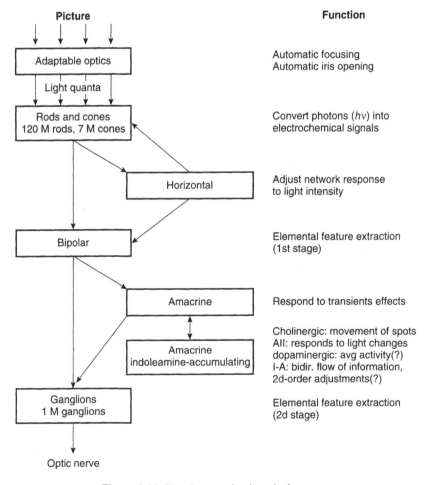

Figure 1-11 Signal processing in retinal neurons.

A substantial effort has been made to understand these elemental features. Experiments have shown that certain retinal neuron circuits respond to dots of light, yet others respond to lines, bands of light, corners, circles, and so on. Another group of retinal circuits responds to motion. Some respond to motion in one direction or another but not in both directions, or to a specific direction and not to any direction [33, 34, 35] and so on. Artificial neural networks mimic this process of feature extraction in handwritten numeric character [36] recognition, visual pattern recognition [37], and speech recognition [38].

1.4.6   Visual Pathways

Most of the optic-nerve fibers derived from the ganglions terminate in the **lateral geniculate nucleus** (LGN) in the brain (Figure 1-12).

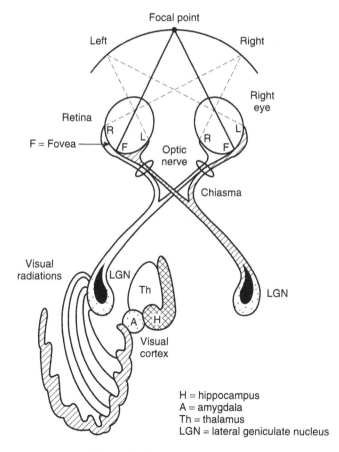

Figure 1-12 Neural net for vision.

The LGN neurons project their axons directly to the **primary visual cortex** via the **optic radiations** region [39, 40]. From there, after several synapses, the messages are sent to destinations adjacent to the cortical areas and other targets deep in the brain. One target area even projects back to the LGN, establishing a feedback path.

Each side of the brain has its own LGN and visual cortex. The optic nerve from the left eye and that from the right eye cross in front of the LGNs at the optic **chiasm**. At the chiasm, part of the left optic nerve is directed to the right side of the brain and the other part to the left side of the brain, and similarly for the right optic nerve. As a result of the optic chiasm, the LGN and the visual cortex on the left side are connected to the two left-half retinas of both eyes and are therefore concerned with the right half of the visual scene; the converse is true for the right LGN and visual cortex.

The pathways terminate in the brain's **limbic system**, which contains the **hippocampus** and the **amygdala**, which have important roles in the memory—in fact, they appear to be the crossroads of memories. Memories from the present and the past and from various sensory inputs meet and associate there, leading to the development of emotions and, perhaps, invention. The amygdala and the hippocampus seem to be coequal concerning memory, especially recognition.

The LGN contains two types of **opponent** neurons, **nonopponent** and **spectrally opponent**. Nonopponent neurons process light intensity information. Spectrally opponent neurons process color information.

The visual cortex registers a systematic map of the visual field so that each small region of the field activates a distinct cluster of neurons that is organized to respond to specific stimuli. There are four types of neurons here. **Simple** neurons respond to bars of light, dark bars or straight-line edges in certain orientations and in a particular part of the visual field. **Complex** neurons respond like simple neurons but independently of the position of lines in the visual field. They also respond to select directions of movement. **Hypercomplex** neurons respond to the stimuli of lines of certain length and orientation. **Superhypercomplex** neurons respond to edges of certain width that move across the visual field, and some respond to corners. The visual cortex is organized into columns where neurons in a given column have similar receptive fields. Thus, one column might respond to vertical lines, another to motion to the right, and so on.

The pathway extends into the **inferior temporal cortex**. Distinct cortical stations are connected in various sequences along the pathway. Neurons here respond to more complex shapes. Each neuron receives data from large segments of the visual world and responds to progressively more complex physical properties such as size, shape, color, and texture until, in the final station, the neurons synthesize a complete representation of the object.

Thus, one concludes with a high degree of confidence that the visual system seems to have a pyramidal hierarchical structure whereby an elemental set of features is extracted first, and from this more complex patterns are extracted, and so on. They are then combined with color information, movement, and their direction and their relative spatial relationship and are finally stored and associated with other features.

1.5   Areas for Further Investigation

1. When the action potential arrives at the axonic ending, determine all mechanisms that dissipate the arriving electrical energy, as in transmission lines. [*Hint:* Some of the energy is dissipated to open the calcium channels, some to move the vesicles closer to the membrane, and some may aid in the production of more neurotransmitters.]

2. Does the axon conduct in one direction only? Is part of the signal used in a feedback mechanism either by back-propagation or by causing a back-propagating molecular reaction? [*Hint:* The hypothesis that a message is sent back to the soma and to the membrane proteins to adjust synaptic weights and threshold may corroborate with Hebbian "learning" and "programming" of the neuron (see also Section 2.4.7).]

3. (a) What are the selection criteria and selection mechanisms in neurons with more than one type of neurotransmitter? (b) Upon arrival of the action potential at the axonic endings, is one neurotransmitter released or are more released in a combination of different proportions? (c) Upon arrival of the action potential at the axonic ending, what determines which neurotransmitter will be released (if more than one) and in what proportions? [*Hint:* Although not experimentally established, let us take a closer look at these questions: The intensity of a stimulus as it arrives at the synapse is coded (in many neurons) in a train of impulses. The frequency of impulses varies from few to hundreds per second. In addition, the number of impulses in the train varies, but all have the same amplitude: the larger the stimulus, the faster the rate of impulses. It may be reasonable to assume that the frequency and amplitude of the arriving signal contribute to the selection of the neurotransmitter and/or the quantity to be released. One may thus test for a hypothesis that I call the "neurotransmitter reso-

nant or tuning fork." Think of the presynapsis as the receiving antenna and the neurotransmitters as tuning forks (or tuned oscillators), each tuned to a different frequency. Then, depending on the arriving frequency, one or more neurotransmitters will directly or indirectly be excited and at different proportions, depending on how close to the frequency they are tuned. In addition, the amplitude of the arriving signal may excite the tuning forks—the neurotransmitters—at different levels. Thus the arriving signal frequency and amplitude may provide answers to the stated questions. The assumption is in alignment with another experimental finding: a neuron that fires rapidly releases more neurotransmitter molecules than a neuron that fires less rapidly. The more neurotransmitter molecules, the more channels open at the postsynaptic membrane, and, therefore, the larger the postsynaptic potential is at the contact.]

4. What is the role of the axonic neurofilaments, or neurofibrils, in the propagation of the signal from the soma and down the axon to the presynapsis of a neuron? [Hint: The axon consists of many filaments that are much smaller than existing probes. Electrical probes used in the lab have a diameter of 0.5 μm. A typical presynapsis is 0.1 to 5 μm. Due to technology limitations, however, it is almost impossible to single out and probe axonic filaments. Are the filaments part of the transmission mechanism, or do they serve as the mechanical structural skeleton of the axon only?]

5. Consider the hypothesis of the electrochemical seeking radar. When action potential is fired, identify the type of the neurotransmitter of a developing neuron and the type of molecular cues released by the target neuron. In addition, what is the time lapsed between the release of the neurotransmitter and the molecular cues? What happens if the molecular cues are altered? Does the developing neuron change path?

6. What happens to all the calcium that enters the presynaptic terminal during the firing process? Obviously it cannot stay there or else there would be an enormous accumulation of calcium over time. [Hint: It is reasonable to assume that there is a calcium pump mechanism at the presynaptic membrane, similar to the sodium pump. That is, there should be a protein with the assignment to capture calcium and abort it from the cell. Which protein is it? What are the dependencies of this protein? How is this protein manufactured? How is the operation of a neuron affected if there is some excess accumulation of calcium in the presynapsis due to malfunctioning of the hypothetical "calcium pump"?]

1.6 Review Questions

1.1. What is the basic building block of the nervous system?

1.2. What are the basic parts of a neuron?

1.3. What is the basic element of the membrane and how is the membrane constructed?

1.4. What is a synapse? Describe the three major parts of it.

1.5. Name two types of synapses.

1.6. When the action potential reaches the synaptic ending, what happens?

1.7. Briefly describe how the action potential is generated.

1.8. Name five membrane proteins.

1.9. Is it true that when the neuron is at rest the voltage across the membrane is zero?

1.10. When the neuron is at rest, what can you say about the concentration of sodium and potassium inside and outside the neuron?

1.11. Is it true that all neurons provide the same functionality?

1.12. Which neurons of the eye are responsible for vision in color and which for vision in gray?

1.13. What is the optic nerve?

1.14. Is it true that visual information is converted to bits (or pixels) that are transmitted from the eye to the brain, as in television? If not, then what happens?

1.15. Is it true that both rods and cones are equally sensitive to light? If not, which one is more sensitive?

1.16. Where in the retina are the cones in higher concentration?

1.17. If cones were not present in the retina, how would a color picture be perceived?

1.18. Name some of the neurons that make up the neural network of the retina.

1.19. What kind of signal preprocessing takes place at the retina?

1.20. How can the eye be adjusted to large differences in light intensity?

For answers, see page 185.

REFERENCES

[1] J. C. Eccles, *The Understanding of the Brain*, McGraw-Hill, New York, 1977.

[2] J. G. Nicholls, A. R. Martin, and B. G. Wallace, *From Neuron to Brain*, 3rd ed., Sinauer Associates, Inc., Publishers, Sunderland, Mass., 1992.

[3] J.-P. Changeux, "Chemical Signals in the Brain," *Sci. Am.*, vol. 269, no. 5, pp. 58–62, 1993.

[4] D. L. Alkon and H. Rasmussen, "A Spatial-Temporal Model of Cell Activation," *Science*, vol. 239, no. 4843, pp. 998–1005, 1988.

[5] P. C. Hinkle and R. E. McCarty, "How Cells Make ATP," *Sci. Am.*, vol. 238, no. 3, pp. 104–123, 1978.

[6] M. Karplus and J. A. McCammon, "The Dynamics of Proteins," *Sci. Am.*, vol. 254, no. 4, pp. 42–51, 1986.

[7] M. Radman and R. Wagner, "The High Fidelity of DNA Duplication," *Sci. Am.*, vol. 259, no. 2, pp. 40–46, 1988.

[8] R. D. Keynes, "Ion Channels in the Nerve-Cell Membrane," *Sci. Am.*, vol. 240, no. 3, pp. 126–136, 1979.

[9] G. E. Hinton, "How Neural Networks Learn from Experience," *Sci. Am.*, vol. 261, no. 9, pp. 144–151, 1992.

[10] M. Conrad, "The Lure of Molecular Computing," *IEEE Spectrum*, pp. 55–60, Oct. 1986.

[11] *Proc. of the Bioelectronic and Molecular Electronic Devices*, Tokyo, Nov. 1985.

[12] F. Carter, ed., *Molecular Electronic Devices*, M. Decker, New York, 1982.

[13] F. S. Ligler, *Fiber Optic Based Biosensor*, Report N92-22458, American Institute of Aeronautics and Astronautics, 1992.

[14] J. W. Yu et al., "Bacteriorhodopsin Film for Processing SAR Signals," *NASA Tech. Briefs*, p. 63, July 1992.

[15] R. Levi-Montalcini and P. Calissano, "The Nerve-Growth Factor," *Sci. Am.*, vol. 240, no. 6, pp. 68–77, 1979.

[16] C. J. Shatz, "The Developing Brain," *Sci. Am.*, vol. 261, no. 9, pp. 61–67, 1992.

[17] D. L. Alkon, "Memory Storage and Neural Systems," *Sci. Am.*, vol. 258, pp. 42–50, 1989.

[18] M. Mishkin and T. Appenzeller, "The Anatomy of Memory," *Sci. Am.*, vol. 256, no. 6, pp. 80–89, 1987.

[19] R. Kandell and R. D. Hawkins, "The Biological Individuality," *Sci. Am.*, vol. 261, no. 9, pp. 78–83, 1992.

[20] G. Cybenko and D. J. Kock, "Revolution or Evolution?" *IEEE Spectrum*, pp. 39–41, Sept. 1992.

[21] O. M. Lubeck et al., *The Performance Realities of Massively Parallel Processors: A Case Study*, Report LA-UR-92-1463, Los Alamos National Laboratory, June 19, 1992.

[22] *Future Electron Devices Jour.*, vol. 2, supplement, p. 53, 1992.

[23] A. I. Cohen, "The Retina and Optic Nerve," in *Adler's Physiology of the Eye: Clinical Applications*, 6th ed., E. Moses, ed., Mosby, St. Louis, 1975.

[24] T. L. Bennett, *Introduction to Physiological Psychology*, Brooks/Cole Publishing, Monterey, Calif., 1982.

[25] R. H. Masland, "The Functional Architecture of the Retina," *Sci. Am.*, vol. 255, no. 6, pp. 102–111, 1986.

[26] C. A. Podgham and J. E. Saunders, *The Perception of Light and Color*, Academic Press, New York, 1975.

[27] J. L. Schnapf and D. A. Baylor, "How Photoreceptor Cells Respond to Light," *Sci. Am.*, vol. 256, no. 4, pp. 40–47, 1987.

[28] L. Stryer, "Cyclic GMP Cascade of Vision," *Ann. Rev. Neurosci.*, vol. 9, pp. 87–119, 1986.

[29] M. H. Pirenne, "Absolute Visual Thresholds," *Jour. Physiol. (London)*, vol. 123, p. 409, 1953.

[30] S. Hecht et al., "Energy, Quanta and Vision," *Jour. Gen. Physiol.*, vol. 25, p. 819, 1942.

[31] T. Sato, T. Kawamura, and E. Iwai, "Responsiveness of Inferotemporal Single Units to Visual Pattern Stimuli in Monkeys Performing Discrimination," *Experimental Brain Res.*, vol. 38, no. 3, pp. 313–319, 1980.

[32] C. Bruce, R. Desimone, and C. G. Gross, "Visual Properties of Neurons in a Polysensory Area in Superior Temporal Sulcus of the Macaque," *Jour. Neurophysiol.*, vol. 46, no. 2, pp. 369–384, 1981.

[33] T. Poggio and Ch. Koch, "Synapses That Compute Motion," *Sci. Am.*, vol. 256, no. 5, pp. 46–52, 1987.

[34] S. V. Kartalopoulos, "Signal Processing and Implementation of Motion Detection Neurons in Optical Pathways," in Proceedings of Globecom'90 Conference, San Diego, Dec. 2–5, 1990.

[35] M. Bongard, *Pattern Recognition*, Spartan Books, New York, 1970.

[36] L. D. Jackel et al., "An Application of Neural Net Chips: Handwritten Digit Recognition," *Proc. ICNN*, San Diego, pp. II-107–II-115, 1988.

[37] K. Fukusima, "A Neural Network Model for Selective Attention in Visual Pattern Recognition," *Biol. Cybernetics*, vol. 55, no. 1, pp. 5–15, 1986.

[38] T. Matsuoka, H. Hamada, and R. Nakatsu, "Syllable Recognition Using Integrated Neural Networks," in Proceedings of IJCNN, Washington, D.C., pp. 251–258, June 18–23, 1989.

[39] H. J. A. Dartnall, ed., *Photochemistry of Vision*, Springer-Verlag, New York, 1972.

[40] H. Darson, ed., *The Eye*, 2d, Academic Press, New York, 1977.

2

ARTIFICIAL NEURAL
NETWORKS: CONCEPTS

2.1 Neural Attributes

In this section we describe the fundamental principles by which neural networks may be mathematically described. These principles emanate from the biological world, and mathematics attempts to describe closely the biological behavior of neurons and their networks.

The basic attributes of neural networks may be divided into the *architecture* and the functional properties or *neurodynamics*. **Architecture** defines the network structure, that is, the number of artificial neurons in the network and their interconnectivity. Neural networks consist of many interconnected neurons, or **processing elements**, with familiar characteristics, such as inputs, synaptic strengths, activation, outputs, and bias. The **neurodynamics** of neural networks defines their properties, that is, how the neural network *learns, recalls, associates*, and continuously *compares* new information with existing knowledge, how it *classifies* new information, and how it develops new classifications if necessary.

Neural networks *process* information but *not with a sequential algorithm*. This process is based on **parallel decomposition** of complex information into basic elements. As composite color can be decomposed into fundamental wavelengths (or frequencies) and amplitudes, then at any time, theoretically speaking, an exact color may be reconstructed. Similarly, a neural network decomposes complex information into its fundamental elements, and these elements and their relationship to each other are stored in the brain's memory banks. For example, when you look at a picture, the brain does not store in its memory a matrix of pixels similar to a scanned version of a picture like a video recorder does, but instead it stores the

elemental features of the picture, such as lines, dots, shapes, colors, and their spatial relationships.

2.1.1   Artificial Neural Networks

Over the past few decades a serious attempt has been made to design electronic circuits that closely resemble biological neural networks and their attributes. Model networks, known as **paradigms** (Greek: something that closely assimilates something else—a typical example or archetype), have been developed and implemented. Some paradigms closely resemble biological neural networks whereas others do not, reflecting the two schools of thought on the matter.

2.1.2   Same Mathematics Again!

All artificial models (paradigms) are described with traditional differential or, in discrete form, difference equations. Even the most sophisticated paradigms, far inferior to the most primitive life, have been designed either to demonstrate certain principles or for limited and specialized applications. Artificial neural networks are serious attempts to understand further how the biological neural network, particularly the brain, works. As we build on this understanding, the human genius will find better paradigms and many applications to better our lives.

Paradoxically, mathematics is quite suitable for a sequential machine, but neural networks *do not* operate sequentially: they do not know equations, series, integrals, and man-made algorithms. Then how can we use traditional math to describe how neural networks work? What kind of math is the neural network using? In other words [1], over what kinds of informational channels and nodes are computations in the brain carried out? We don't exactly know. This cannot stop progress, however, and since the computer is one of the best tools available today, we have to keep going forward and always be searching for the answer to these questions.

To demonstrate the flaws of our math and tools, use a computer to divide 100 by 3 *exactly*. You obtain $33.333333 + \epsilon$, where ϵ is a very small number not exactly known. Now, if our math tools were exact, we should be able to add the resulting numbers and reconstruct 100. However, $33.333333 + 33.333333 + 33.333333 + 3\epsilon$ is not equal to 100 because ϵ is not known exactly. On the other hand, we can cut a string 100 cm long into three exactly equal pieces by simply folding the string into exactly three equal parts. Hence, using our brain, we have done something that the most accurate computer cannot do.

2.2   Modeling

Serious efforts to create a model of a neuron have been underway during the last 100 years, and remarkable progress has been made [2]. To develop an artificial neural network (ANN), one develops a mathematical model that best describes the biological system's functionality. A computer can then simulate the model fairly quickly, and some degree of confidence may be gained with regard to its operation and functionality. Changes may then be made to the model either to enhance its performance or to simplify it. To create a model that emulates a biological system, however, one must first study and understand that system in every detail. Mathematics is a human invention to describe nature's phenomena. Modeling is our expression to approximate nature's creations. Nature preceded mathematics. Hence, if your mathematical model fails, look for faults in the model, not in nature.

Visual information processing (see Chapter 1) is one of the most complex processes in the brain, and therefore the organization of the optical pathway has influenced neural network models. It has been established that visual information (e.g., picture or scene analysis) is processed in stages. Simple forms, such as edge orientation and contrast, are analyzed in the early stages, and more complex features are analyzed in later stages of the optical pathway (between the eye and the inner parts of the brain). Motion and color are also analyzed during picture analysis. This hierarchical picture processing has led to layered organized models, and the parallel processing of a picture has led to massive parallel processing models.

In the next chapter certain key paradigms are described in a chronological order of development, wherever possible, so that their evolution is also demonstrated. Here, the terms *model* and *paradigm* are used equivalently and interchangeably.

2.3   Basic Model of a Neuron

We now look into the fundamental unit or building block of the artificial neural network, the neuron (or processing element) itself. The processing element is also called an *artificial neuron*; this term, however, is used here only with the understanding that it does not, even closely, describe the biological neuron.

The general neuron has a set of n **inputs** x_j, where the subscript j takes values from 1 to n and indicates the source of the input signal. Each input x_j

is **weighted** before reaching the main body of the processing element by the **connection strength** or the weight factor w_j (i.e., x_j is multiplied by w_j). In addition, it has a **bias** term w_0, a threshold value Θ that has to be reached or exceeded for the neuron to produce a signal, a nonlinearity function F that acts on the produced signal (or **activation**) R, and an **output** O after the nonlinearity function: O constitutes input to other neurons. When the neuron is part of a network of many neurons, it is referred to as a **node**. For m nodes in a network, an additional subscript, i, is needed to distinguish a single neuron. Inputs, weights, activation signals, output, threshold, and nonlinear function are written as x_{ij}, w_{ij}, R_i, O_i, Θ_i, F_i, respectively. The basic model of a neuron is illustrated in Figure 2-1. Figure 2-2 attempts to compare the artificial model with the biological neuron [3].

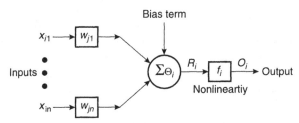

Figure 2-1 Basic neuron model.

The transfer function of the basic model is described by the relation

$$O_i = Fi \left(\sum_{j=1}^{n} w_{ij} x_{ij} \right), \qquad (2.1)$$

and the neuron's firing condition is

$$\sum_{j=1}^{n} w_{ij} x_{ij} \geq \Theta_i, \qquad (2.2)$$

where the index i represents the neuron in question and j represents the inputs from other neurons. Figure 2-3 illustrates the workings of a neuron.

The purpose of the nonlinearity function is to ensure that the neuron's response is bounded—that is, the actual response of the neuron is conditioned, or damped, as a result of large or small activating stimuli and thus is controllable. In the biological world, conditioning of stimuli is continuously done by all sensory inputs. For example, it is well known that to perceive a sound as twice as loud, an actual increase in sound amplitude of about 10 times must take place; hence, the almost logarithmic response of the ear. Biological neurons condition their output response in a similar

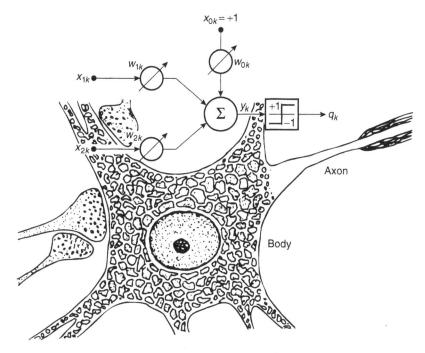

Figure 2-2 Basic neuron model.

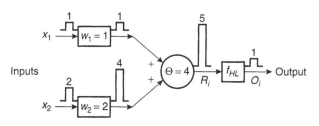

Figure 2-3 Workings of a neuron.

manner, so this concept is consistent with the biological neuron. But the nonlinearity function used in many paradigms is not necessarily a close replica of the biological one; often it is merely used for mathematical convenience. Thus, different nonlinearity functions are used, depending on the paradigm and the algorithm used. Some nonlinearities used are depicted pictorially in Figure 2-4.

The two most popular nonlinearities are the **hard limiter** and the **sigmoid** (each is described in more detail in Chapter 4). The nonlinearities depicted in Figure 2-4 are all bounded—they have an upper and/or lower

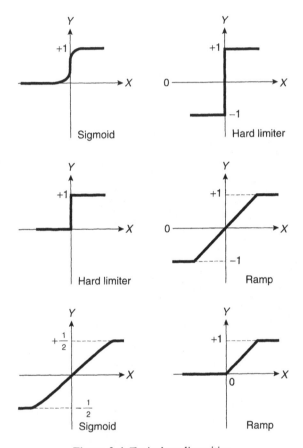

Figure 2-4 Typical nonlinearities.

limit such as ±1, $\pm\frac{1}{2}$. In actual networks the user chooses the value of the bounds. The sigmoid is very popular because it is monotonic, is bounded, and has a simple derivative: $f'(s) = kf(s)[1 - f(s)]$; however, it is nonlinear. The hard limiter, on the other hand, is not monotonic (it has a discontinuity at the origin) and thus is not easily differentiable; however, it is linear within its upper and lower bounds. Hence, as long as the neuron operates within the bounds, the derivative of $f(s)$ is a constant, $f'(s) = k$.

2.4 Learning in Artificial Neural Networks

Learning in neural networks is highly important and is undergoing intense research in both biological and artificial networks. The fundamental questions that behaviorists try to answer are: How do we learn? Which is the most efficient process for learning? How much and how fast can we learn? What are the roadblocks in learning?

Research in learning has been conducted on animals of different intelligence levels, on humans of different ages and intelligence levels, on marine life, and on more primitive life. Learning is not a unique process; there are different learning processes, each suitable to different species. Not all learning processes are equally efficient. Behaviorists will have to determine which is the most suitable and most efficient for a particular species. In artificial neural networks, the concepts of learning processes have been borrowed from the behaviorist's lab and ported in actual electronic circuitry. The neural network engineer selects the most efficient type of learning and integrates it with the most suitable artificial neural network.

Generally speaking, learning is the process by which the neural network adapts itself to a stimulus, and eventually (after making the proper parameter adjustments to itself) it produces a desired response. Learning is also a continuous classification process of input stimuli; when a stimulus appears at the network, the network either recognizes it or it develops a new classification. In actuality, during the process of learning, the network adjusts its parameters, the **synaptic weights**, in response to an input stimulus so that its actual output response converges to the desired output response. When the actual output response is the same as the desired one, the network has completed the learning phase; in other words, it has "acquired knowledge."

The paradigms developed so far consist of artificial neurons; the neurons may be interconnected in different ways, however, and the learning process is not the same for them all. Paradigms observe **learning rules** described by mathematical expressions called **learning equations**. Learning equations describe the learning process for the paradigm, which in actuality is the process for self-adjusting its synaptic weights. As different learning methodologies suit different people, so do different learning techniques suit different artificial neural networks.

2.4.1 Supervised Learning

During the training session of a neural network, an input stimulus is applied that results in an output response. This response is compared with an a priori desired output signal, the **target** response. If the actual response differs from the target response, the neural network generates an **error signal**, which is then used to calculate the adjustment that should be made to the network's synaptic weights so that the actual output matches the target output. In other words, the error is minimized, possibly to zero. The error minimization process requires a special circuit known as a **teacher** or **supervisor**, hence the name **supervised learning**.

The notion of a teacher comes from biological observations. For example, when learning a language, we hear the sound of a word (from a teacher). The sound is stored in the memory banks of our brain, and we try to reproduce the sound. When we hear our own sound, we mentally compare it (actual output) with the stored sound (target sound) and note the error. If the error is large, we try again and again until it becomes significantly small; then we stop.

With artificial neural networks the amount of calculation required to minimize the error depends on the algorithm used; clearly, this is purely a mathematical tool derived from optimization techniques. Such techniques are extensively used in neural network paradigms, and the reader is encouraged to review them. Some parameters to watch are the time required per iteration, the number of iterations per input pattern for the error to reach a minimum during the training session, whether the neural network has reached a global minimum or a local one, and, if a local one, whether the network can escape from it or it remains trapped.

2.4.2   Unsupervised Learning

In contrast to supervised learning, **unsupervised learning** does not require a teacher; that is, there is no target output. During the training session, the neural net receives at its input many different excitations, or input patterns, and it arbitrarily organizes the patterns into categories. When a stimulus is later applied, the neural net provides an output response indicating the class to which the stimulus belongs. If a class cannot be found for the input stimulus, a new class is generated. For example, show a person a set of different objects. Then ask him/her to separate them into groups, or classifications, such that objects in a group have one or more common features that distinguishes them from another group. When this is done, show the same person another object and ask him/her to place the object in one of the groups. If it does not belong to any of the existing groups, a new group may be formed.

Even though unsupervised learning does not require a teacher, it requires guidelines to determine how it will form groups. Grouping may be based on shape, color, or material consistency or on some other property of the object. Hence, if no guidelines have been given as to what type of features should be used for grouping the objects, the grouping may or may not be successful. Similarly, to classify more comprehensive patterns efficiently, neural networks, although unsupervised initially, may need some feature-selecting guidelines. In some experiments the selecting criteria are embedded in the neural network design (i.e., they have been designed to extract certain features based on the type of the input patterns).

2.4.3   Reinforced Learning

Reinforced learning requires one or more neurons at the output layer and a teacher that, unlike supervised learning, does not indicate how close the actual output is to the desired output but whether the actual output is the same with the target output or not. During the learning phase an input stimulus is applied and an output response is obtained (consider one output for simplicity). The teacher does not present the target output to the network, but presents only a "pass/fail" indication. Thus, the error signal generated during the training session is binary: pass or fail.

If the teacher's indication is "bad," the network readjusts its parameters and tries again and again until it gets its output response right. During this process there is no indication if the output response is moving in the right direction or how close to the correct response it is. Hence, the process of correcting synaptic weights follows a different strategy than the supervised learning process.

Some parameters to watch are the following: the time per iteration and the number of iterations per pattern to reach the desired output during the training session, whether the neural network reaches a global or local minimum, and when in a local pattern if it can get out or if it is trapped. When reinforced learning is used as a training technique, certain boundaries should be established so that the trainee should not keep trying to get the correct response ad infinitum.

2.4.4   Competitive Learning

Competitive learning is another form of supervised learning that is distinctive because of its characteristic operation and architecture. In this scheme, several neurons are at the output layer. When an input stimulus is applied, each output neuron competes with the others to produce the closest output signal to the target. This output then becomes the dominant one, and the other outputs cease producing an output signal for that stimulus. For another stimulus, another output neuron becomes the dominant one, and so on. Thus, each output neuron is trained to respond to a different input stimulus. Competitive learning can also be viewed as a *random specialization* process. When an ANN with competitive learning is part of a greater ANN system, then, because of connectivity issues, this random specialization may not always be desirable. In this case, one might try reinforced learning.

Competitive learning is frequently encountered in groups of people where each member of the group was selected and trained to perform specific tasks based on the principle of the right person at the right time at the right place.

2.4.5 The Delta Rule

The Delta rule is based on the idea of continuous adjustments of the value of the weights such that the difference of error (delta) between the desired (or target) output value and the actual output value of a processing element is reduced. This is also known as the Widrow-Hoff learning rule (see the Adaline paradigm in Chapter 4) or as the Least Mean Square (because it minimizes the mean square error).

2.4.6 Gradient Descend Rule

The values of the weights are adjusted by an amount proportional to the first derivative (the gradient) of the error between the desired (or target) output value and the actual output value of a processing element, with respect to the value of the weight. The goal is to decrease (descend) the error function, avoiding local minima and reaching the actual or global minimum (Figure 2-5).

2.4.7 Hebbian Learning

In 1949, Donald Hebb stated that when an axon of cell A is near enough to excite a cell B and repeatedly or persistently takes place in firing it, some growth process or metabolic change takes place in one or both cells such that A's efficiency, as one of the cells firing B, is increased. Thus, the synaptic strength (known as weight w) between cell A and cell B is modified according to the degree of correlated activity between input and output. This type of learning is called **Hebbian learning**, a term encountered frequently in ANNs. **Anti-Hebbian learning** refers to artificial neural networks where the synaptic contacts are inhibitory only.

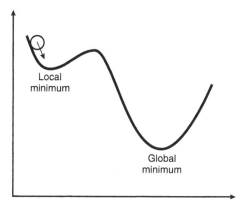

Figure 2-5 Descent to a minimum—will it
reach the global minimum?

2.5   Characteristics of ANNs

Generally speaking, the neural net is an adaptive communication network
that communicates a "cost function" for a desired output. Mathematically
speaking, a neural network represents a dynamic system that can be mod-
eled as a set of coupled differential equations. As we know from feedback
control theory, a system like this depends on the values of the equation
parameters; small changes in parameters may result in stability, instability
(oscillations), or even catastrophic instability (chaos).
   Neuronal networks are characterized by

1. Collective and synergistic computation (or neurocomputing).

   • Program is executed collectively and synergistically.
   • Operations are decentralized.

2. Robustness.

   • Operation is insensitive to scattered failures.
   • Operation is insensitive to partial inputs or inputs with inaccura-
     cies.

3. Learning.

   • Network makes associations automatically.
   • Program is created by the network during learning.

- Network adapts with or without a teacher; no programmer intervention.

4. Asynchronous operation; biological neural nets have no explicit clock to synchronize their operation. A number of ANNs require a clock.

2.6   Important ANN Parameters

The performance of the neural network is described by the figure of merit, which expresses the number of recalled patterns when input patterns are applied that are complete, partially complete, or noisy. A 100% performance in recalled patterns means that for every trained input stimulus signal, the network always produces the desired, or target, output pattern. When designing an artificial neural network, one should be concerned with the following:

1. Network *topology*
2. *Number of layers* in the networks
3. *Number of neurons* or nodes per layer
4. *Learning* algorithm to be adopted (in the supervised case only)
5. *Number of iterations* per pattern during training
6. *Number of calculations per iteration*
7. *Speed to recall* a pattern
8. *Network performance*, as defined earlier
9. *Network plasticity* (i.e., the number of neurons failing and the degree of functionality of the ANN)
10. *Network capacity*, or the maximum pattern signals that the network can recall
11. Degree of *adaptability* of the ANN (i.e., to what extent the ANN is able to adapt itself after training)
12. *Bias* terms (occasionally set a priori to some fixed value, such as +1)
13. *Threshold* terms (occasionally set to some a priori fixed value, such as 0 or 1)

14. *Boundaries* of the synaptic weights (for best performance and noise immunity, boundaries should be determined based on the actual implementation of the ANN)

15. *Choice* of the nonlinearity function and the range of operation of the neuron.

16. *Network noise immunity* (i.e., the degree of corruption of an input stimulus signal or the degree of signal loss (i.e., partial signal) that produces the desired target output pattern)

17. *Steady-state* or final values of the synaptic weights (this is the program of the ANN)

2.7   Artificial Neural Network Topologies

Artificial neural networks comprise many neurons, interconnected in certain ways to cast them into identifiable topologies. Some of the most used topologies are illustrated in Figure 2-6 (circles represent neurons). From the figure one distinguishes single-layer and multilayer networks. Typically, the layer where the input patterns are applied is the **input** layer, the layer where the output is obtained is the **output** layer, and the layers between the input and output layers are the **hidden** layers. There may be one or more hidden layers, which are so named because their outputs are not directly observable.

2.7.1   Modeling ANNs

Modeling neural networks is a human attempt to understand and evaluate nature. Modeling means to develop a set of mathematical expressions that, to some extent, faithfully describes the neuron and the network.

Mathematical analysis of an ANN can tell us the following about a network:

- *Complexity*—how large the ANN can be in order to execute a task

- *Capacity*—how many bits of information can be stored in the ANN

- *Paradigms choice*—which ANN implementation is more suitable for the application

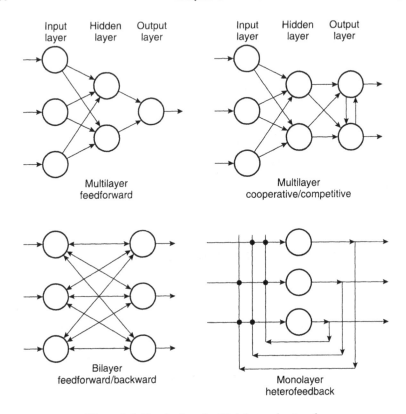

Figure 2-6 Topologies of artificial neural networks.

- *Performance*—which ANN performs best
- *Learning efficiency*—how fast an ANN "learns"
- *Response*—how fast an ANN provides an output from the time a stimulus is present
- *Reliability*—whether the ANN can reach the same desired solution for the same stimulus
- *Noise sensitivity*—how accurately an ANN provides the desired output at the presence of noise
- *Failure sensitivity*—how accurately an ANN associates if it partially fails

2.7.2 ANN Learning and Program

In artificial neural networks the mathematical description of how the connection strengths w_{ij} evolve during the training session constitutes the

learning algorithm. The final, steady-state values of all w_{ij} define the **program** of the ANN.

The types of learning have been borrowed from the biological world. The two major categories of learning in ANNs are the **unsupervised** and the **supervised** [4–6] (see also Section 2.4).

The meaning of *teacher* in supervised learning is an artifact. By teacher is meant that, during learning, there is additional circuitry that compares the desired output with the target output. That is, when the stimulus pattern is applied at the input, the desired output is known a priori. The actual output from the ANN and the desired output are applied at a comparator that produces an error signal. This error is processed according to a learning algorithm and, in an attempt to minimize the error, adjustments on the values of the connection strengths w_{ij} are made. This process requires many iterations until the ultimate minimum error is reached. In terms of the actual circuitry, today's teachers have been implemented in various ways. The most popular teacher is microprocessor based; this is very convenient because, after all, the learning algorithm is an iterative sequential procedure. Figure 2-7 illustrates a simple neural network with a teacher. In the figure,

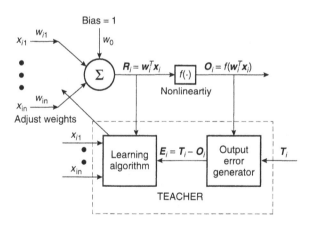

Figure 2-7 Model of a neuron with a teacher.

$w_{ij} = [w_{i1}, w_{i2}, \ldots, w_{in}] =$ weight vector of the inputs of the ith neuron

$x_{ij} = [x_{i1}, x_{i2}, \ldots, x_{in}] =$ input vector of the ith neuron

$R_i = w^T x =$ output of neuron i prior to nonlinearity

$O_i =$ output from neuron i after nonlinearity
     $(O_i = f(\sum_{j=1}^{n} w_{ij} x_{ij}))$

T_i = teacher's training, or target, signal (this, along with the input signal, produces the error or (learning) signal used only during training)

$E_i = T_i - O_i$ = output error used during learning

Δw_{ij} = change of weights during training (when training has been completed, this difference is zero or a minimum).

In general, the change of weights is proportional to a learning signal and to the stimulus at the neuron. Then learning for neuron i can be expressed as

$$\frac{\delta w_{ij}(t)}{\delta t} = \mu E_i(O_i, \ T_i)x_i(t), \tag{2.3}$$

where μ is a small positive constant known as the **learning rate**.

Since weights are computed with a digital computer, Eq. (2.3) is more useful in discrete-time form:

$$w_{ij}(k+1) = w_{ij}(k) + \mu E_i(O_i(k), T_i(k))x_i(k). \tag{2.4}$$

Thus, the rule for learning can be expressed as

$$w_{ij}(k+1) = w_{ij}(k) + \text{correction term}, \tag{2.5}$$

where k is the iteration step number. Learning has been completed when the correction term is zero.

Unsupervised learning, also known as **self-organizing**, does not require a teacher. In subsequent sections we examine ANNs with both supervised and unsupervised learning.

Other learning categories, well known to behavioral psychologists, exist, such as:

- Competitive learning
- Cooperative learning
- Reinforced learning
- Error-correcting learning
- Markovian (stochastic) learning
- Hard-wired system (a priori knowledge)

2.8   Learning Algorithms

A **learning algorithm** is a mathematical tool that outlines the method and speed for an ANN to reach the steady state of its parameters, weights, and thresholds successfully. Typically, one starts with an **error function** (or energy function), which is expressed in terms of thresholds and weights of the neural network. The objective is to reach a minimum error that corresponds to a set of weights. When the error is zero, or conveniently small, the steady state of the network and of the weights is reached. The steady-state weights define the program and the ANN model. Thus, ANN learning is focused on a particular optimization algorithm, suited to the ANN model.

The selection of the error function and the optimization method is important since it may promote stability, instability, or a solution trapped in a local minimum.

During learning, the error function decreases and the weights are updated. The decrease (or descent to stability) may be accomplished with different optimization techniques (optimization techniques are found in abundance in the literature), including the Delta rule, Boltzmann's algorithm, the back-propagation learning algorithm, simulation annealing, and the Markovian technique. In Chapter 4 we will study some of these techniques.

Hebbian learning was introduced in Section 2.4.7. Now we consider unsupervised learning. Hence, the vector T_i does not exist. In addition, considering the bipolar function sgn($\cdot$) as the nonlinearity, then $R_i = O_i$. Starting with initial weights that have small random values around zero, with a learning rate value (positive small), and a known input pattern, we calculate the output from

$$O_i(k) = f\left(\sum_{i=1}^{n} w_{ij}(k)x_{ij}\right), \tag{2.6}$$

where $k = 1, 2, \ldots,$ is the iteration number.

The next updated weights are calculated from

$$\Delta w_i = \mu O_i(k)x_{ij}, \tag{2.7}$$

$$w_i(k+1) = w_i(k) + \mu O_i(k)x_{ij}. \tag{2.8}$$

This process continues until the output signal and/or the weights do not change. Then we continue with the next input pattern, and so on.

2.9 ANN Discrimination Ability

The neural network is trained to recognize pattern signals. In other words, the ANN should be able to discriminate between the applied patterns at its inputs and then produce the desired output response. In several applications an ANN has to identify the applied pattern and the group to which the pattern belongs. For example, suppose that the patterns $(+1+1)$, $(-1+1)$, $(+1-1)$, and $(-1-1)$ have been divided into two groups: one group is $(+1+1)$ and $(-1+1)$ and the other is $(+1-1)$ and $(-1-1)$. Now, let an ANN be trained such that it produces an output response of 1 whenever one of the input patterns $(+1+1)$ or $(-1-1)$ is applied and -1 when one of the other two input patterns $(-1+1)$ or $(+1-1)$ is applied.

Discriminating among four patterns or two groups of patterns may only seem like a trivial problem that can be solved more simply than using an ANN. As the number of patterns and groups increases, however, ANNs may start showing their superiority over conventional techniques, considering the amount of processing required.

The number of patterns with which an ANN is able to discriminate is called its **discriminating ability**. It is measured by the maximum number of points that it can separate, or clearly identify, and to which it can provide a unique response. This ability of ANNs is extensively used in pattern recognition. A rudimentary discrimination test is the simple Exclusive-OR. This test raised Minsky and Papert's criticism on Rosenblatt's initial Perceptron paradigm: it was not able to pass the Exclusive-OR test (later multilayer Perceptrons did, however). The discriminating ability of an ANN, based on its linear or nonlinear characteristics, characterizes the ANN as **linear, multilinear, or nonlinear.**

2.9.1 Linearly Separable ANNs

To describe **linearly separable** ANNs, think of the binary patterns $(+1+1)$, $(-1+1)$, $(+1-1)$, and $(-1-1)$ and an ANN that has to produce either a 1 when one of the input patterns $(-1+1)$, say the O group, is applied or a 0 when one of the patterns $(+1-1)$, $(+1+1)$, or $(-1-1)$, say the X group, is applied. Mapping these four patterns in a two-dimensional x_2, x_1 space, the *input space*, we obtain four symmetrical points around the origin; here the dimension is 2 since the input patterns are two inputs and have two literals; input patterns with three literals (e.g., 011), should be mapped in three-dimensional input space, and so on. Now, a straight line can separate the two-dimensional plane into two half-planes such that each half has one of the two groups (Figure 2-8). A straight line is described by the general equation $y = Ax + B$. For example, the straight line described by the function $x_2 = 1.1x_1 + 0.8$ separates the x_1x_2 plane into two half-planes, each containing one of the two desired groups. Based on this, if we have an artificial neural network that can identify or separate the four points into the two desired groups, then we have a pattern recognition ANN.

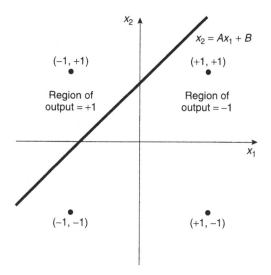

Figure 2-8 Graphical representation of a linearly separable ANN.

Now we can construct a neural network that is described by the linear function $x_2 = Ax_1 + B$, where A and B are functions of the ANN parameters. Then, if we manage to design an ANN with parameters such that $A = 1.1$ and $B = 0.8$, the neural network described by the function $x_2 = 1.1x_1 + 0.8$ will produce at its output the desired response for each of the four patterns when applied at its input. Obviously, this is a very simple example, and there is an infinite number of values for A and B that can produce the desired response.

The parameters of an ANN that can best solve the preceding problem are calculated as follows. Consider a two-input neuron. A critical threshold condition occurs (i.e., the neuron fires, yielding 1) when the threshold of the neuron is reached or exceeded; if not, the neuron produces a 0 output:

$$O_i = x_1 w_{i1} + x_2 w_{i2} - \Theta_i = 0. \tag{2.9}$$

This leads to

$$x_2 = -\left(\frac{w_{i1}}{w_{i2}}\right)x_1 + \frac{\Theta_i}{w_{i2}} = Ax_1 + B, \tag{2.10}$$

where

$$-\frac{w_{i1}}{w_{i2}} = \text{slope of a straight line}$$

and

$$\frac{\Theta_i}{w_{i2}} = \text{intercept of a straight line with } x_2.$$

From the last two relationships, the parameters Θ_i, w_{i1}, and w_{i2} may be evaluated. For $A = 1.1$ and $B = 0.8$, and setting Θ to the small threshold value of 0.2, we find $w_{i1} = 2.5$ and $w_{i2} = -2.75$. Notice that one value is negative. This is resolved by giving it a positive value and by making one input (x_1) excitatory ($+$) and the other (x_2) inhibitory ($-$). In most applications, the values of w_{ij} are implemented with resistive networks; hence they are positive only. The minus sign is taken care of by using the inhibitory input ($-$) of the summing junction of the artificial neuron.[*]

This illustration is oversimplified. Actual networks have many neurons and more than one layer; hence, the equations are more complex. In addition, there are many more input patterns. Consequently, it is more tedious to determine the network's discrimination ability than simply drawing a straight line on the x_1x_2 plane.

2.9.2   Multilinear ANNs

In multilinear ANNs the ANN has to separate into two or more groups of points on the x_2x_1 plane. The ANN then consists of a set of linear functions, where each function has a different slope and intercept, as illustrated in Figure 2-9. In actual ANN problems the points represent patterns plotted in a multidimensional space ($x_1, x_2, \ldots, x_n$). It is difficult to illustrate the n-dimensional space, but you may be able to visualize it (with that amazing bioneural net).

The example in Figure 2-10, though somewhat complex for the simple Exclusive-OR function that is performed, illustrates how a feedforward multilinear ANN performs a task it has been trained to do. Circled numbers

---

[*] When implementing neurons, typically operational amplifiers are used where the excitatory input corresponds to the $+$ input and the inhibitory input corresponds to the $-$ input of the op amp.

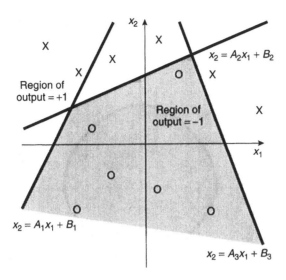

Figure 2-9 Graphical representation of a multilinearly separable ANN.

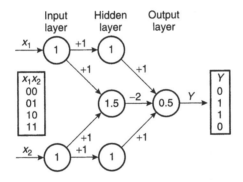

Figure 2-10 A neural network implementation of Exclusive-OR.

indicate threshold values, and numbers over the arrows indicate weight values.

2.9.3 Nonlinear Separable ANNs

In nonlinear separable ANNs the ANN is described by a nonlinear function that, depending on the nonlinearities, may be quite complex and difficult to solve. Figure 2-11 shows a nonlinear ANN. The mathematical analysis is beyond the scope and interest of this tutorial.

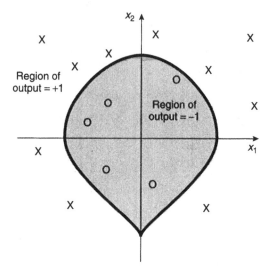

Figure 2-11 Graphical representation of a non-linearly separable ANN.

2.10   ANN Adaptability

One of the major features of biological neural networks is their continuous learning. Thus, it is desirable to maintain this capability in artificial neural networks. We'll see this feature in certain paradigms. Continuous learning implies continuous update of the neuron's weights, however; this may present some technical limitations for many paradigms. Hence, adaptability, although a highly desirable feature for many paradigms, is identified by its limits in the world of electronics.

2.11   The Stability-Plasticity Dilemma

Stability of an ANN denotes that its weights have reached the steady state. Additional learning implies that the weights will change and this causes the ANN to lose its memory or its program. To avoid loss of memory, additional learning should be avoided. How good is an ANN that loses its future adaptability? Adaptability of an ANN has been related to plasticity of materials;

that is, the material can undergo deformations without losing its characteristics and properties. Thus, we are presented with a difficult design requirement whereby the network must exhibit stability yet maintain plasticity. This is known as the **stability-plasticity dilemma**, which is stated as follows: How can a learning system be designed to remain plastic or adaptable enough to learn new things whenever they might appear and yet remain stable enough to preserve previously learned knowledge? What prevents the new learning from washing away the memories of previous learning? How does the system know when and how to switch to its stable model to achieve stability without rigidity and to its plastic model to achieve plasticity without chaos? The stability-plasticity dilemma has been one of the main concerns in the development of ANN paradigms (see Section 3.8) [7, 8].

To visualize the importance of the stability-plasticity dilemma, assume that you present to an ANN three different classes of objects: rocks, pieces of wood, and pieces of fabric. Assume that training of the ANN has been completed and that the ANN thereafter recognizes these three categories without faults (stability). Now assume that over time, the rocks presented to the ANN for identification have different sizes and consistency (e.g., sand, pebbles, boulders), the pieces of wood have different dimensions, and the pieces of fabric are made of different materials (e.g., wool, cotton, silk). The (plasticity) question is, Does the ANN have the know-how, flexibility, and capacity to group the rocks, wood, and fabric into subcategories? Concerning stability-plasticity, can the ANN do the aforementioned without forgetting the original three classifications?

2.12   Review Questions

2.1. Is it true that neural networks process information based on a sequential algorithm?

2.2. Describe the basic model of a neuron.

2.3. Name some of the most used nonlinearities.

2.4. What do we mean by "learning" in neural networks?

2.5. What is supervised learning and how is it different from unsupervised learning?

2.6. How does a neural network learn during supervised learning?

2.7. From a mathematical point of view, what is the process of learning in supervised learning?

2.8. Consider Hebbian learning; what can you say about the synaptic strength between two cells?

2.9. Name some of the characteristics of artificial neural networks.

2.10. Consider 20 objects on a table with a straight line across it. A neural network can recognize and separate the objects into two categories: those above the straight line and those below the line. What could you say about that network?

2.11. Consider that among different objects on a table some of them are similar and form a cluster. What could you say about the neural network that can recognize the cluster?

2.12. We want to design a highly stable neural network. What can you say about its plasticity?

For answers, see page 186.

REFERENCES

[1] R. Jackendoff, "Languages of the Computation Mind," in *The Computer and the Brain: Perspectives on Human and Artificial Intelligence*, J. R. Brink and C. R. Haden, eds., pp. 171–190, North Holland, New York, 1989.

[2] L. A. Akers et al., "VLSI Implementations of Neural Systems," in *The Computer and the Brain: Perspectives on Human and Artificial Intelligence*, J. R. Brink and C. R. Haden, eds., pp. 125–157, North Holland, New York, 1989.

[3] S. V. Kartalopoulos, "Tutorial in Fuzzy Logic and Neural Networks in Communication Systems: Concepts and Applications," in Tutorial Notes at IEEE Globecom '93, Houston, Nov. 29, 1993.

[4] P. Werbos, "Neurocontrol and Supervised Learning: An Overview and Evaluation," in *Handbook of Intelligent Control: Neural, Fuzzy and Adaptive Approaches*, pp. 65–90, Van Nostrand Reinhold, New York, 1992.

[5] J. A. Anderson, "Neural-Network Learning and Mark Twain's Cat," *IEEE Communications Mag.*, vol. 30, no. 9, pp. 16–22, 1992.

[6] S. I. Gallant, *Neural Network Learning and Expert Systems*, MIT Press, Cambridge, Mass., 1993.

[7] S. Grossberg, "How Does the Brain Build a Cognitive Code?" *Psychol. Rev.*, vol. 89, pp. 529–572, 1980.

[8] G. A. Carpenter and S. Grossberg, "The ART of Adaptive Pattern Recognition by a Self-Organizing Neural Network," *Computer*, vol. 21, pp. 77–88, March 1988.

3

NEURAL NETWORK
PARADIGMS

Characteristic artificial neural networks, inspired from the biological world, have been developed and are known as **paradigms**. The search for the best representative paradigms—the paradigm that truly emulates the biological neural network—is still under way. Herein, the terms *artificial neural networks* (ANNs), *neural network models*, and *paradigms* will be used synonymously.

A typical paradigm is structured in layers of neurons. Some have one layer—*single-layer neural networks* (SLNN)—and some have more—*multilayer neural networks* (MLNN). In Chapter 2 we illustrated the topologies of neural networks. Based on these topologies, the layer where input patterns are applied is the **input layer**. The layer from which the output response is obtained is the **output layer**. Intermediate layers are called **hidden layers** because their outputs are not readily observable. This hierarchical organization in layers can also be seen in biological neural networks (see Chapter 1).

In Figure 3-1, an artificial neural network is shown; circles represent neurons and arrows represent communication paths between neurons. Each arrow is also associated with a synaptic strength or weight value (not shown but implied). Note that arrows connect neurons from one layer to the next and do not leapfrog layers. Although it occurs in biological neural networks, the mathematical analysis would be too complicated if leapfrogging were allowed.

In general, a neural network may be thought of a sophisticated signal processor. The processing ability of this network, however, does not depend on serial algorithms executed by sequential von Neumann machines. In a neural network the program is **distributed** across the network and stored at the synapses of each neuron. During the learning phase, synaptic

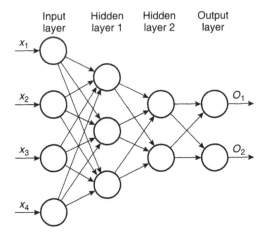

Figure 3-1 Feedforward multilayer neural network.

weights and threshold values are adjusted until they yield the desired outputs. In the general case, the strength of each synapse (i.e., the synaptic weight) and the threshold value of each neuron at steady state constitute the network's program. Thus, every neuron takes part in a massive parallel program execution. In today's paradigms the synaptic weights are adjusted automatically by a supervisory computer or by a direct feedback mechanism during learning (see Chapter 2). Interestingly, early paradigms used manual potentiometers to set the synaptic values and thresholds. Although tedious, they proved the point and stimulated enormous interest.

This chapter describes many key paradigms while keeping the mathematics as simple as possible.

3.1   McCulloch-Pitts Model

Warren McCulloch, a neurobiologist, and Walter Pitts, a statistician, presented the first mathematical model [1] of a single idealized biological neuron in 1943. Known as the **McCulloch-Pitts model**, it is quite simple, with no learning or adaptation, and has been the basic building block that inspired and stimulated subsequent work in developing paradigms [2]. McCulloch and Pitts's seminal paper was followed by others expanding the ideas in pattern recognition [3].

In this model each input receives a stimulus x_j that is weighted (multiplied) by some value w_{ij} (see Section 2.7.2) that represents the synaptic strength. All weighted inputs are summed, and if the combined input reaches a certain threshold level, a response is generated, which is further modulated by a **nonlinear transfer function** f. The output is then expressed by

$$O_i = f\left(\sum_{j=1}^{N}(x_{ij}w_{ij}) - \Theta_i\right), \qquad (3.1)$$

where x_{ij} is the incoming signal or stimulus at input j on the ith neuron, f is the nonlinearity, and O_i is the output response of the ith neuron. In this model the bias term Θ_i and the weights w_{ij} are assumed to have reached steady state. Constant weight values imply that all learning or adaptation has been completed (Figure 3-2).

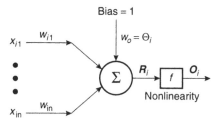

Figure 3-2 Model of an artificial neuron.

3.2 The Perceptron

The McCulloch-Pitts model is a simple open-loop system with a sole purpose: to model a single neuron. No mechanism exists here to compare the actual expected output response, and thus no weight adjustment and no learning take place. The need for feedback was quickly recognized, particularly at a time when feedback control theory was moving in the direction of adaptive control. Thus, it attracted the interest of many researchers, who built on the McCulloch-Pitts model and developed the next-generation paradigms with learning and adaptation. Such a model is the Perceptron by Frank Rosenblatt [4, 5].

3.2.1 Original Perceptron

The Perceptron is a paradigm that requires supervised learning. It is a pattern classification system that recognizes abstract and geometric patterns from optical input patterns. It can make limited generalizations and can properly categorize patterns despite noise in the input. Its learning mechanism depends on the error difference between target and actual output data from the network during the learning phase.

Rosenblatt's original paradigm is described in terms of three units (or levels) (Figure 3-3): the sensory unit, S, where an optical stimulus is applied; the association unit, A, where learning is known a priori (i.e., synaptic weights are fixed); and the response unit, R, where training takes place and the output response is obtained. The sensory input is a two-dimensional matrix of 400 photodetectors upon which a lighted picture with geometric black-and-white patterns impinges. The photodetectors provide a binary (0) electrical signal (i.e., no gray scale is supported) if the input stimulus signal exceeds a certain threshold. Thus, the sensory input maps the two-dimensional array of discrete sensors to a linear array. These photodetectors were connected randomly with the association unit, A.

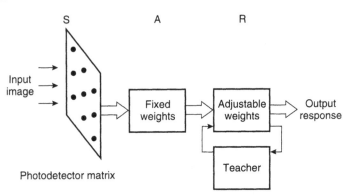

Figure 3-3 Original Perceptron architecture.

The association unit consisted of a set of subcircuits called **feature demons** or **predicates**. The feature demons were hard-wired to detect specific features of a pattern and were equivalent to the **feature detectors** of the retina neural networks (see Chapter 1). Each predicate examined some or all of the responses of the sensory unit for a particular feature (straight line, corner, etc.). The results from the predicate units were also binary (i.e., 0 or 1). The third unit, the response, contains the **pattern recognizers** or **perceptrons**. The weights of the input and demon layers are all fixed, whereas the weights on the output layer are trainable.

For the transfer function to condition the inputs, Rosenblatt used the hard-limiting nonlinearity

$$f_{HL}(y) = \begin{cases} 1 & \text{for } y > 0, \\ 0 & \text{for } y \leq 0. \end{cases} \tag{3.2}$$

In addition, the bias term was set to 1 and a bias weight $w_0 = \theta$ is included as part of the input vector.

When a Perceptron has been trained to perform a pattern recognition task, synaptic weights, the threshold values, and sets of input patterns cannot change. For a different set of input patterns a different Perceptron has to be trained. Thus, different sets of patterns yield different Perceptrons. This was viewed as a deficiency of the model. Another deficiency of the early Perceptron was that it failed to pass a benchmark test, the linear separation. It could not differentiate between two linearly separable sets of patterns (see Chapter 2); that is, it could not perform a simple Exclusive-OR function. The Perceptron was severely criticized by Minsky and Papert [6], who believed that many of the claims about pattern recognition and learning capabilities of the Perceptron were exaggerated.

Nevertheless, the early Perceptron deficiency was recognized and other Perceptrons were designed that eventually solved the initial Exclusive-OR problem. One such is the **back-coupled error correction** model, which included a feedforward adaptive filter and a binary output signal (Figure 3-3). During training of the Perceptron, the input patterns and target output (T) are applied. From the response obtained, an error signal is calculated that is used to adjust the weights of the R units.

During training of the Perceptron, a stimulus excites its inputs and an output O is produced. This output is compared with the closest-matched target output T, and their difference (or error signal) E is then used to adjust the value of the weights, based on a learning algorithm (see Figures 2-7 and 3-4). The difference (E) between the actual output (O) and the target output (T) is expressed as

$$E = T - O. \tag{3.3}$$

Change of synaptic weights is calculated from

$$\Delta w = \mu[T - f(w(k)x)]x \tag{3.4}$$

or

$$w(k + 1) = w(k) + \mu[T - f(w(k)x)]x. \tag{3.5}$$

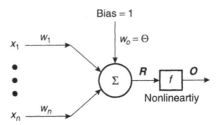

Figure 3-4 Single Perceptron model.

3.2.2 Perceptron Learning Procedure

Before training the Perceptron (or any paradigm), one should check the following:

1. Choose a set of input vectors $\{x\}$.
2. Choose a set of target outputs $\{O\}$ (one target output for each input vector).
3. Choose a small positive value of the learning rate, μ, and (if needed) a criterion and the step the learning rate will change.
4. Select the nonlinearity; if the sigmoid is selected, then also select the gain (a constant) of the function.
5. Decide on the termination procedure: define a small acceptable error value (it may be zero) for the actual output. When this error is reached, the iteration process terminates. Another termination procedure sets the maximum number of iterations; however, the latter does not always warranty steady-state solutions.

When this is done,

1. Initialize thresholds and weights: set $w_j(0)$ and Θ to small random values.
2. Apply an input pattern x_p and the corresponding target output T_p, where p is the number of patterns in the set.
3. Calculate the actual output O from

$$O(k) = f[\sum_{j=0}^{N} w_j(k)x_j(k)$$

or, in vector notation,

$$O(k) = f[w^T(k)x].$$

4. Adapt weights using the iterative relationship

$$w(k+1) = w(k) + \mu[T(k) - w(k)x(k)]x(k) \qquad \text{for } 0 \le k \le N-1.$$

The desired output has been reached when the weights stop changing.

5. Repeat steps 2–4.

Assuming n input variables, there are 2^n rows in the truth table that yield 2^{2^n} combinations of logic output functions. The number of implementable logic functions is bounded by

$$\frac{2^{n(n-1)}}{2} < NLF(n) \le 2 \sum_{i=0}^{n} \binom{2^n - 1}{i} < 2^{n^2}. \qquad (3.6)$$

That is, for large n the number of implementable functions is extremely small.

Example 3.1

Consider a four-input single-neuron net (hence, the subscript i may be deleted) to be trained with the input vector x and an initial weight vector given by

$$x = \begin{bmatrix} +1 \\ -2 \\ 0 \\ 1.5 \end{bmatrix}, \qquad w = \begin{bmatrix} +1 \\ -1 \\ 0.5 \\ 0 \end{bmatrix}.$$

For simplicity, the learning constant is set to 1, and the bipolar function sgn($\cdot$) is chosen as the nonlinearity. Then the first iteration output signal is

$$O(1) = \text{sgn}\,[w(1)x] = \text{sgn}\left(\begin{bmatrix} +1 & -1 & 0.5 & 0 \end{bmatrix} \begin{bmatrix} +1 \\ -2 \\ 0 \\ 1.5 \end{bmatrix} \right)$$

$$= \text{sgn}\,(3) = +1,$$

and the first iteration updated weights are

$$w(2) = w(1) + \mu(O(1))x$$

$$= \begin{bmatrix} +1 \\ -1 \\ 0.5 \\ 0 \end{bmatrix} + \begin{bmatrix} +1 \\ -2 \\ 0 \\ 1.5 \end{bmatrix} = \begin{bmatrix} +2 \\ -3 \\ 0.5 \\ 1.5 \end{bmatrix}.$$

Now, repeat the previous two steps iteratively until the weights reach a steady state (i.e., they do not change in subsequent iterations).

3.2.3   Logic Operations with Simple-Layer Perceptrons

The simple Perceptron may be viewed as

1. A discriminant function for two-class pattern recognition problems (see Section 2.9).
2. A binary logic unit. The same Perceptron, depending on the weight values, may implement some logic functions but not all. For $n = 2$ it may may be an AND, OR, and NOT, but not an XOR (see Figure 3-5).

In addition, other interesting, yet simple, logic functions may be implemented, such as the **plurality** and the **majority** functions. The plurality function is defined to be true ($+1$) if more of its inputs are true ($+1$) than false, false (-1) if more of its inputs are false (-1) than true, and unknown (0) if an equal number of its inputs are true and false. The majority function on n Boolean inputs is defined to be true ($+1$) when most of the inputs are true, false (-1) when most of its inputs are false, and unknown (0) if most of the inputs are unknown. The majority function is often confused with the plurality function, and occasionally a similar implementation is falsely provided. Although a plurality function may be implemented with a simple Perceptron, a majority function can be implemented with a multiple Perceptron, as we shall see in the next section. As an example, if we try the input vector 0, 0, and $+1$ at the last Perceptron of Figure 3-5, we obtain the output $+1$ as the true response of the plurality function (as defined earlier) but not a 0 output of the majority function. As an exercise, design a four- and a five-input plurality circuit and verify the plurality function and disprove the majority function.

3.2.4   Multilayer Perceptron

Since Rosenblatt's original Perceptron was introduced, other Perceptron models have been developed. In general, multilayer Perceptron (MLP) nets are composed of many simple perceptrons in a hierarchical structure forming a feedforward topology (see Chapter 2) with one or more layers (**hidden layers**) between the input and output layers (see Figure 3-6, page 70). The number of hidden layers and the number of neurons per layer are not fixed. Each layer may have a different number of neurons, depending on the application. The developer will have to determine how many layers and how many neurons per layer should be selected (typically that is either an educated guess or a cut-and-try process) for the application.

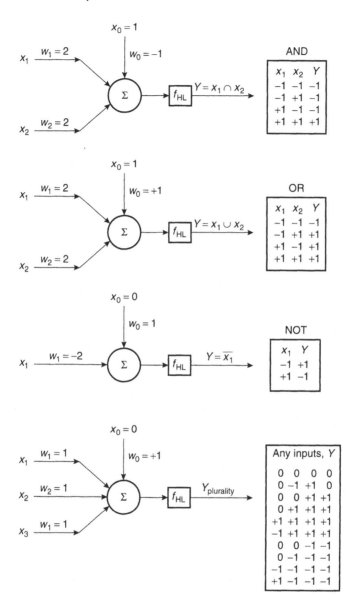

Figure 3-5 Logic functions with Perceptrons.

A single-layer Perceptron forms half-plane decision regions, a two-layer Perceptron can form convex (polygon) regions, and a three-layer Perceptron can form arbitrarily complex decision regions in the input space (see Section 2.9.1).

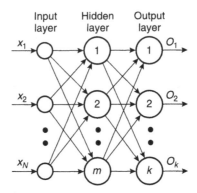

Figure 3-6 Layer definition in MLP.

Different learning algorithms have been used with MLPs, the most common being the Delta and the Back Propagation.

In MLPs sigmoidal nonlinearity may also be used:

$$f_s(R) = (1 + e^{-kR})^{-1}, \tag{3.7}$$

where k, the gain of the sigmoid, varies monotonically from $-\infty$ to $+\infty$. One of the advantages of the sigmoid is that it is differentiable, and thus it simplifies the search for the optimum solution.

The MLP can be used to implement arbitrary Boolean logic functions (two layers are sufficient) to partition the pattern space, to classify patterns (two to three layers are sufficient), and to implement nonlinear transformations for functional approximation problems (two to three layers are sufficient).

We have indicated the number of layers needed. However, no indication is provided as to the optimal number of nodes per layer. There is no formal method to determine this optimal number; typically, one uses trial and error.

3.2.5   Delta Learning Algorithm

The Delta learning algorithm is based on the least-square-error minimization method. The objective with this method is to express the difference of the actual and target outputs in terms of the inputs and weights. We start with the least-squared error (E) between the target output (T) and actual output (O) defined by

$$E = \tfrac{1}{2}(T_i - O_i)^2 = \tfrac{1}{2}[T_i - f(w_i x_i)]^2, \tag{3.8}$$

where w_i is the matrix representation of the weights; x_i, O_i, T_i are the vector representations of the input, actual output, and target output, respectively, of the ith neuron; and f is the activation function, or nonlinearity.

The error gradient vector is

$$\nabla E = -(T_i - O_i)f'(w_i x_i)x_i. \tag{3.9}$$

Since we are seeking minimization of the error (hence the negative sign), we consider

$$\Delta w_i = -\mu \nabla E, \tag{3.10}$$

where μ is a positive constant. Hence, Δw_i becomes

$$\Delta w_i = \mu(T_i - O_i)f'(w_i x_i)x_i. \tag{3.11}$$

Applying discrete mathematics, we update the weight vector, using

$$w_i(k+1) = w_i(k) + \mu(T_i - O_i)f'(w_i x_i)x_i. \tag{3.12}$$

If we assume that the sigmoid nonlinearity with a constant $k = 1$ is used, then the gradient is approximated by the relation

$$f'(w_i x_i) = \tfrac{1}{2}(T_i - O_i^2). \tag{3.13}$$

Thus,

$$w_i(k+1) = w_i(k) + \frac{\mu}{2}(T_i - O_i)(T_i - O_i^2)x_i.$$

Example 3.2

Consider a four-input net with a training input vector and initial weights as

$$x_i = \begin{bmatrix} +1 \\ -1 \\ +1 \\ -1 \end{bmatrix}, \qquad w_i = \begin{bmatrix} +1 \\ -1 \\ 0 \\ -1 \end{bmatrix}.$$

In addition, the desired or target output is -1, the learning rate $\mu = 0.1$, and the sigmoid is used as the nonlinearity function. Then

$$w(1)x = \begin{bmatrix} 1 & -1 & 0 & -1 \end{bmatrix} \begin{bmatrix} +1 \\ -1 \\ +1 \\ -1 \end{bmatrix} = 3,$$

$$O(1) = f(3) = 0.95,$$

$$f'(w(1)x_i) = \tfrac{1}{2}[T_i - (O_i(1))^2]$$

$$= \tfrac{1}{2}[1 - (0.85)^2] = 0.138,$$

and
$$w(2) = w(1) + \mu[T - O(1)]f'[w(1)x_i]x_i$$

$$= \begin{bmatrix} +1 \\ -1 \\ 0 \\ -1 \end{bmatrix} + 0.1(-1 - 0.85)0.138 \begin{bmatrix} +1 \\ -1 \\ +1 \\ -1 \end{bmatrix}$$

$$= \begin{bmatrix} +0.975 \\ -0.975 \\ -0.025 \\ +1.025 \end{bmatrix}.$$

Now, with the new weight vector calculate the output signal, and if the error is larger than a desired value, repeat the above problem until the desired minimum error is reached.

3.3   ADALINE and MADALINE Models

3.3.1   ADALINE

Bernard Widrow and his colleagues [7–10] developed a three-level model called ADALINE (ADaptive LInear NEuron) and a MADALINE (Many ADALINE) model. The ADALINE has only one neuron in the middle level of the network (Figure 3-7). In the figure,

$w_j = [w_1, w_2, \ldots, w_n]$ = weight vector of the inputs

$x_j = [x_1, x_2, \ldots, x_n]$ = input vector

$R = w^T x$ = output of the neuron before to the nonlinearity

$O = \text{sgn}(\sum_{j=1}^{n} w_j x_j)$ = output from the neuron after the nonlinearity

T = teacher's training, or target, signal (this along with the input signal produces the error or (learning) signal used only during training)

$E = T - R$ = output error used during learning.

The basic ADALINE model consists of trainable weights. Inputs are two valued ($+1$ or -1), and weights are signed (positive or negative). Initially, the weights are assigned random values. The weighted sum of the inputs, including a bias term, is applied to a quantizer transfer function

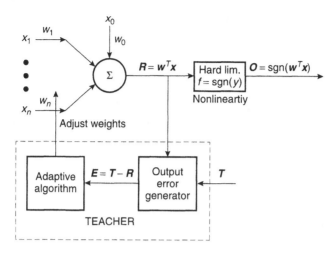

Figure 3-7 ADALINE model with teacher.

that restores the outputs to $+1$ or -1. The ADALINE model compares the actual output R with the target output T, and based on the mean-square learning algorithm the weights are adjusted, where the error function is

$$E = T - R. \tag{3.14}$$

The idea is to adjust the weights so that the mean-square error is minimized:

$$\frac{\delta w_{ij}}{\delta t} = \alpha \delta a_i \frac{a_i}{|a|^2}, \tag{3.15}$$

where α is a constant, typically $0 < \alpha < 1$.

To teach an ADALINE model, one uses the following learning algorithm [11], known as **Widrow-Hoff learning**:

1. Assign random synaptic weight values in the range -1 to 1.

2. Apply the selected input and the target output to the model.

3. Calculate the error signal (the difference between the weighted sum before the quantizer and the target output).

4. Adjust each weight, based on the preceding equations, so that the error is reduced by $1/n$, where n is the number of weights.

5. Repeat the process until the error becomes zero.

6. Repeat the process for the next set of inputs.

Experimental results indicate that an ADALINE will typically converge to a stable solution in five times as many learning trials as there are weights.

3.3.2 MADALINE

The MADALINE model uses many ADALINEs in parallel with a single output unit that has a value based on some selecting rules. For example, if the majority vote is used as a rule, then the output has a true/false answer: a 1 if at least 51% of the inputs have the value 1 (true), or else -1 (false). If the AND rule is used [11], then the output will be at 1 (true) if all inputs are at 1, and so on. In the latter case, think of two parallel ADALINEs where their outputs are inputs to an AND gate and the inputs to both ADALINEs are the same (Figure 3-8).

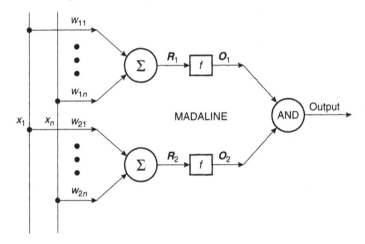

Figure 3-8 Two ADALINE MADALINE.

The ADALINE-MADALINE model has been applied effectively in communications systems in adaptive equalizers and in adaptive echo cancellation, among others. The self-learning capabilities of the MADALINE paradigm composed of 26 adaptive ADALINEs has been demonstrated with a simulated truck backer-upper example [12, 13].

3.4   Winner-Takes-All Learning Algorithm

The winner-takes-all algorithm is suited to cases of competitive unsupervised learning. One assumes that there is a single layer of N nodes and that each node has its own set of weights w_n. An input vector x is applied to all nodes, and each node provides an output $O_n = \sum_j w_{nj} x_j$. The node with the best response to the applied input vector x is declared the winner according to the winner selection criterion:

$$O_n = \max_{i=1,2,\ldots,N} (w_n x). \tag{3.16}$$

Now, the change in weights is calculated according to

$$\Delta w_n = \alpha(k)(x - w_n) \tag{3.17}$$

or

$$w_n(k + 1) = w_n(k) + \alpha(k)(x - w_n), \tag{3.18}$$

where $\alpha(k)$ is a small positive scalar known as the **learning rate**. This scalar may be decreasing at each iteration as learning progresses, or it may be a constant fixed value throughout the learning process. If $\alpha(k)$ is selected to decrease, the rate of decrease depends on the speed of convergence to the optimum solution and on the termination procedures.

The last equation indicates that weights change proportionally to the difference $x - w_n$; that is, the winning weight vector is the closest to the input x.

In Figure 3-9, the concept of a competitive single-layer neural network with three nodes and three inputs is illustrated, where the first node is winning (solid arrows).

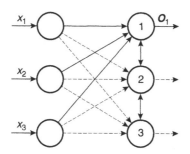

Figure 3-9 Competitive learning with node 1 winning.

3.5 Back-Propagation Learning Algorithm

The back-propagation (BP) algorithm was developed by Paul Werbos [14] in 1974 and rediscovered independently by Rumelhart [15] and Parker [16]. Since its rediscovery, the back-propagation algorithm has been widely used as a learning algorithm in feedforward multilayer neural networks [17, 18, 19]. The BP is applied to feedforward ANNs with one or more hidden layers, as shown in Figure 3-10.

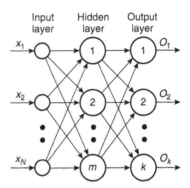

Figure 3-10 Feedforward MLP.

Based on this algorithm, the network learns a distributed associative map between the input and output layers.

What makes this algorithm different than the others is the process by which the weights are calculated during the learning phase of the network. In general, the difficulty with multilayer Perceptrons is calculating the weights of the hidden layers in an efficient way that result in the least (or zero) output error; the more hidden layers there are, the more difficult it becomes. To update the weights, one must calculate an error. At the output layer this error is easily measured; this is the difference between the actual and desired (target) outputs. At the hidden layers, however, there is no direct observation of the error; hence, some other technique must be used to calculate an error at the hidden layers that will cause minimization of the output error, as this is the ultimate goal.

3.5.1   Learning with the Back-Propagation Algorithm

The back-propagation algorithm is an involved mathematical tool; however, execution of the training equations is based on iterative processes, and thus is easily implementable on a computer.

During the training session of the network, a pair of patterns is presented (X_k, T_k), where X_k is the input pattern and T_k is the target or desired pattern. The X_k pattern causes output responses at each neuron in each layer and, hence, an actual output O_k at the output layer. At the output layer, the difference between the actual and target outputs yields an error signal. This error signal depends on the values of the weights of the neurons in each layer. This error is minimized, and during this process new values for the weights are obtained. The speed and accuracy of the learning process—that is, the process of updating the weights—also depends on a factor, known as the *learning rate.*

Before starting the back-propagation learning process, we need the following:

- The set of training patterns, input, and target

- A value for the learning rate

- A criterion that terminates the algorithm

- A methodology for updating weights

- The nonlinearity function (usually the sigmoid)

- Initial weight values (typically small random values)

The process then starts by applying the first input pattern X_k and the corresponding target output T_k. The input causes a response to the neurons of the first layer, which in turn cause a response to the neurons of the next layer, and so on, until a response is obtained at the output layer. That response is then compared with the target response, and the difference (the error signal) is calculated. From the error difference at the output neurons, the algorithm computes the rate at which the error changes as the activity level of the neuron changes. So far, the calculations were computed forward (i.e., from the input layer to the output layer). Now, the algorithm steps back one layer before the output layer and recalculates the weights of the output layer (the weights between the last hidden layer and the neurons of the output layer) so that the output error is minimized. The algorithm next calculates the error output at the last hidden layer and computes new values for its weights (the weights between the last and next-to-last hidden layers). The algorithm continues calculating the error and computing new weight values, moving layer by layer backward, toward the input. When the input is reached and the weights do not change, (i.e., when they have reached a steady state), then the algorithm selects the next pair of input-target patterns and repeats the process. Although responses move in a forward direction, weights are calculated by moving backward, hence the name back propagation.

3.5.2   Mathematical Analysis

Consider a feedforward network with the following parameters:

L layers and N_l nodes in layer l,

$w_{l,j,i}$ = weight between node i of layer $l - 1$ and node j of layer l,

$O_{l,j}(x_p)$ = actual output (for pattern x_p of jth node in layer l (after nonlinearity)),

$T_{L,j}(x_p)$ = expected, or target, output (for pattern x_p of jth node in layer L),

$\alpha_{l,j}(x_p)$ = activation output (for pattern p) for node j in layer l (prior to nonlinearity),

P = training patterns and x_p the pth training pattern.

To illustrate the back-propagation learning procedure, assume that node i of the $(l + 1)$th layer receives signals from node j in the lth layer via the weights w_{ij}^l (Figure 3-11).

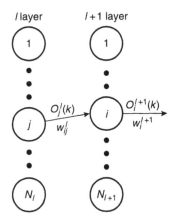

Figure 3-11 Learning procedure
with back propagation at a node.

N_l nodes in the lth layer, the output signal from node i of the $(l + 1)$th node, and the kth input pattern to the network are expressed by

$$O_i^{l+1}(k) = f\left(\sum_{j=1}^{N_l} w_{ij}^l O_j^l(k) - \theta_i^{l+1}\right)$$

$$= f\left(\sum_{j=1}^{N_l+1} w_{ij}^l O_j^l(k)\right),$$

where the threshold term θ_i^{l+1} has been included in the summation.

If the sigmoid function $f(x) = 1/(1 + \exp(-\beta x))$ is used, its derivative is

$$f'(x) = \beta f(x)(1 - f(x)).$$

The total error, E, for the network and for all patterns K is defined as the sum of squared differences between the actual network output and the target (or desired) output at the output layer L:

$$E = \sum_{k=1}^{K} E_k = \sum_{k=1}^{K} \left(\frac{1}{2} \sum_{i=1}^{N_L} [T_i(k) - O_i^L(k)]^2 \right).$$

The goal is to evaluate a set of weights in all layers of the network that minimize E. The learning rule is specified by setting the change in the weights proportional to the negative derivative of the error with respect to the weights:

$$\Delta w_{nm}^l \approx -\frac{\partial E_k}{\partial w_{nm}^l}.$$

To calculate the dependence of the error E_k on the nmth weight of a neuron in the lth layer, we use the chain rule:

$$\frac{\partial E_k}{\partial w_{nm}^l} = \frac{\partial E_k}{\partial O_i^L(k)} \frac{\partial O_i^L(k)}{\partial w_{nm}^l}.$$

Then

$$-\frac{\partial E_k}{\partial w_{nm}^l} = \sum_{i=1}^{N_L} (T_i(k) - O_j^L(k)) \frac{\partial O_i^L(k)}{\partial w_{nm}^l}.$$

If we introduce the sigmoid function and its derivative into the latter relationship and for $l = L - 1$ (i.e., weights of the output layer), then

$$-\frac{\partial E_k}{\partial w_{nm}^l} = (T_n - O_n^L)\beta O_n^L(1 - O_n^L)O_m^{L-1}.$$

Thus, the procedure for adjusting weights of the output layer is

$$\Delta w_{nm}^L = \eta[(T_n - O_n^L)O_n^L(1 - O_n^L)]O_m^{L-1},$$

where η is a proportionality factor known as the learning rate.

However, if $l \neq L - 1$, then O_m^{L-1} still depends on w_{nm}^l, and the error dependency on weights, again by applying the chain rule, is

$$-\frac{\partial E_k}{\partial w_{nm}^l} = \sum_{i=1}^{N_L} (T_i - O_i^L)f'(O_i^L) \sum_{j=1}^{N_{L-1}+1} w_{ij}^{L-1} \frac{\partial O_j^{L-1}}{\partial w_{nm}^l}.$$

Now, if $l = L - 2$ (i.e., weights of neurons in the last hidden layer), then the latter is expressed by

$$-\frac{\partial E_k}{\partial w_{nm}^l} = \sum_{i=1}^{l}(T_i - O_i^L)f'(O_i^L)w_{in}^{L-1}f'(O_n^{L-1})O_m^{L-2}$$

$$= f'(O_m^{L-1})\left[\sum_{i=1}^{N}(T_i - O_i^L)f'(O_i^L)w_{in}^L\right]O_m^{L-2}.$$

Consequently, the procedure for adjusting the weights of the last hidden layer is

$$\Delta w_{nm}^{L-2} = \eta[f'(O_n^{L-1})\sum_{i=1}^{N_L}(T_i - O_i^L)f'(O_i^L)w_{in}^L]O_{in}^{L-2}.$$

The latter is summarized as

$$\Delta w_{ij}^l = \eta\delta_i^l O_j^{l-1},$$

where, for the weights at the output layer,

$$\delta_i^L = (T_i - O_i^L)O_i^L(1 - O_i^L),$$

and, for the weights of the hidden layers,

$$\delta_i^l = \left(\sum_{r=1}^{N_l}\delta_r^{l+1}w_{ri}^{l+1}\right)O_i^l(1 - O_i^l).$$

The process of computing the gradient and adjusting the weights is repeated until a minimum error is found. In practice, one develops an algorithm termination criterion so that the algorithm does not continue this iterative process forever.

It is apparent that for nodes in layer l the computation of δ_i^l depends on the errors computed at layer $l+1$; that is, the computation of the differences is computed backwards.

3.5.3 Applications

Before applying the algorithm, one needs to

1. Decide on the function of the network to be performed (i.e., recognition, prediction, or generalization).
2. Have a complete set of input and output training patterns.
3. Determine the number of layers in the network and the number of nodes per layer.

4. Select the nonlinearity function (typically a sigmoid) and a value for the learning rate.

5. Determine the algorithm termination criteria.

The learning algorithm can now be applied as follows:

1. Initialize all weights to small random values.

2. Choose a training pair $(x(k), T(k))$.

3. Calculate the actual outputs from each neuron in a layer starting with the input layer and proceeding layer by layer toward the output layer L:

$$O_j^l(k) = f \left(\sum_{m=0}^{N_{l-1}} w_{jm}^l O_m^{l-1} \right).$$

4. Compute the gradient δ_i^l and the difference Δw_{ij}^l for each input of the neuron in a layer starting with the output layer and backtracking layer by layer toward the input.

5. Update the weights.

6. Repeat steps 2–5.

3.5.4   Criticism

Although widely used, the back-propagation algorithm has not escaped criticism. The method of backwards calculating weights does not seem to be biologically plausible; neurons do not seem to work backward to adjust the efficacy of their synaptic weights. Thus, the back-propagation learning algorithm is not viewed by many as a learning process that emulates the biological world but as a method to design a network with learning.

Second, the algorithm uses a digital computer to calculate weights. When the final network is implemented in hardware, however, it has lost its plasticity (see Section 3.7). This loss is in contrast with the initial motivation to develop neural networks that emulate brainlike networks and are adaptable (plastic) enough to learn new patterns. If changes are necessary, a computer calculates anew the weight values and updates them. This means that the neural network implementation still depends on a digital computer.

The algorithm suffers from extensive calculations and, hence, slow training speed. The time required to calculate the error derivatives and to update the weights on a given training exemplar is proportional to the size of the network. The amount of computation is proportional to the number of weights. In large networks, increasing the number of training patterns causes the learning time to increase faster than the network. The computational speed inefficiency of this algorithm has triggered an effort to explore techniques that accelerate the learning time by at least a factor of 2 [20, 21, 22]. Even these accelerated techniques, however, do not make the back-propagation learning algorithm suitable in many real-time applications.

3.6   Cerebellum Model Articulation Controller (CMAC)

The cerebellum model articulation controller (CMAC) was developed by James Albus [23] in an attempt to design a controller that stems from the functionality of the brain.

The CMAC [24, 25] is, in many respects, similar to the functionality of the back-propagation learning algorithm. They both need supervision to learn and they both associate an input pattern to an output response. They have a fundamental difference, however. The CMAC uses a different learning algorithm, the Widrow least-mean-square learning algorithm (or Delta learning rule), which results in the steepest descent to the error minimum:

$$w_{ij}(k + 1) = w_{ij}(k) + \beta(O_i - T_i),$$

where β is the learning rate with a value between 0.2 and 0.8.

One of the salient characteristics of the CMAC is its fast learning speed, which, compared with the back-propagation learning algorithm, is faster by orders of magnitude. In addition, the CMAC inputs and outputs operate with binary-valued signals (1 or 0). Hence, the CMAC circuitry is easily implemented with relatively fast and low-power CMOS circuitry.

3.7   Adaptive Resonance Theory (ART) Paradigm

The adaptive resonance theory (ART) paradigm, developed by Steven Grossberg and Gail Carpenter [26, 27, 28] (for a comprehensive description of the ART paradigm see [29]), is consistent with cognitive and behavioral

models. This is an unsupervised paradigm that, based on competitive learning, finds categories autonomously and learns new categories if needed.

The adaptive resonance model was developed to solve the problem of
instability of feedforward systems [30], particularly the stability-plasticity
dilemma (Section 2.11). The key idea of ART is that the stability-plasticity
dilemma can be resolved by a system in which the network includes bottom-
up (input-output) competitive learning combined with top-down (output-
input) learning.

The architecture of the ART has two main layers: the first is the in-
put/comparison layer with N nodes, and the second is the output/recognition
layer with M nodes (Figure 3-12). The two layers are interacting; in other
words, there is extensive feedforward and feedback connectivity. In addition, there is an intermediate layer, an adaptive filtering network between
the input and output circuits. Moreover, for each layer there are control
signals that control the data flow.

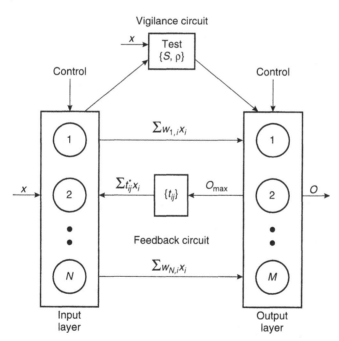

Figure 3-12 Representation of the ART model.

During training of the network, a pattern enters the network through
the input layer, where it is encoded and passed to the output layer over
weighted connections of the adaptive filtering network. Here, system dy-

namics initially follow the course of competitive learning with bottom-up
activation leading to a constant-enhanced category representation, and the
top layer stabilizes to the nearest learned category. Then, signals are recalled from learned memory and sent back from the output layer to the first
layer via a top-down adaptive filter. The input layer, therefore, has two
inputs: the read input and the reflected one.

For an n-input node layer the vigilance threshold is set to a small
positive number, $0 < \rho < 1$, and the feedforward connections are set to a
small number based on the relationship

$$w_i = \frac{1}{1+n}. \tag{3.19}$$

When an input vector is presented to the inputs, the weighted sum of an input
node is passed to the output layer. At the output layer the weighted sum of
the input is compared with the classifications (weighted sum) represented
at each node at the output layer. The network finds the output closest to
the input pattern and suppresses the remaining output nodes. The result
(closest output) is passed back to the input layer over a second set of
weighted connections t_{ij}.

The input layer then compares the "feedback" signal with the actual
input. The resulting comparison vector and current input vector are then
passed to a vigilance circuit where a test is performed of the similarity ratio
of the input and comparison vectors, expressed by

$$S = \frac{\sum t_{ij} x_i}{\sum x_i},$$

and the vigilance threshold ρ. If they agree (i.e., if $S > \rho$), then the ART
has identified the correct category. If they do not agree (i.e., $S < \rho$), then
the ART tries the next best match, and so on. In doing so, the ART trains
itself continuously and keeps updating its weights. Eventually, the layers
"resonate." This autonomous training is suitable for dynamic processes
where data change over time.

In brief, when an input vector **a** enters the bottom layer it is forwarded
to the top layer through an adaptive filter; here system dynamics initially
follow the course of competitive learning (Figure 3-12), with bottom-up
activation leading to a constant-enhanced category representation at F2
and the top layer stabilizing to the nearest learned category. Then signals
are recalled from learned memory and sent back from F2 to F1 via a top-
down adaptive filter to the first level. The first level F1, therefore, has two
inputs—the read input and the reflected one. It then compares the two, and

if the error signal (mismatch) exceeds a predetermined threshold it repeats the up-and-down again. This continues until the signal error is less than the predetermined error. Thus, Grossberg's architecture learns to recognize input vectors.

This feedback process allows the ART module to overcome both sources of instability as follows. First, the ART system carries out a matching process by an auxiliary subsystem controlled by ART dynamics. If an input does not match one of the chosen categories, the selected category is quickly rendered inactive, before past learning is disrupted, and the search ensues. If the match is good enough, the input is accepted as an exemplar of the chosen category. Second, once an input is accepted and learning proceeds, the top-down filter continues to play a different kind of stabilizing role; namely, top-down signals that represent past learning meet the original input signals at F1. Thus, the F1 activity pattern is a function of the past as well as the present, and a blend of the two, rather than the present input alone, is learned by the weights in both adaptive filters. This dynamic matching during learning leads to stable coding, even with fast learning.

3.7.1 The ART Algorithm

1. Initialization:

$$t_{ij}(0) = 1, \quad w_{ij} \frac{(0)=1}{1+N}, \quad 0 \le \rho \le 1,$$
$$0 \le i \le N - 1, 0 \le j \le M - 1.$$

2. Apply new input vector x.

3. Compute output:

$$O_j = \sum_{i=0}^{N-1} w_{ij}(k)x_i, \quad 0 \le j \le M - 1.$$

4. Select best matching exemplar:

$$O_j^* = \max_j [O_j].$$

5. Calculate ratio:

$$S = \frac{\|TX\|}{\|X\|} = \frac{\sum_{i=0}^{N-1} t_{ij}^*(k)x_i}{\sum_{i=0}^{N-1} x_i}.$$

6. Test: If $S \ge \rho$, GO TO 8, else GO TO 7.

7. Disable best match: set output of best match node to 0. GO TO 3.

8. Adapt best match:

$$w_{ij}^*(k+1) = \frac{t_{ij}^*(k)x_i}{0.5 + \sum_{i=0}^{N-1} t_{ij}^*(k)x_i},$$

$$t_{ij}^*(k+1) = t_{ij}^*(k)x_i.$$

9. Repeat: enable any disabled nodes, then GO TO 2.

3.8 Hopfield Model

In 1982, John J. Hopfield, working at the California Institute of Technology and at AT&T Bell Laboratories, conceptualized a model [31, 32] conforming to the asynchronous nature of biological neurons. As such it was a more abstract, fully interconnected, random and asynchronous network in contrast to the Perceptron, which required a clock to synchronize its circuit operation, similar to a digital computer. In general, the Hopfield network is an *autoassociative fully connected* network of a single layer of nodes [33, 34]. It is also a *symmetrically weighted* network. The network takes two-valued inputs: binary (01) or bipolar (+1 − 1); the bipolar makes the mathematical analysis easier.

Hopfield's model basic unit was a processing element with two outputs, one noninverting and one inverting (Figure 3-13). The outputs of each processing element can be coupled back to the inputs of any other processing element except itself. The connections are resistive (a resistor in parallel to a capacitor) and represent the connection strength (weight), w_{ij}. Since there are no negative resistors, excitatory connections use positive outputs, and inhibitory connections use inverted outputs. Connections are made excitatory when the output of a processing element is the same as the input; they are inhibitory when the inputs differ from the output of the processing element. Although both outputs are shown in Figure 3-13 to be fed back, one of the two will eventually make the connection. The sigmoid was used as the nonlinearity. A connection between processing elements i and j is associated with a connection strength w_{ij} that, if positive, represents the case where if unit i is on, unit j is also on (i.e., a kind of an excitatory synapse). If the connection strength is negative, it represents the situation that unit j is not on when unit i is on. Moreover, the weights are symmetric: the connection strength w_{ij} is the same as w_{ji}.

Hopfield described his model in terms of an energy function that depends on the state of interconnected neurons j with i, the state of firing V,

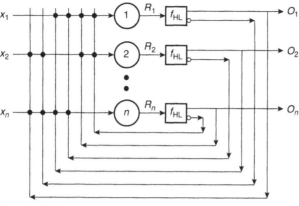

f_{HL} = hard limiter

● = possible summing junction

Figure 3-13 Basic Hopfield paradigm.

and their strength of connections, w_{ij}:

$$E = -\frac{1}{2} \sum_{i \neq j} \sum w_{ij} V_i V_j. \tag{3.20}$$

He stated that changes in V_i decrease E monotonically until a minimum is reached. The latter is mathematically verified by differentiating E over V_i:

$$\frac{\delta E}{\delta V_i} = -\sum_{j \neq i} w_{ij} V_j. \tag{3.21}$$

Equation (3.21) produces all minima, local and global. We are not interested in local minima, however, because they do not necessarily represent true results (targets). Thus, the neural network must be able to escape local minima and settle at the global minimum, that is, produce true results.

The Hopfield network has found interesting applications whereby the weighted sum of the inputs is computed and the outputs quantized. Based on this, an analog-to-digital converter has been demonstrated [35].

3.8.1 Mathematical Analysis

For an n-neuron single-layer Hopfield network, the output before nonlinearity R_i of the ith neuron is

$$R_i = \sum_{j}^{n} w_{ij} O_j + x_i - \Theta_i \qquad \text{for } i = 1, 2, \ldots, n, \tag{3.22}$$

where x_i is the external input to the ith node, O_j are the outputs from the neurons (after the nonlinearity), Θ_i is the threshold value of the ith neuron, and w_{ij} are the connection weights.

Equation (3.22), in vector notation, for one neuron is

$$R_i = w_i^T O + x_i - \Theta_i \qquad \text{for } i = 1, 2, \ldots, n, \tag{3.23}$$

where the weight vector and the output vectors of the ith neuron are

$$w_{ij} = \begin{bmatrix} w_{i1} \\ w_{i2} \\ \cdot \\ \cdot \\ \cdot \\ w_{in} \end{bmatrix}, \qquad O = \begin{bmatrix} O_1 \\ O_2 \\ \cdot \\ \cdot \\ \cdot \\ O_n \end{bmatrix}. \tag{3.24}$$

Taking all nodes into consideration, we write

$$R = WO + x - \Theta, \tag{3.25}$$

where

$$R = \begin{bmatrix} R_1 \\ R_2 \\ \cdot \\ \cdot \\ \cdot \\ R_n \end{bmatrix}, \quad x = \begin{bmatrix} x_1 \\ x_2 \\ \cdot \\ \cdot \\ \cdot \\ x_n \end{bmatrix}, \quad \text{and} \quad \Theta = \begin{bmatrix} \Theta_1 \\ \Theta_2 \\ \cdot \\ \cdot \\ \cdot \\ \Theta_n \end{bmatrix}, \tag{3.26}$$

where the weights can be expressed in an $n \times n$ symmetric matrix (i.e., $w_{ij} = w_{ji}$) with diagonal terms $w_{ii} = 0$:

$$W = \begin{bmatrix} w_1^T \\ w_2^T \\ \cdot \\ \cdot \\ \cdot \\ w_n^T \end{bmatrix}, \tag{3.27}$$

and w_i^T is in n-vector form.

Now, if the activation function is sgn($\cdot$), the outputs O_i take values $(+1, -1)$. The response of the network will be $O_i = -1$ if $R_i < 0$ or $O_i = +1$ if $R_i > 0$.

To study the stability properties of the network, one starts with the energy function

$$E = -\tfrac{1}{2} O^T W O - x^T O + \Theta^T O, \tag{3.28}$$

or, in expanded form,

$$E = -\frac{1}{2} \sum_{\substack{i=1 \\ i! = j}}^{n} \sum_{\substack{j=1 \\ i! = j}}^{n} w_{ij} O_i O_j - \sum_{i=1}^{n} x_i O_i + \sum_{i=1}^{n} \Theta_i O_i. \quad (3.29)$$

The energy gradient vector is

$$\nabla E = -\frac{1}{2}(W^T + W)O - x^T + \Theta^T. \quad (3.30)$$

During learning, outputs are updated asynchronously (i.e., only one at a time, here the ith). Then

$$\Delta O = \begin{bmatrix} 0 \\ \cdot \\ \cdot \\ \cdot \\ \Delta O_i \\ 0 \\ \cdot \\ \cdot \\ \cdot \\ 0 \end{bmatrix}. \quad (3.31)$$

The energy increment reduces to the form

$$\Delta E = (-w_i^T O - x_i^T + \Theta_i) \Delta O_i \quad (3.32)$$

or

$$\Delta E = -\left(\sum_{j=1}^{n} w_{ij} O_j + x_i - \Theta_i \right) \Delta O_i \quad \text{for } j \neq i. \quad (3.33)$$

3.8.2 The Hopfield Learning Algorithm

1. Assign random connection weights with values $w_{ij} = +1$ or -1 for all $i \neq j$ and 0 for $i = j$ (i.e., all diagonal terms are zero—a condition for asynchronous updates).

2. Initialize the network with an unknown pattern: $x_i = O_i(k)$, $0 \leq i \leq N - 1$, where $O_i(k)$ is the output of node i at time $t = k = 0$ and x_i is an element at input i of an input pattern, $+1$ or -1; that is, the input pattern consists of the $+1$ and -1 symbols, and the threshold of the nodes is zero.

3. Iterate until convergence is reached, using the relation

$$O_i(k+1) = f\left(\sum_{i=0}^{N-1} w_{ij} O_i(k)\right), \qquad 0 \le j \le N-1, \quad (3.34)$$

where the function $f(\cdot)$ is a hard-limiting nonlinearity. Repeat the process until the node outputs remain unchanged. The node outputs then best represent the exemplar pattern that best matches the unknown input.

4. Go back to step 2 and repeat for the next x_i, and so on.

3.8.3   Discrete-Time Hopfield Net

For a discrete-time recurrent Hopfield network (Figure 3-14), the ith output is

$$O_i(k+1) = f_{\mathrm{HL}}(R_i(k)), \qquad\qquad (3.35)$$

where

$$R_i(k) = \sum_{j=1}^{N} w_{ij} O_j(k) + x_i - \Theta_i \qquad\qquad (3.36)$$

and k is the index of the recursive process. The recursion starts with the initialization vector $O(0)$, and the first iteration results in $O_i(1)$.

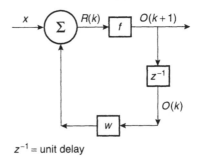

z^{-1} = unit delay

Figure 3-14 Discrete-time Hopfield model.

3.9   Competitive Learning Model

Competitive learning was described in Section 2.4.4 as a learning methodology. Here, the paradigm that was based on competitive learning is described.

The Competitive Learning model [36] was developed to show how a stream of input patterns to a network can adaptively tune the weights in the pathways from the input layer to the output layer. The input layer consists of adaptive filters called the long-term memory level (LTM) and the output layer consists of a maximal filter called the coding level. Initially, the input layer traces are randomly chosen. Then, during learning, the presentation of normalized patterns at the inputs passes through an adaptive filter before the maximal filter output is chosen by a winner-take-all network. The winning population then triggers associative pattern learning within the vector of LTM traces, which sent its inputs through the adaptive filter. Such a competitive learning model is a particular type of the adaptive vector quantization scheme that possesses Bayesian processing properties.

The rules and process of competitive learning are summarized as follows:

- The units in a given layer are broken into a set of nonoverlapping clusters.

- Each unit within a cluster inhibits every other unit within a cluster. The clusters are working on the winner-take-all concept.

- Every element in every cluster receives inputs from the same lines. The largest input achieves its maximum value, and all other units in the cluster are pushed to the minimum value. The maximum value is set arbitrarily to 1, the minimum value to 0.

- A unit learns if and only if it wins the competition with other units in its cluster.

- A stimulus pattern x_j consists of a binary pattern in which each element of the pattern is either active or inactive. An active element is assigned the value 1 and an inactive element is assigned the value 0.

- Each unit has a fixed amount of weight (all weights are positive) that is distributed among its input lines. The weight on the line connecting unit i on the lower (or input) layer to unit j on the upper layer is designated w_{ij}.

- The fixed total amount of weight for unit j is designated $\sum_i w_{ji} = 1$.

- A unit learns by shifting weight from its inactive to its active input lines. If a unit does not respond to a particular pattern, no learning takes place in that unit. If a unit wins the competition, then each of its input lines gives up some proportion g of its weight, and that weight is then distributed equally among the active input lines.

The competitive learning module can operate with or without an external teaching signal b; learned changes in the adaptive filter can proceed indefinitely or can cease after a finite time interval. If there is no teaching signal at a given time, the net input vector to the output layer is the sum of signals arriving via the adaptive filter. Then, if the category representation network is designed to make a choice, the node that automatically becomes active is the one whose weight vector best matches the signal vector, the external signal x, which may or may not overrule the past in the competition.

In cognitive psychology, competitive learning is used to model categorical perception.

3.10   Memory-Type Paradigms

3.10.1   Random Access Memory (RAM)

Random access memory (RAM) is not an ANN paradigm. Understanding the RAM operation, however, will strengthen the understanding of other paradigms that emanate from RAM concepts.

The RAM is a stack of storage bins or *locations*. An 8-bit bin is known as a *byte*. Locations are numbered in ascending order, from 0 to a very large number (a power of 2), and typically in the thousands or millions of bytes. A 64-kbyte memory has 64,000 bytes or 64K $\times$ 8 = 512,000 bits. The bit is the smallest single quantity in a byte; it contains a 1 or a 0. Hence, RAMs store binary numbers. Thus, a RAM looks macroscopically like a matrix of bits, 64,000 rows by 8 columns. Memories other than those that store binary numbers are not readily available, yet. However, some proposals for analog memories have been made.

A RAM consists of the bit matrix, the data bus, the address bus, the address decoder, and the control bus (clock, read, and write signals). The data bus consists of eight paths, each of which is connected to one column of the matrix. The address bus consists of paths where a binary number is applied; the decimal value of the binary number is as large as the number of rows in the matrix. For a 64,000-byte RAM a 16-bit address bus is needed. When a 16-bit binary code is applied at the address bus, the decoder circuit of the RAM decodes the address and activates one of the decoder output signals that correspond to the decimal value of the address; this signal enables the corresponding row. For example, if a binary code has the decimal value of 3093, the 3093rd row will be enabled (Figure 3-15).

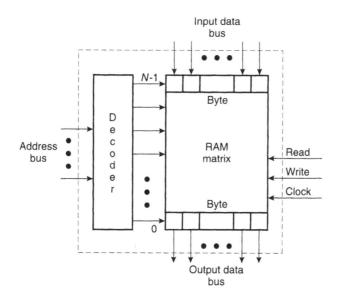

Figure 3-15 RAM model.

The RAM is used to write information in or read information out one byte at a time. Writing in a RAM may be paralleled with learning; reading out may be paralleled with association or recall. Write or read is accomplished by utilizing the control signals as follows:

Write: The byte to be written in the memory is put on the data bus, the location number on the address bus. The 8 data bits are presented simultaneously on all locations, but only the addressed location is enabled. Then the write signal is presented, and at the rising edge of the clock the byte is written in the addressed memory location.

Read: For a read operation, the location number is put on the address bus, and the read signal is enabled. Then at the rising edge of the clock, the contents of the addressed location become available on the data bus.

Other types of RAM are read only memory (ROM), electrically programmable read only memory (EPROM), and electrically erasable programmable read only memory (EEPROM). The name of each variation describes its functionality. For example, in ROM, once written it reads only—it cannot write in again.

In principle, RAM memories may be viewed as one-directional associating (or mapping) networks where each address pattern corresponds to a unique memory location where data patterns are stored. Hence, each address pattern is associated with a pattern stored in a RAM location. Learning takes place during writing in the RAM and association takes place during reading. The decoder circuit of a RAM is the first associating network; when an address pattern is presented, its associated decoder output is activated. Then the activated decoder output selects the corresponding RAM location and the associated output pattern in that location is obtained.

Comparing RAMs with ANNs, there are fundamental differences and pros and cons that must be considered in any application:

- With RAMs one does not have to deal with weights, and there is no iterative process during learning, as in neural networks.

- The contents of the RAM are easily updated, and hence so is the association between input-output patterns.

- ANNs require much processing time during learning, and reprogramming is either not feasible or requires an external processor and field-programmable devices to update the weights.

- The RAM decoder is an a priori network; in other words, it is prewired and there is no learning capability in the RAM decoder.

- The RAM cannot provide correct outputs from partial inputs.

- RAMs have greater capacity (millions of bytes versus a few thousand patterns), greater speed (nanoseconds versus microseconds), and smaller size (one small integrated circuit versus few) than ANNs.

3.10.2 Content Addressable Memory (CAM)

The content-addressable memory (CAM) is also a matrix memory as is RAM/ROM. There is a fundamental difference, however, in the read operation [37, 38, 39]. Typically, during the learning phase, initial patterns are written in the CAM. During recall, one wants to check whether some pattern at the input matches a pattern in the CAM. Then the data pattern is presented at the data bus at all locations simultaneously. If there is a match, the CAM provides a confirmation signal and the address where it is stored (Figure 3-16). Hence, the CAM provides a match or no-match indication in a single operation.

The CAM function may be accomplished with RAM by using an iterative algorithm: read out a location of the RAM and compare the output with the pattern under test; if it does not match, read the next location, and so on, until either a match is found or all locations are read. This iterative process, however, requires many operations, which many applications cannot afford.

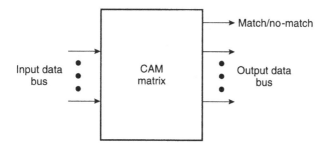

Figure 3-16 Basic CAM architecture.

The CAM may be viewed as associating (or mapping) data to address; that is, for every data in the memory there corresponds some unique address. Also, it is viewed as a data correlator; input data is correlated with stored data in the CAM. Notice that stored patterns must be unique (i.e., different patterns in each location). If the same pattern is in more than one location in the CAM, then, although the correlation will be correct, the address will be ambiguous.

3.10.3   Bidirectional Associative Memory (BAM)

The architecture of the bidirectional associative memory (BAM) [40, 41, 42] is not a matrix but a two-layer neural network, F_A and F_B. The BAM is a heteroassociative, nearest-neighbor, pattern-matching network that encodes binary or bipolar pattern pairs using Hebbian learning. It thus associates patterns from a set A to patterns from a set B, and vice versa (Figure 3-17). When a pattern from the A set of data is presented to the F_A input, the network associates with and recalls a pattern from data set B. The reverse is also true; when a pattern from the B set of data is presented to the F_B input, the network associates with and recalls a pattern from data set A, hence the name bidirectional associative memory. A variation of the BAM that exhibits adaptivity is known as ABAM [43] (for adaptive BAM).

The training phase of a BAM, during which the neural network makes weight adjustments to learn to associate k pairs of patterns A_k and B_k in each direction, requires vector and matrix manipulation. The weight matrix W, an $n \times m$ matrix, is calculated as

$$W = \sum_{k=1}^{m} A_k^T B_k.$$

During recall, when a pattern A_k is presented at the F_A inputs, the $B_k(R)$ pattern is retrieved. The final pattern $B_k(O)$ is obtained by passing

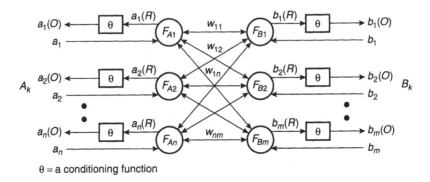

θ = a conditioning function

Figure 3-17 BAM architecture.

the pattern $B_k(R)$ through a conditioning function θ that limits the outputs to $+1$ or -1. The conditioning function is estimated as

$$[\theta_k] = \sum_{j=1}^{n} \theta_{k,j} = \sum_{j=1}^{n} \left(\sum_{i=1}^{n} a_{i,k}^T w_{ij} \right),$$

where $a_{i,k}$ is the ith element of the input pattern A_k, and $[\theta]$ is a scalar. Now:

If $[\theta_k] > 0$, then $B_{k+1}(O)$ values $\geq +1$ become $+1$ and values $< +1$ become -1.

If $[\theta_k] \leq 0$, then $B_{k+1}(O)$ values > -1 become $+1$ and values ≤ -1 become -1.

If $[\theta_k] = 0$, then $B_{k+1}(O)$ values ≥ 0 become $+1$ and values < 0 become -1.

Similarly, when a pattern B_k is presented at the F_B inputs, the $A_k(O)$ pattern is retrieved by passing the pattern $A_k(R)$ through the conditioning function θ that conditions the outputs to $+1$ or -1. The conditioning function is estimated as

$$[\theta_k] = \sum_{j=1}^{n} \theta_{k,j} = \sum_{j=1}^{n} \sum_{i=1}^{m} b_{i,k}^T w_{ij},$$

where $b_{i,k}$ is the ith element of the input pattern B_k, and $[\theta]$ is a scalar. Now:

If $[\theta_k] > 0$, then $A_{k+1}(O)$ values $\geq +1$ become $+1$ and values $< +1$ become -1.

If $[\theta_k] < 0$, then $A_{k+1}(O)$ values > -1 become $+1$ and values ≤ -1 become -1.

If $[\theta_k] = 0$, then $A_{k+1}(O)$ values ≥ 0 become $+1$ and values < 0 become -1.

Examples 3.3 and 3.4 illustrate the foregoing concepts.

Example 3.3: Calculate the weights of 2×2 BAM

Consider the two pairs of patterns (with bipolar symbols):

$$A_1 = (+1, +1, -1) \quad \text{and} \quad B_1 = (-1, +1, -1, +1)$$

and

$$A_2 = (+1, -1, +1) \quad \text{and} \quad B_2 = (+1, -1, +1, -1).$$

Then

$$A_1^T B_1 = \begin{bmatrix} +1 \\ +1 \\ -1 \end{bmatrix} [-1, +1, -1, +1] = \begin{bmatrix} -1 & +1 & -1 & +1 \\ -1 & +1 & -1 & +1 \\ +1 & -1 & +1 & -1 \end{bmatrix}$$

and

$$A_2^T B_2 = \begin{bmatrix} +1 \\ -1 \\ +1 \end{bmatrix} [+1, -1, +1, -1] = \begin{bmatrix} +1 & -1 & +1 & -1 \\ -1 & +1 & -1 & +1 \\ +1 & -1 & +1 & -1 \end{bmatrix}.$$

The sum of the two matrices is

$$W = \sum_{k=1}^{2} A_k^T B_k = \begin{bmatrix} 0 & 0 & 0 & 0 \\ -2 & +2 & -2 & +2 \\ +2 & -2 & +2 & -2 \end{bmatrix}.$$

Example 3.4: Given the BAM of Example 3.3 and a pattern $A_1 = (+1, +1, -1)$, recall pattern B_1

$$B_1(R) = A_1 W = (+1, +1, -1) \begin{bmatrix} 0 & 0 & 0 & 0 \\ -2 & +2 & -2 & +2 \\ +2 & -2 & +2 & -2 \end{bmatrix}$$

$$= (-4, +4, -4, +4).$$

Now apply the conditioning function $(-4, +4, -4, +4) = 0$ to all the elements of the $B_1(R)$ vector, and those elements that are > 0 set to $+1$, those < 0 set to -1. When this is done, the $B_1(O)$ pattern $(-1, +1, -1, +1)$ is obtained, as expected.

A BAM may be thought of as two CAMs connected such that the output from one is the input to the other (Figure 3-18). The dynamic heteroassociative memory [44] is based on the 2-CAM BAM concept.

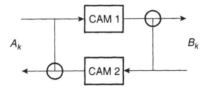

Figure 3-18 Conceptual 2-CAM BAM.

3.10.4 Temporal Associative Memory (TAM)

The temporal associative memory (TAM) [45, 46, 47] is a two-layer, nearest-neighbor ANN (Figure 3-19). It uses unsupervised learning, and functionally it is a cyclic sequential encoder with feedback paths; it learns to associate bipolar or binary sequential patterns, as A_1 with A_2, A_2 with A_3, A_3 with $A_4, \ldots, A_{n-1}$ with A_n, and A_n with A_1.

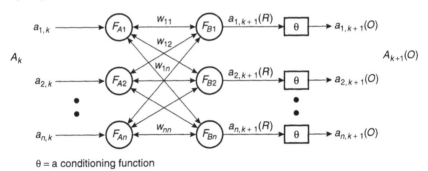

θ = a conditioning function

Figure 3-19 TAM architecture.

The stability of this network needs to be verified over the complete cycle [40] of patterns; compared with the stability of static ANNs, where one pattern is presented and the obtained output is verified. Thus, the TAM needs n sequential verifications, for n patterns, to determine that the network is stable.

The architecture of the TAM is a two-layer neural network, F_A and F_B, similar to the BAM network. Notice the bidirectional interconnectivity between the two layers. For simplicity, inputs and outputs are shown in one direction only.

The training phase of a TAM during which the neural network learns to associate consecutive pairs (A_k, A_{k+1}) of patterns in each direction requires similar vector and matrix manipulation as the BAM. For example, for n

sequential patterns $A_1, A_2, \ldots, A_n$ the weight matrix W is calculated as

$$W = \sum_{k=1}^{n-1} A_k^T A_{k+1} + A_n^T A_1.$$

Then, during recall, when a pattern $A_k = a_{1,k}, \ldots, a_{n,k}$ is presented at the F_A inputs, the $A_{k+1}(R) = a_{1,k+1}(R), \ldots, a_{n,k+1}(R)$ pattern is retrieved. The final pattern $A_{k+1}(O)$ is obtained by passing the pattern $A_{k+1}(R)$ through a conditioning function, as in the BAM model, and conditioning it to $+1$ or -1.

The conditioning function is estimated as

$$[\theta_k] = \sum_{j=1}^{n} \theta_{k,j} = \sum_{j=1}^{n} \sum_{i=1}^{n} a_{i,k}^T(O) w_{ij},$$

where $a_{i,k}$ is the ith element of the input pattern A_k, and $[\theta]$ is a scalar. Now:

If $[\theta_k] > 0$, then $A_{k+1}(R)$ values $\geq +1$ become $+1$ and values $< +1$ become -1.

If $[\theta_k] < 0$, then $A_{k+1}(R)$ values > -1 become $+1$ and values ≤ -1 become -1.

If $[\theta_k] = 0$, then $A_{k+1}(O)$ values ≥ 0 become $+1$ and values < 0 become -1.

See Examples 3.5 and 3.6.

Example 3.5: Calculate the weights of a TAM

Consider the three patterns (with bipolar symbols)

$$A_1 = (+1, +1, -1), \quad A_2 = (-1, +1, -1), \quad \text{and}$$
$$A_3 = (+1, -1, +1).$$

Then

$$A_1^T A_2 = \begin{bmatrix} +1 \\ +1 \\ -1 \end{bmatrix} [-1, +1, -1] = \begin{bmatrix} -1 & +1 & -1 \\ -1 & +1 & -1 \\ +1 & -1 & +1 \end{bmatrix},$$

$$A_2^T A_3 = \begin{bmatrix} -1 \\ +1 \\ -1 \end{bmatrix} [+1, -1, +1] = \begin{bmatrix} -1 & +1 & -1 \\ +1 & -1 & +1 \\ -1 & +1 & -1 \end{bmatrix},$$

and

$$A_3^T A_1 = \begin{bmatrix} +1 \\ -1 \\ +1 \end{bmatrix} [+1, +1, -1] = \begin{bmatrix} +1 & +1 & -1 \\ -1 & -1 & +1 \\ +1 & +1 & -1 \end{bmatrix}.$$

The sum of the three matrices is

$$W = \sum_{k=1}^{2} A_k^T A_{k+1} i + A_3^T A_1 = \begin{bmatrix} -1 & +3 & -3 \\ -1 & -1 & +1 \\ +1 & +1 & -1 \end{bmatrix}.$$

Example 3.6: Given the TAM of Example 3.5 and a pattern
$A_1 = (+1, +1, -1)$, generate the next pattern A_2

$$A_2(R) = A_1 W = (+1, +1, -1) \begin{bmatrix} -1 & +3 & -3 \\ -1 & -1 & +1 \\ +1 & +1 & -1 \end{bmatrix}$$
$$= (-3, +1, -1).$$

Now, calculate the conditioning function:

$$[\theta] = (-3, +1, -1) = -3 < 0.$$

Hence, elements of the $A_2(R)$ vector with values > -1 will
be set to $+1$ and ≤ -1 will be set to -1. Thus, $(-3, +1, -1)$
is conditioned to $(-1, +1, -1)$, as expected.

Similarly, a TAM may be thought of as a CAM in a feedback configuration (Figure 3-20); when A_k is presented at the input, A_{k+1} is obtained
at the output, which is fed back to obtain A_{k+2}; and so on.

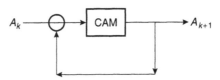

Figure 3-20 Conceptual TAM using a
CAM with feedback.

3.11   Linear Associative Memory (LAM)

In 1972, James Anderson focused on the development of a linear model,
called a **linear associator memory** (LAM). This model was based on

the Hebbian principle that connections between neuronlike elements are strengthened every time they are activated (Figure 3-21).

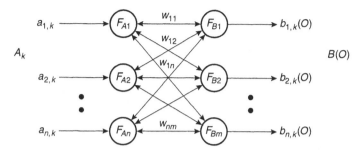

Figure 3-21 LAM architecture.

An extension to the linear associator is the **brain-in-the-box** model. Anderson describes this model as follows: an activity pattern inside the box receives positive feedback on certain components that has the effect of forcing it outward. When its elements start to limit (when it hits the wall of the box), it moves into a corner of the box where it remains for eternity. The box resides in the state-space (one axis for each neuron) of the network and represents the saturation limits for each state.

The LAM, pioneered by Anderson [48], Kohonen [49], and Nakano [50], stores a p set of pattern pairs (A^p, B^p) as a correlation matrix in one direction. During learning, the weight matrix is calculated as

$$w_{ij} = \sum_{p=1}^{m} a_i^p b_j^p \qquad (3.37)$$

or, in vector form,

$$W = \sum_{p=1}^{m} A_p^T b_p.$$

During recall, presentation of pattern A_p yields an output vector X proportional to B_p, as follows:

$$X_p = A^{(p)} W_i = \sum_i a_i^{(p)} w_{ij} = \sum_i a_i \left(\sum_q a_i^{(p)} b_j^{(p)} \right)$$

$$= \sum_q \left(\sum_i a^{(p)} a_i^{(q)} \right) b_j^{(q)} = \sum_q (a^{(p)} a^{(q)}) b_j^{(q)} \qquad (3.38)$$

If the vectors $a^{(p)}$ are mutually orthogonal,

$$A_i A_j^T = 0 \quad \text{for every } 1 \neq j, \qquad (3.39)$$

then the last sum in the equation reduces to a single term, with

$$X_j = \|a^{(p)}\|^2 b_j^{(p)}. \tag{3.40}$$

That is, the output vector X is directly proportional to the desired output vector $b^{(p)}$. Now if all the vectors A_k are normalized to unit length,

$$\sum_{i=1}^{n} (a_i^p)^2 = 1 \quad \text{for every } p = 1, 2, \ldots, m, \tag{3.41}$$

then the output $X_j = A_k$; that is, the desired output has been recalled.

3.12   Real-Time Models

Most of the paradigms described require external control of system dynamics. The term *real-time* describes neural network paradigms that require no external control of system dynamics, and they process information as soon as it arrives without any delay other than the inherent system delay that is characteristic of any electrical and/or chemical process due to the system's time constants. Differential (not difference) equations constitute the language of real-time models. To clarify this, consider a differential circuit made with differential operational amplifiers. This circuit will start differentiating the input signal autonomously and in real time. The only delay is some RC time constant. If differentiation should be implemented by a controlled system (e.g., a digital system), the input should be sampled, the samples converted into binary numbers, the binary numbers stored, and subtraction performed between two samples by a circuit and the difference stored; when all this is done, take the stored binary differences, convert them into an analog pulse, and pass all pulses through a smoothing filter to reconstruct a continuous signal that represents the first derivative of the input signal. All these operations take place in synchronism with a square-wave oscillator as the synchronizing mechanism. Because of the clock, again in a strict sense, the operation of the circuit is sequential—so much for nonsequential algorithmic execution of neural networks. Real-time models today may or may not have an external teaching input, and learning may or may not be terminated after a finite time interval.

3.13   Linear Vector Quantization (LVQ)

The linear vector quantization (LVQ) is a classifier paradigm, developed by Teuvo Kohonen, that adjusts the boundaries between categories to minimize misclassification. An LVQ net has a single layer of nodes (see also winner-takes-all) where each node responds to a class or subclass of patterns. During training, for each input pattern, the LVQ finds (Figure 3-22) the output node with the best match to the training pattern. If the training pattern's class differs from the output node's class, then it finds the next-best match. If the next-best match has the correct class, the LVQ moves the best-match node farther from the training pattern and moves the next-best match node closer to it. This process, known as competitive learning, in effect moves the boundary between classes closer to the optimum position.

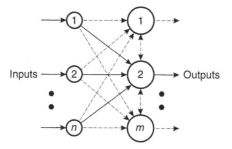

Figure 3-22 Learning vector quantization.

LVQ is used for optical character recognition, converting speech into phonemes, and other applications.

3.14   Self-Organizing Map (SOM)

The self-organizing map (SOM) is a clustering algorithm developed by Teuvo Kohonen [51]. It creates a map of relationships among input patterns. The map is a reduced representation of the original data (Figure 3-23). A SOM net resembles an LVQ net. Both have a single layer of nodes and use a distance metric to find the output node closest to a given input pattern, like the LVQ does. Unlike the LVQ, however, SOM output nodes do not correspond to known classes but to unknown clusters that the SOM finds in the data autonomously.

During training, the SOM finds the output node that has the least distance from the training pattern. It then changes the node's weights to increase the similarity to the training pattern, and it influences the weights of the neighboring nodes even though they have only random relationships to the training pattern. Different patterns trigger different winners that influence different neighbors. The overall effect is to move the output nodes

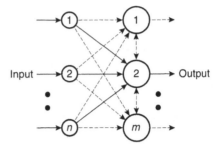

Figure 3-23 Self-organizing map.

to "positions" that map the distribution of the training patterns. After training, each node's weights model the features that characterize a cluster in the data.

3.15 Probabilistic Neural Network (PNN)

The probabilistic neural network (PNN) is a classifier paradigm [52] that instantly approximates the optimum boundaries between categories. This paradigm assumes that the training data are a true representative sample. This network has two hidden layers (see Figure 3-24). The first contains a dedicated node for each training pattern; the second contains a dedicated node for each class. The two hidden layers are connected on a class-by-class basis; that is, the multiple examples of the class in the first are connected only to a single matching node in the second.

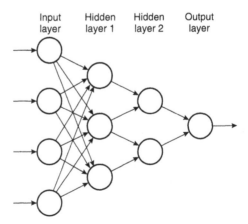

Figure 3-24 PNN network.

During training, PNN uses the training patterns to estimate the class probability distributions; each new input is classified according to the weighted average of the closest training examples. PNN simply stores the training patterns, avoiding the iterative process. It therefore learns very fast, but large data sets require large networks.

3.16 Radial Basis Function (RBF)

The radial basis function (RBF) is a classification and functional approximation paradigm developed by M. J. D. Powell [53]. It consists of two layers whose output nodes form a linear combination of the basis (or kernel) functions computed by the hidden layer nodes (see Figure 3-25). The basis functions (nonlinearity) in the hidden layer produce a significant nonzero response to input stimulus only when the input falls within a small localized region of the input space. This paradigm is also known as a *localized receptive field network.*

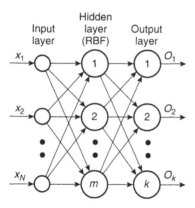

Figure 3-25 RBF model.

The most common nonlinearities used in RBF are the sigmoidal and the Gaussian kernel functions. The latter is of the form

$$u_{1,j} = \exp\left[\frac{(x - w_{1,j})(x - w_{1,j})}{2\sigma_j^2}\right], \qquad j = 1, 2, \ldots, N_l, \quad (3.42)$$

where $u_{1,j}$ is the output of the ith node in the first layer, x is the input pattern, $w_{1,j}$ is the weight vector for the jth node in the first layer, σ_j^2 is the normalization parameter for the jth node, and N_l is the number of nodes in the first layer. The output (second layer with N_2 nodes) is

$$O_j = w_{2,j}^T u_1, \qquad j = 1, 2, \ldots, N_2, \qquad (3.43)$$

where O_j and $w_{2,j}$ are the output and the weight vectors, respectively, of the jth output node, and u_1 is the vector of outputs from the first layer (augmented with an additional component of value 1, replacing the bias term; see Section 3.3).

When Gaussian kernel functions are used, each node produces an identical output for inputs within a fixed radial distance from the center of the kernel $w_{j,i}$; that is, they are radially symmetric, and hence the name RBF. The overall network forms a linear combination of the nonlinear basis function of Eq. (3.42), and hence it performs a nonlinear transformation from R^{N_1} to R^{N_2} (by forming a linear combination of the nonlinear basis functions in Eq. (3.42)).

RBF Learning Algorithm

- Start training the hidden layer with an unsupervised learning algorithm.

- Continue training the output layer with a supervised learning algorithm.

- Simultaneously apply a supervised learning algorithm to the hidden and output layers to fine-tune the network.

3.17   Time-Delay Neural Net (TDNN)

Consider a tapped delay line, that is, a shift register. Consider also a multilayer Perceptron where the tapped outputs of the delay line are applied at its input (see Figure 3-26). This network constitutes a time-delay neural net (TDNN). The output has a finite temporal dependence on the input

$$u(k) = F[x(k), x(k-1), \ldots, x(k-n)], \qquad (3.44)$$

where F is the typical nonlinearity function. When this function is a weighted sum, then the TDNN is equivalent to a **finite impulse response** (FIR) filter. Based on the network architecture of the TDNN, when the output is fed back, via a unit delay, into the input, the net is equivalent to an infinite impulse response (IIR) filter (Figure 3-27). Notice that FIR and IIR filters are implemented routinely with digital signal processors (DSPs).

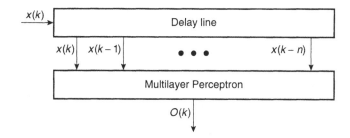

Figure 3-26   TDNN.

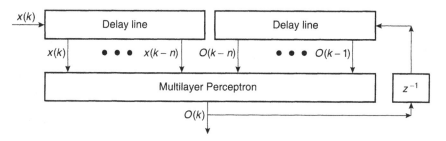

Figure 3-27   TDNN with output feedback.

3.18   Cognitron and Neocognitron Models

Fukushima developed the Cognitron [54] in 1975 and the larger-scale Neo-cognitron [55, 56] in 1980. The Neocognitron is a hierarchical multilayer network consisting of a cascade of many layers. The neurons in each layer can receive analog nonnegative inputs. The nonlinearity of each neuron is a positive ramp starting at zero; $f = x$ for $x \geq 0$ and $f = 0$ for $x < 0$.

The Neocognitron can learn to recognize sets of patterns. Learning can proceed with or without a teacher. During the learning phase the neurons of the lower layers of the network extract elemental features of the pattern, which are passed to the next layer, where gradual integration of the features takes place from layer to layer. At the highest layer (output layer), each neuron responds to a specific pattern only. Hence, for N patterns, N output neurons are needed. Locally, the computations are based on competitive learning and use combinations of contributory and inhibitory dynamics. This feature extraction process, known as *progressively redundant elemental feature coding*, is met in biological pattern recognition (see Section 1.4), and on this basis future recognition is accomplished in the Neocognitron.

Thus, recognition is performed on the basis of similarity of pattern shape and not on the exact positioning or size of the pattern. As a result, pattern deformations or shifts in position do not affect the recognition process. The latter classifies the Neocognitron as a *translation-invariant* and *size-invariant pattern recognition* network.

3.19   Simulated Annealing

A class of probabilistic weight-change laws appears in neural models under the name **simulated annealing** [57–61]. This technique is primarily for combinatorial optimization problems with many variables [62]. A combinatorial optimization problem seeks to find some configuration of parameters $\bar{X} = (X_1, \ldots, X_N)$ that minimizes some function $f(\bar{X})$ known as the cost function. In ANNs the configuration parameters are associated with the set of weights and the cost function is associated with the error function.

The main idea of simulated annealing stems from a method widely used in statistical mechanics, the Metropolis algorithm [63]. This algorithm approximately describes a many-body system—namely, a material that anneals into a solid as temperature is slowly decreased. To describe this technique, consider the slope of a hill that has local valleys and a ball moving down the hill (Figure 3-28); the local valleys are local minima, and the bottom of the hill is the universal minimum. It is possible that the ball may stop at a local minimum and never reach the universal one (see Figure 3.28). In ANNs this would correspond to a set of weights that corresponds to that local; however, this is not the desired solution. To avoid situations of this kind, simulation annealing perturbs the ball such that, if it is trapped in a local minimum, it escapes from it and continues falling until it reaches the global minimum (i.e., the optimum solution). At that point, further perturbations cannot move the ball to a lower position.

The annealing algorithm (its mathematical description is beyond the scope of this text) needs four basic components:

1. A configuration: the possible problem solution over which we search for a good answer (in ANNs this is the optimum steady-state weights).

2. The move set: a set of allowable moves that permits us to escape from local minima and reach all feasible configurations.

3. The cost function.

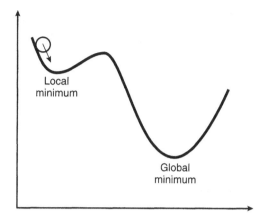

Figure 3-28 Simulation annealing—ball and hill.

4. A cooling schedule: a starting cost function and rules to determine when it should be lowered and by how much, and when annealing should be terminated.

The methods and ideas here are so closely tied to those of neural networks that the two approaches are often linked. This link is perhaps closest in the Boltzmann machine [64], which uses a simulated annealing algorithm to update weights in a binary network similar to the additive model studied by Hopfield [65].

3.20   Boltzmann Machine

One early optimization technique used in ANNs is based on the Boltzmann machine [66, 67]. The Boltzmann learning machine is surprisingly simple. The learning cycle has two phases (positive and negative) that alternate, followed by a progressive weight adjustment. During the positive phase, we cycle through the entire set of input-output pattern pairs. Each pair is clamped into the input and output units, and the rest of the network is then annealed (i.e., starting with a high temperature and gradually cooling down the thermal equilibrium at a temperature of 1°C), allowing the hidden neurons to evolve according to Metropolis dynamics. Once the system is close to equilibrium, we keep running it for a few more cycles, during which time each connection keeps a record of how often the two units it joins are on at the same time. After all of the input-output pairs have been presented in this way, each connection will have recorded a value ρ, which is the fraction of time during the positive phase in which the two connected nodes are on at the same time at thermal equilibrium. The negative phase is identical except that only the inputs are clamped; the output units are allowed to settle into whatever states they like. During this phase the entire network evolves according to Metropolis dynamics.

3.21   Other Paradigms

3.21.1   Restricted Coulomb Energy (RCE)

The restricted Coulomb energy (RCE) paradigm is a three-layer, feedforward neural network based on Coulomb's law, developed by the Nestor Company. Coulomb's law states that the potential energy due to a distribution of charge on the surface of a sphere is, for points outside the sphere, the same as would be produced by the same total charge at the sphere's center. Therefore, no potential maxima or minima exist in a charge-free region.

The RCE is an equilibrium neural network model that avoids the problem of spurious max and min associated with other models. It does so by depositing "memories" as if they were charges in some high-dimensional feature space; that is, a pattern input to the RCE excites one or more of the memories. A test charge, corresponding to a pattern input to the network, can be attracted only to sites where other charges are located. Thus, the problem of spurious memories does not exist in the RCE.

3.21.2   Culbertson's Model

Culbertson's concern was visual pattern recognition. In 1950, he compiled an artificial retina from many layers of neurons with the properties that any figures projected onto the retina were processed by taking them through all transformations necessary to provide a comparison with a set of "templates" (standard set of figures). The first transformation is linear, the second for dilation, the third for expansion, and the last for rotation.

3.21.3   Encephalon Project

The Encephalon project is based on holographic memories and Hebb's principle, which states that when two neurons fire, the efficacy of the connection between them is increased. The Encephalon consists of three units: the **cortical column**, the **basal ganglia** (for motor activities), and the **reticular information**. It decentralizes control and avoids lengthy training, nor does it use weights at the synaptic inputs.

The Encephalon gives an instant readout of the state of a multidimensional machine with the concept of holographic memories; when you look at an object from any angle, you still recognize that object. The Encephalon duplicates that effect by creating a circuit element called the *cortical column*, which can be ganged with other columns to store each viewpoint from which an object might be observed. Through the use of relatively simple electronic devices to store patterns in this highly distributed network of cortical columns, an object can be recognized regardless of its orientation. This allows the Encephalon to associate the patterns it learns with other patterns it may have in memory automatically. The Encephalon does not require repeated presentations of training data, nor does it make any distinction between learning and recall. The architecture is constantly associating new data with previously learned information.

3.21.4   Cellular Neural Network (CNN)

In 1988, the cellular neural network (CNN) architecture was introduced [68, 69], based on cellular automata; that is, every cell in the network is connected only to its neighbor cells (Figure 3-29). The basic circuit unit of the CNN is the **cell**. For example, $C(2, 3)$ in Figure 3-29 is a cell. Cells not directly connected together affect each other indirectly due to propagation effects of the network dynamics. Mathematical analysis of CNNs is based on electronic circuit analysis, where each cell consists of

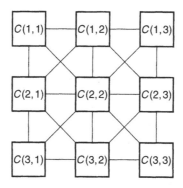

Figure 3-29 A 3 × 3 CNN.

linear capacitors and resistors, linear and nonlinear controlled sources, and independent sources. This analysis differs from the familiar neural network one outlined so far, and it will not be repeated here. However, the interested reader is referred to [68] and [69]. CNNs have been used in a variety of ways, particularly in image processing and pattern recognition and in an array computer [70].

3.21.5   Logicon Projection Network (LPN)

The Logicon projection network (LPN) [71] is a learning process, developed by scientists at Logicon, that amalgamates unsupervised and supervised training during the learning phases. It uses a feedforward network with a hidden layer between the input and output layers. The reason is that with unsupervised training the network learns rather quickly but not very accurately, whereas with supervised training it learns slowly but with fewer errors. An unsupervised method is first applied, such as Kohonen, ART, or RCE, to initialize the weights of the network to some gross values quickly, and then a supervised method such as back propagation is used to fine-tune the weight values. Since the back propagation starts from some "almost acceptable" solution, the network is claimed to converge quickly to a global minimum. Logicon claims that the LPN method outperforms others. In a handwritten character recognition experiment, Logicon claims that a network with the LPN learning method can learn the 26 characters of the alphabet with 100% accuracy from 520 training images, 20 different images per character, in 70 iterations, where each handwritten character has a 20-by-40-pixel image. This LPN performance is compared with back propagation, which can achieve 50% accuracy after 200,000 iterations. Logicon also claims that this network does not have to be reinitialized if more knowledge is to be added. Moreover, a network with some knowledge may be added to another network with different knowledge to obtain the sum of both.

3.21.6   Probabilistic RAM (pRAM-256)

The pRAM-256 Very Large Scale-Integrated (VLSI) neural network processor [72] was developed for general use by the Electrical Engineering Department of King's College, London. It has 256 (pRAM) reconfigurable neurons, each with six inputs. Its on-chip learning unit utilizes reinforced learning where learning can be global, local, or competitive. Synaptic weights are stored in external static RAM. The pRAM embodies both stochastic and nonlinear aspects of biological neurons in a manner that allows for hardware exploitation.

3.21.7 Neural Accelerator Chip (NAC)

The neural accelerator chip (NAC) was developed and integrated in a silicon chip in 1992 by the Information Defence Division of Australia's Defence Science and Technology Organization. It is a systolic array composed of 16 10-bit integer processing elements that can be cascaded in two dimensions with control signals synchronizing the operations. Neuron activation levels and their respective synaptic weights are stored in external RAM.

Each processing element multiplies its input by one of 16 weights preloaded into its dual-ported registers and accumulates the results to 23-bit precision at a rate of 500 million operations per second. Four ports allow processing elements to input weights, activation levels, and partial results from adjacent processing elements or other cascaded NACs, and to output results as well. Outputs are limited to 10 bits by a switchable nonlinear function that simulates the threshold function inherent in real biological systems.

The NAC can be hard-wired to implement a variety of neural network paradigms—feedforward and feedback—as well as standard operations such as two-dimensional convolutions.

A two-layer network may be constructed for image detection. The first layer detects edges in the image, and the second layer evaluates the disparity between frames among the detected features. The output is a real-time readout of the distance between a moving camera and a detected object of interest.

3.22 Review Questions

3.1. Name three different layers of a neural network.

3.2. If the program of a computer is a set of sequential instructions stored in a matrix memory (RAM), what is the program of a neural network, and where is it stored?

3.3. What is the fundamental model of a neuron in a neural network?

3.4. Is it true that the Perceptron does not require supervised learning? If yes, what does it require?

3.5. What is the building block of the Perceptron?

3.6. During learning of a Perceptron, the input is I, the target output is T, the obtained output is O, and the nonlinearity function is F. Express the error signal.

3.7. What is the Delta learning algorithm?

3.8. What is the pitfall using an optimization algorithm?

3.9. Is it true that the MADALINE paradigm consists of many Perceptrons?

3.10. Is it true that the winner-takes-all paradigm can have many inputs and one output only?

3.11. What learning is used in the winner-takes-all paradigm?

3.12. Consider a multilayer perceptron, where the back-propagation algorithm is applied during learning. Is it true that the error obtained between the actual output O and the target output T is used to make changes of the weights at the input stage?

3.13. What was the motivation to develop the CMAC?

3.14. What type of learning does the ART use, and what kind of problems is it best for?

3.15. How many layers does the Hopfield paradigm have?

3.16. If a pattern is presented at the inputs of a content-addressable memory, what is the most basic output message expected?

3.17. What is the basic functional difference between a RAM and a CAM (during a read operation)?

3.18. Is it true that input patterns may be applied at the outputs of a BAM?

3.19. What is the functional equivalent of the TAM network?

3.20. What is the main function of the LVQ network?

3.21. Why is simulated annealing used in many paradigms?

For answers, see page 187.

REFERENCES

[1] W. W. McCulloch and W. Pitts, "A Logical Calculus of the Ideas Imminent in Nervous Activity," *Bull. Math. Biophys.*, vol. 5, pp. 115–133, 1943.

[2] J. von Neumann, *The Computer and the Brain*, Yale University Press, New Haven, Conn., 1958.

[3] W. Pitts and W. S. McCulloch, "How We Know Universals: The Perception of Auditory and Visual Forms," *Bull. Math. Biophys.*, vol. 9, pp. 27–47, 1947.

[4] F. Rosenblatt, "The Perceptron: A Probabilistic Model for Information Storage and Organization in the Brain," *Psychol. Rev.*, vol. 65, no. 6, pp. 386–408, 1958.

[5] F. Rosenblatt, *Principles of Neurodynamics*, Spartan Books, Washington, D.C., 1962.

[6] M. L. Minsky and S. Papert, *Perceptrons: An Introduction to Computational Geometry*, MIT Press, Cambridge, Mass., 1969.

[7] B. Widrow, "Generalization and Information Storage in Networks of Adaline 'Neurons'," in *Self Organizing Systems*, M. C. Yovitz, G. T. Jacobi, and G. D. Goldstein, eds., pp. 435–461, Spartan Books, Washington, D.C., 1959.

[8] B. Widrow and S. D. Stearns, *Adaptive Signal Processing*, Prentice Hall, Englewood Cliffs, NJ, 1985.

[9] B. Widrow and M. A. Lehr, "30 Years of Adaptive Neural Networks: Perceptron, Madaline and Backpropagation," *Proc. IEEE*, vol. 78, pp. 1415–1442, Sept. 1990.

[10] B. Widrow and R. Winter, "Neural Nets for Adaptive Filtering and Adaptive Pattern Recognition," *Computer*, vol. 31, pp. 25–39, 1988. Also in *An Introduction to Neural and Electronic Networks*, S. F. Zonetzer, J. L. Davis, and C. Lau, eds., pp. 249–271, Academic Press, New York, 1990.

[11] B. Widrow and M. E. Hoff, "Adaptive Switching Circuits," in *IRE WESCON Convention Record*, Part 4, pp. 96–104, Institute of Radio Engineers, New York, 1960.

[12] D. Nguyen and B. Widrow, "The Truck Backer-Upper: An Example of Self-Learning in Neural Networks," in *Neural Networks for Control*, W. T. Miller III, S. Sutton, and P. J. Werbos, eds., pp. 287–299, MIT Press, Cambridge, Mass., 1990.

[13] D. Nguyen and B. Widrow, "The Truck Backer-Upper: An Example of Self-Learning in Neural Networks," in Proceedings of IEEE International Joint Conference on Neural Networks (IJCNN), Washington, D.C., pp. 359–363, 1989.

[14] P. Werbos, "Beyond Regression: New Tools for Prediction and Analysis in the Behavioral Sciences," Ph.D. dissertation, Harvard University, 1974.

[15] D. Rumelhart, G. Hinton, and R. Williams, "Learning Representations by Backpropagating Errors," *Nature*, vol. 323, pp. 533–536, 1986.

[16] D. Parker, *Learning Logic*, Invention Report, S81-64, File 1, Office of Technology Licensing, Stanford University, Stanford, Calif., 1982.

[17] F. J. Pineda, "Generalization of Backpropagation to Recurrent and Higher Order Networks," in *Neural Information Processing Systems*, D. Z. Anderson, ed., pp. 602–611, American Institute of Physics, New York, 1988.

[18] R. Hecht-Nielsen, "Counterpropagation Networks," *Appl. Optics*, vol. 26, no. 23, pp. 4979–4984, 1987.

[19] R. C. Fry, E. A. Rietman, and C. C. Wong, "Back-Propagation Learning and Nonidealities in Analog Neural Network Hardware," *IEEE Trans. Neural Networks*, vol. 2, no. 1, pp. 110–117, 1991.

[20] S.-B. Cho and J. H. Kim, "A Fast Back-Propagation Learning Method Using Aitken's Δ^2 Process," *Int. Jour. Neural Networks*, vol. 2, no. 1, pp. 37–42, 1991.

[21] S. Becker and Y. Le Cun, "Improving the Convergence of Back-Propagation Learning with Second-Order Methods," *Proc. of the 1988 Connectionist Models Summer School*, pp. 29–37, 1989.

[22] D. B. Parker, "Optimal Algorithms for Adaptive Networks: Second-Order Backpropagation, Second-Order Direct Propagation, and Second-Order Hebbian Learning," in *Proc. of the IEEE International Conference on Neural Networks*, vol. II, pp. 593–600, 1987.

[23] J. S. Albus, "A New Approach to Manipulator Control: The Cerebellum Model Articulation Controller (CMAC)," *Trans. ASME, Jour. of Dyn. Sys. Meas. and Control*, vol. 97, pp. 220–227, Sept. 1975.

[24] G. Burgin, "Using Cerebellar Arithmetic Computers," *AI Expert*, pp. 32–41, June 1992.

[25] W. T. Miller III et al., "CMAC, an Associative Neural Network Alternative to Backpropagation," *Proc. IEEE*, vol. 78, p. 10, Oct. 1990.

[26] G. A. Carpenter and S. Grossberg, "The ART of Adaptive Pattern Recognition by a Self-Organizing Neural Network," *Computer*, vol. 21, pp. 77–88, March 1988.

[27] G. A. Carpenter and S. Grossberg, "ART2: Stable Self-organization of Pattern Recognition Codes for Analog Input Patterns," *Appl. Optics*, vol. 26, pp. 4919–4930, 1987.

[28] G. A. Carpenter and S. Grossberg, "ART3: Hierarchical Search Using Chemical Transmitters in Self-organizing Neural Pattern Recognition Architectures," *Neural Networks*, vol. 3, pp. 129–152, 1990.

[29] G. A. Carpenter and S. Grossberg, "A Massively Parallel Architecture for a Self-organizing Neural Pattern Recognition Machine," *Computer Vision, Graphics, and Image Processing*, vol. 37, pp. 54–115, 1987.

[30] S. Grossberg, "On the Development of Feature Detectors in the Visual Cortex with Applications to Learning and Reaction-diffusion Systems," *Biol. Cybernetics*, vol. 21, pp. 145–159, 1976.

[31] J. J. Hopfield, "Neural Networks and Physical Systems with Emergent Collective Computational Abilities," *Proc. Nat. Acad. Sci. (USA)*, vol. 79, pp. 2554–2558, April 1982.

[32] S. U. Hedge, J. L. Sweet, and W. B. Levy, "Determination of Parameters in a Hopfield/Tank Computational Network," in *Proceedings of the IEEE International Conference on Neural Networks*, pp. II-291–II-298, July 1988.

[33] J. J. Hopfield, "Neurons with Graded Response Have Collective Computational Properties Like Those of Two-State Neurons," *Proc. Nat. Acad. Sci. (USA)*, vol. 81, pp. 3088–3092, May 1984.

[34] J. J. Hopfield and D. W Tank, "Neural Computation of Decisions in Optimization Problems," *Biol. Cybernetics*, vol. 52, pp. 141–152, 1985.

[35] D. W. Tank and J. J. Hopfield, "Simple Neural Optimization Networks: An A/D Converter, Signal Decision Circuit, and a Linear Programming Circuit," *IEEE Trans. Circuits and Systems*, vol. CAS-33, no. 5, pp. 533–541, May 1986.

[36] D. E. Rumelhart and D. Zipser, "Feature Discovery by Competitive Learning," *Cognitive Sci.*, vol. 9, pp. 75–112, 1985.

[37] T. Kohonen, *Content-Addressable Memories*, Springer-Verlag, Berlin, 1984.

[38] D. Bursky, "Content-Addressable Memory Does Fast Matching," *Electric. Design*, pp. 119–121, Dec. 1988.

[39] Advanced Micro Devices, Product Description: "The Am95C85 Content Addressable Data Manager," AMD, July 1987.

[40] B. Kosko, "Bidirectional Associative Memories," *IEEE Trans. Systems, Man, and Cybernetics*, vol. SMC-18, pp. 42–60, 1988.

[41] B. Soffer et al., "Holographic Associative Memory Employing Phase Conjugation," *Proc. SPIE*, vol. 684, pp. 2–6, 1986.

[42] B. Soffer et al., "Associative Holographic Memory with Feedback Using Phase-Conjugate Mirrors," *Optics Lett.*, vol. 11, pp. 118–120, 1986.

[43] B. Kosko, "Adaptive Bidirectional Associative Memories," *Appl. Opt.*, vol. 26, no. 23, pp. 4947–4959, 1987.

[44] M. H. Hassoun, "Dynamic Heteroassociative Neural Memories," *Neural Networks*, vol. 2, pp. 275–287, 1989.

[45] S.-I. Amari, "Neural Theory of Association and Concept Formation," *Biol. Cybernetics*, vol. 26, pp. 175–185, 1972.

[46] J. Buchman and K. Schulten, "Storing Sequences in Biased Patterns in Neural Networks with Stochastic Dynamics," in *Neural Computers*, NATO ISI Series, vol. E41, R. Ecmiller and C. v. d. Malsburg, eds., pp. 231–242, Springer-Verlag, Berlin, 1988.

[47] I. Guyon, L. Personnaz, and G. Dreyfus, "Of Points and Loops," in *Neural Computers*, NATO ISI Series, vol. E41, R. Ecmiller and C. v. d. Malsburg, eds., pp. 261–269, Springer-Verlag, Berlin, 1988.

[48] J. Anderson, "A Simple Neural Network Generating an Interactive Memory," *Math. Biosc.*, vol. 14, pp. 197–230, 1972.

[49] T. Kohonen, "Correlation Matrix Memories," *IEEE Trans. Computers*, vol. C-21, pp. 353–359, 1972.

[50] N. Nakano, "Association: A Model of Associative Memory," *IEEE Trans. Systems, Man, and Cybernetics*, vol. SMC-2, pp. 381–388, 1972.

[51] T. Kohonen, *Self-Organization and Associative Memory*, Springer-Verlag, Berlin, 1984.

[52] D. F. Specht, "Probabilistic Neural Networks and the Polynomial Adaline as Complimentary Technique for Classification," *IEEE Trans. Neural Networks*, vol. 1, no. 1, pp. 111–121, 1990.

[53] M. J. D. Powell, "Radial Basis Function for Multi-Variable Interpolation: A Review," in Proceedings of IMA Conference on Algorithm for the Approximation of Function and Data, RMCS, Shrivenham, 1985 (or Report #DAMTP/NA12, Dept. of Applied Mathematics and Theoretical Physics, University of Cambridge), 1985.

[54] K. Fukushima, "Cognitron: A Self-Organizing Multilayer Neural Network," *Biol. Cybernetics*, vol. 20, pp. 121–136, 1975.

[55] K. Fukushima, "Neocognitron: A Self-Organizing Neural Network Model for a Mechanism of Pattern Recognition Unaffected by Shift in Position," *Biol. Cybernetics*, vol. 36, pp. 193–202, 1980.

[56] K. Fukushima and S. Miyake, "Neocognitron: A New Algorithm for Pattern Recognition," *Pattern Recognition*, vol. 15, no. 6, pp. 455–469, 1982.

[57] R. A. Rutenbar, "Simulated Annealing Algorithms: An Overview," *IEEE Circuits and Devices Mag.*, pp. 19–26, Jan. 1989.

[58] P. J. M. van Laarhoven and H. L. Aarts, *Simulated Annealing: Theory and Applications*, D. Reidel Publishing, Norwell, Mass., 1987.

[59] B. Hajek, "A Tutorial Survey of Theory and Applications of Simulated Annealing," in *Proceedings of the 24th IEEE Conference on Decision and Control*, pp. 755–760, Dec. 1985.

[60] S. Kirkpatrick, C. D. Gelatt, and M. P. Vecchi, "Optimization by Simulated Annealing," *Science*, vol. 220, no. 4598, pp. 671–680, 1983.

[61] R. V. V. Vidal, ed., *Applied Simulated Annealing*, Springer-Verlag, New York, 1988.

[62] E. M. Reinhold, J. Nevergelt, and N. Deo, *Combinatorial Algorithms: Theory and Practice*, Prentice Hall, Englewood Cliffs, N.J., 1977.

[63] N. Metropolis et al., "Equations of State Calculations by Fast Computing Machines," *Jour. Chem. and Phys.*, vol. 21, pp. 1087–1091, 1953.

[64] D. H. Ackley, G. E. Hinton, and T. J. Sejnowski, "A Learning Algorithm for Boltzmann Machines," *Cognitive Sci.*, vol. 9, pp. 147–169, 1985.

[65] J. J. Hopfield, "Neural Networks and Physical Systems with Emergent Collective Computational Abilities," *Proc. Nat. Acad. Sci. (USA)*, vol. 79, pp. 2554–2558, 1982.

[66] G. E. Hinton, T. J. Sejnowski, and D. H. Ackley, "Boltzmann Machines: Constraint Satisfaction Networks that Learn," *S.I.A.M. Jour. Control and Optim.*, vol. 24, pp. 1031–1043, 1986.

[67] H. J. Sussmann, *On the Convergence of Learning Algorithms for Boltzmann Machines*, Tech. Report 88-03, Rutgers Center for Systems and Control, 1988.

[68] L. O. Chua and L. Yang, "Cellular Neural Networks: Theory," *IEEE Trans. Circuits and Systems*, vol. 35, no. 10, pp. 1257–1272, 1988.

[69] L. O. Chua and L. Yang, "Cellular Neural Networks: Applications," *IEEE Trans. Circuits and Systems*, vol. 35, no. 10, pp. 1273–1290, 1988.

[70] T. Roska and L. O. Chua, "The CNN Universal Machine: An Analogic Array Computer," *IEEE Trans. Circuits and Systems*, vol. 40, no. 3, pp. 163–173, 1993.

[71] R. C. Johnson, "Logicon Breeds Neural Hybrid," *Electr. Eng. Times*, pp. 31–32, Jan. 17, 1994.

[72] pRAM-256 Data Sheet, Dept. Electronic and Electrical Engineering, King's College, London, UK.

4

FUZZY LOGIC

4.1 Propositional Logic

In crisp logics, such as binary logic, variables are either true or false, black or white, 1 or 0. An extension to binary logic is multivalue logic, where variables may have many crisp values. Propositional logic, on the other hand, is defined with uncertain terms, as illustrated in Example 4.1.

Example 4.1

> If it is about 2:00 P.M., and if I did not have lunch at about noon, and if I had a fair breakfast at about 8:00 A.M., then I am a little hungry. If I had lunch at about 1:00, however, and it is now about 3:00 P.M., regardless of whether I had breakfast, then I am not very hungry, but if it is past 7:00 P.M., then I'm somewhat hungry.

Although I have not defined in crisp, definite terms what the exact times are, nor have I defined "fair breakfast," "a little hungry," "not very hungry," or "somewhat hungry" (interpretations vary among people), you understood my meaning.

Consider a generalized logic that includes not only crisp values but all possible values between 1 and 0. Moreover, there is some degree of *fuzziness* about the exact value in {1, 0}; each input value is fuzzy. The logic to infer a crisp outcome from fuzzy input values is **fuzzy logic** [1, 2].

Example 4.2

In an upcoming race it is expected that, from past experience, all runners finish the race in four groups, with each group at different speed. The first group finishes in the "shortest" time, the second with a "moderate-to-shortest" time, the third with a "moderate-to-longest" time, and the fourth group with the "longest" time. In addition, if we record the times of each runner in each group, we'll notice that each group has a particular distribution of times or speeds. Now, we are asked to predict the outcome of a race based on three variables: height of runner, speed of runner, and ground conditions. These variables have been further divided, based on some requirements or common sense, into "slow," "moderate," and "fast" for the variable "speed"; "tall" and "short" for the variable "height"; and "wet," "damp," and "dry" for the variable "ground condition." Now, on this basis and with some rules (not yet defined), we must predict in which of the four groups the runner will finish if he or she is moderately fast and tall and if the ground is wet.

4.2   The Membership Function

A relationship is defined to express the **distribution of truth** of a variable. For example, "small" may be defined as a distribution around a value x; hence, any value within the distribution may be interpreted as "small," although with different degrees of truth or confidence.

Theoretically, a fuzzy set F of a universe of discourse $X = \{x\}$ is defined as a mapping, $\mu_F(x) : X \to [0, \alpha]$, by which each x is assigned a number in the range $[0, \alpha]$, indicating the extent to which x has the attribute F. Thus, if x is the number of vehicles in a queue, "small" may be considered as a particular value of the fuzzy variable "queue," and each x is assigned a number in the range from 0 to ∞, $\mu_{\text{small}}(x) \in [0, \alpha]$, that indicates the extent to which that x is considered to be small: $\mu_{\text{small}}(x) \in [0, \alpha]$ is called a **membership function**. When the membership function has been normalized (i.e., $\alpha = 1$), then $\mu_F(x) : X \to [0, 1]$ and the fuzzy logic is called **normal**. From now on, only normal fuzzy logic is considered. For the extreme case, where the distribution is of "zero" width, the membership function is reduced to **singularities**; in other words, the fuzzy logic reduces to a crisp logic. If the singularities are of two possibilities, we then have binary logic.

Recall Example 4.2. The distributions for "speed" would correspond to the membership function for "slow," "moderate," and "fast." Similarly, the same would apply for "wet" and "dry" for the variable "ground condition," and so on.

The normalization of the fuzzy set $\tilde{F}$ is expressed by

$$\sup_{x \in X} \mu_{\tilde{F}}(x) = 1. \tag{4.1}$$

Normalization of a set of numbers (or of a function) is achieved by dividing each number of the set by the largest one, the supremum. Then the largest number in the set becomes equal to 1 and this is what relation (4.1) expresses. For example, the set of numbers (30, 50, 80, 100, 70, 40) is normalized to $(0.3, 0.5, 0.8, 1.0, 0.7, 0.4)$ if we divide each number by 100, the supremum in the set.

Let X be a time-invariant set of objects x. A fuzzy set $\tilde{F}$ in X may be expressed by a set of ordered pairs:

$$\tilde{F} = [(x, \mu_{\tilde{F}}(x)) | c \in X], \tag{4.2}$$

where $\mu_{\tilde{F}}$ is the membership function that maps X to the membership space M, and $\mu_{\tilde{F}}(x)$ is the grade of membership (or degree of truth) of x in $\tilde{F}$. The latter is equivalent to $A = $ true (or $A = 1$) in binary logic; in fuzzy logic $A = $ true is expressed by the degree of truth or the grade of membership for some value of x. In addition, when M contains the values 0 and 1 only, then $\tilde{F}$ is nonfuzzy and $\mu_{\tilde{F}}$ is the characteristic function of a nonfuzzy set. Hence, binary and multivalue logics (i.e., crisp logics) are extreme subcases of fuzzy logic.

As an example, let runners' speeds be $X = \{1, 2, 3, 4, 5, 6, 7, 8, 9, 10\}$, where x is the speed. Speeds around 1 km/h are considered *Slow* $(\tilde{A})$, around 4 km/h *Moderate* $(\tilde{B})$, and around 7 km/h *Fast* $(\tilde{C})$. Thus, Slow, Moderate, and Fast are not crisply defined. Then the normalized fuzzy sets for Slow and Fast may be described in pairs as

$$\tilde{A} = \{(0, 0), (0.5, 1), (1, 1), (3, 0)\}$$

and

$$\tilde{C} = \{(5, 0), (7, 1), (8, 1)\}$$

(Figure 4-1). Here, for simplicity, piecewise linear membership functions have been assumed. However, membership functions may be continuous curves of many different shapes.

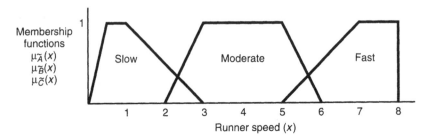

Figure 4-1 Membership functions (normalized) for Slow, Moderate, and Fast.

Exercise 4.2

Using Figure 4-1, find the grade of membership of $\mu_{\tilde{A}}(1)$, $\mu_{\tilde{A}}(2)$, $\mu_{\tilde{B}}(4)$, and $\mu_{\tilde{C}}(6)$.

For those thinking "Booleanly," view the membership functions as fuzzified variables of a multivariable logic. In our example of the runners, if the three crisp variables (trivalent logic) were defined as Fast = 7 km/h, Slow = 2 km/h, and Moderate = 4 km/h, then speeds between 1 and 4 and between 4 and 7 are not defined. Now, *fuzzification* of the three crisp variables, as in Figure 4-1, causes spreading of the variables with a distribution profile that suits the problem at hand, and thus all speeds are included. If a runner runs at 2.5 km/h (see Figure 4-1), this speed belongs to variable Slow with 0.25 and to Moderate with 0.5 confidence (overlapping is common, and many times desirable, in fuzzy logic).

4.3   Fuzzy Logic

In Boolean logic the function of Boolean operators (or gates) AND, OR, and INVERT is well known. For instance, by "gating" the value of two variables using an AND, we get $11 \rightarrow 1$, $10 \rightarrow 0$, $01 \rightarrow 0$, or $00 \rightarrow 0$. In fuzzy logic, the values are not crisp, and their fuzziness exhibits a distribution described by the membership function. Hence, if we try to "gate" two fuzzy variables, what will the output be? This question has been addressed by various fuzzy logics. Here, we consider min-max logic. In simple terms, if we consider "union" (equivalent to OR), the outcome is equal to the input variable with the greatest value, $\max(x_1, x_2, \ldots, x_n)$. That is, if $A = 0.5$, $B = 0.7$, and $C = A$ OR B, then $C = \max(0.5, 0.7) = 0.7$. If we consider "intersection" (equivalent to AND), the outcome is equal to the least value of the input variables, $\min(x_1, x_2, \ldots, x_n)$. In this case, if $C = A$ AND B, then $C = \min(0.5, 0.7) = 0.5$. If we consider "complement" (equivalent to NOT), then the outcome is the complement of 1, or $\bar{x} = 1 - x$. If $C = \bar{B}$, then, $C = 1 - 0.7 = 0.3$.

Example 4.3

Consider the fuzzy logic expression $\mu_A(x_1)$ AND $\mu_B(x_2)$ evaluated at $x_1 = 2$ and $x_2 = 4$ to be $\mu_A(x_1 = 2) = 0.72$ and $\mu_B(x_2 = 4) = 0.45$. Thus, the output of the expression is $\min\{0.72, 0.45\} = 0.45$. Similarly, if the fuzzy expression was $\mu_A(x_1)$ OR $\mu_B(x_2)$, then the output of the expression is $\max\{0.72, 0.45\} = 0.72$. Furthermore, the complement of $\mu_A(x_1 = 2)$ is $1 - 0.72 = 0.28$.

4.4 Fuzzy Rule Generation

In most fuzzy problems the rules are generated based on past experience. Concerning problems that deal with **fuzzy engines** or **fuzzy control**, one should know all possible input-output relationships even in fuzzy terms. The input-output relationships, or **rules**, are then easily expressed with **if** ... **then** statements, such as

If A_1 and/or B_1, then H_{11}, else.

If A_2 and/or B_1, then H_{21}, else.

If A_1 and/or B_2, then H_{12}, else.

If A_2 and/or B_2, then H_{22}.

Here "and/or" signifies logical union or intersection, the A's and B's are fuzzified inputs, and the H's are actions for each rule.

The case where rules are expressed by a single input variable—if A_1 then H_1, if A_2 then H_2, ..., if A_n then H_n—represents a simple translation (or transformation) of input variables to the output. However, the most common fuzzy logic problems involve more than one variable. The set of *if...then* rules with two input variables is tabulated in Table 4-1.

The *if...then* rule becomes more difficult to tabulate if the fuzzy statements are more involved (i.e., have many variables), such as *if A and B and C or D, then H*. Tabulation is greatly simplified if one follows a statement decomposition process. For example, consider the original problem

Table 4-1. Fuzzy Rule Tabulation

A_1	H_{11}	H_{12}
A_2	H_{21}	H_{22}
	B_1	B_2

statements of the form

$$\textit{If } A_i \textit{ and } B_j \textit{ and } C_k, \textit{ then } H_{ijk}.$$

This statement is decomposed as

$$\textit{If } A_i \textit{ and } B_j, \textit{ then } H_{ij}.$$

$$\textit{If } H_{ij} \textit{ and } C_k, \textit{ then } H_{ijk}.$$

H_{ij} is an intermediate variable. This process is illustrated in Table 4-2.

Table 4-2. Decomposition Process of Three Variables

A_1	H_{11}	H_{12}		C_1	H_{111}	H_{121}	H_{211}	H_{221}
A_2	H_{21}	H_{22}		C_2	H_{112}	H_{122}	H_{212}	H_{222}
	B_1	B_2			H_{11}	H_{12}	H_{21}	H_{22}

Example 4.4

The original statement *if A_1 and B_2 and C_1, then H_{121}* is decomposed into *if A_1 and B_2, then H_{12}*, and *if H_{12} and C_2, then H_{121}*. From Table 4-2, left side, the intersection of A_1 and B_2 yields the intermediate variable H_{12}; from the right-side table, H_{12} and C_1 yields the response H_{121}.

This decomposition process may easily be extended to many variables.

Example 4.5

Consider a vehicular throttle control system that opens and closes at various degrees, depending on changing road slope and desired speed, to maintain the desired speed. For simplicity, many other parameters are not taken into account.
    The conditions of the problem are

If the slope is greater than 25°, and
if the current speed is high, and
if the speed desired is higher,
then open the throttle a lot to increase speed.

or
If the slope is between 15° and 25°, and
if the current speed is high, and
if the speed desired is medium,
then open throttle a little.

or
If the slope is between 2° and 4°, and
if the current speed is high, and
if the speed desired is medium,
then close throttle a little.
and so on.

These statements constitute the fuzzy logic rules. The first group constitutes rule 1, the second, rule 2, and so on. From these rules, the key variables are "slope" (S), "current speed" (V_c), "desired speed" (V_d), and "throttle" (Thr). More important in this problem, however, are the slope difference (ΔS), the difference between current and desired speed (ΔV), and the opening difference of the throttle (ΔThr). Typically, we partition these differences in fuzzy ranges such as "small," "medium," and "large." In our example,

$\Delta S : \pm$ 0–10° small, around 15° medium, around 30° large.

$\Delta V : \pm$ 0–10 km/h small, around $\pm$15 km/h medium, and around $\pm$30 km/h large.

ΔThr: around $\pm$5% small, around $\pm$10% medium, around $\pm$20% large.

Each of these ranges has a profile; positive changes may have profiles that differ from negative changes. Some positive profiles are illustrated in Figures 4-2, 4-3, and 4-4.

In addition, we modify the propositional statements (rules) accordingly:

Rule 1
   If the slope changes by medium, and
   if the speed changes by small,
   then the throttle opening changes by medium.

or
Rule 2
   If the slope changes by small, and
   if the speed changes by small,
   then the throttle opening changes by small.

or

Rule 3

   If the slope changes by large, and
   if the speed changes by small,
   then the throttle opening changes by large.

and so on.

Here "and" implies logical union ($\cup$). The fuzzy logic equation (general rule) of the problem is thus

$$\Delta Thr = \Delta S \cup \Delta V. \qquad (4.3)$$

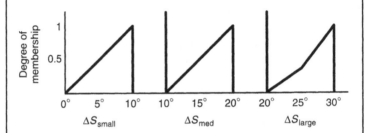

Figure 4-2 Membership functions for ΔS.

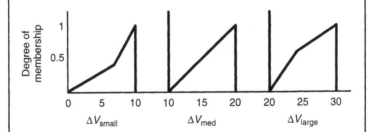

Figure 4-3 Membership functions for ΔV.

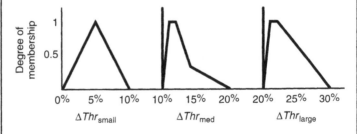

Figure 4-4 Membership functions for ΔThr.

4.5   Defuzzification of Fuzzy Logic

The defuzzification process is an important step. Based on this step, the output action may or may not be successful. It is not uncommon to have, based on the rules and membership functions, two (or more) answers to a question; see Figure 4-1 where $\mu_{slow}(2.5) = 0.25$ and $\mu_{moder.}(2.5) = 0.5$. In general, defuzzification is the process where the membership functions are sampled to find the grade of membership; then the grade of membership(s) is used in the fuzzy logic equation(s) and an outcome region is defined. From this, the output is deduced.

Several techniques have been developed to produce an output. The three most used are:

maximizer, by which the maximum output is selected,

weighted average, which averages weighted possible outputs,

centroid (and its variations), which finds output's center of mass.

Example 4.6

This oversimplified example demonstrates how the principles discussed so far can be used to make inferences. Assume that the membership functions for slope difference (ΔS), speed difference (ΔV), and throttle difference (ΔThr) are as in Example 4.5 and that, at a given time, the vehicle is moving from horizontal to a positive slope of 18°, the current speed of the car is 60 km/h, and the desired speed is 65 km/h. Hence, ΔS is 18°, and ΔV is 5 km/hr. Based on rule 1, the fuzzy logic equation, and the membership relationship (4.3) for ΔS_{medium}, ΔV_{small}, and ΔThr_{medium}, the process to infer the proper outcome is illustrated in Figure 4-5.

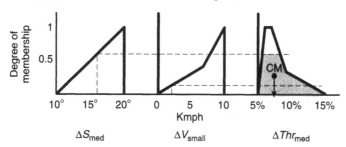

Figure 4-5 Membership functions and defuzzification of throttle control problem.

In summary, the key steps for solving a fuzzy problem are as follows:

1. Define the fuzzy problem in detail.

2. Identify all important variables and their ranges.

3. Determine membership profiles for each variable range.

4. Determine rules (propositional statements), including action needed.

5. Select the defuzzification methodology.

6. Test the system for correct answers; if needed, go back to step 3.

4.6 Time-Dependent Fuzzy Logic

4.6.1 Crisp Logics

Traditional combinatorial logic is a static logic. It provides a logic output 1 or 0 based on the binary values at the inputs. Sequential logic takes combinatorial logic a step further; it considers events or states in sequential order. It is a process/state-based logic that, based on current states and input/output parameters, determines the *next* state. This may be encapsulated in an *if...then, else* statement: *if* {this happens}, *then* {do this}, *else* {do that}. The next state is merely the next "step" of a process that takes place at a later, unspecified, time. The state diagram in Figure 4-6 substantiates exactly this point: the next state {A, B, or C} in the state diagram depends on the current state {A, B, or C} and input {1 or 0}, whereby the dimension of time is *not* significant *nor* explicitly indicated. For instance, state A will change to state B only when the input will be 1; when the input will become 1, however, is not known.

Combinatorial or sequential logic does not address many knowledge-intensive and real-time processes [3] where temporal reasoning plays an important role. The logic that extends the traditional logic and predicate calculus to include the *notion* of time is called **temporal logic** [4–11]. However, combinatorial, sequential, and temporal logics are crisp and the parameter and variable values are true/false, exactly 1 or 0.

4.6.2 Fuzzy Logics

Fuzzy logic, as described so far, may be considered a generalized combinatorial or sequential logic; however, the passage of time is not necessarily of the essence. In fuzzy control an *if...then, else* approach [12] is also followed, where again the passage of time is not of the essence.

As with combinatorial and sequential processes, there are real-time fuzzy processes where temporal reasoning is important. However, existing fuzzy control approaches [13, 14] are not result-related, they are algorithmically oversimple, and they do not reflect real-time evaluation of the control objectives. To overcome this difficulty, different approaches have been proposed [15], but again, time is not explicit in these approaches.

In the next section fuzzy logic is extended to include time-dependent membership functions. This logic is called **temporal fuzzy logic** (TFL) [16, 17]. Pictorially, TFL may be viewed as filling the matrix of logics (Figure 4-7). In the figure, B_L = Boolean/multivalue logic, T_L = temporal logic, and F_L = fuzzy logic.

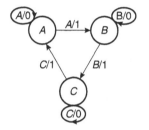

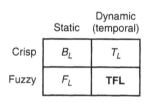

Figure 4-6 Typical state diagram.   Figure 4-7 Matrix of logics.

4.7 Temporal Fuzzy Logic (TFL)

The notion of time in knowledge-based systems goes back to antiquity; Plato's τά πάντα ρεῖ (everything flows) meant that everything is changing in form and substance with the passage of time. Although this statement is philosophically inspired, it has universal truth and has been well understood and experienced in many areas in technology and everyday life. Hence, it was reasonable that sooner or later the notion of time would find its way into areas other than physics and mathematics, where time is explicitly included in the equations of motion. One such area is linguistics. Recently, the uncertainty of *time interval* in linguistic expressions has led to a temporal representation that considers time intervals as primitives [18] and to the development of a fuzzy temporal reasoning process [19] (i.e., in many respects, a logic of fuzzy time intervals). For example, "I'll see you at 3:00 P.M.," "I'll see you in the afternoon," or "I'll see you later" define different levels of certainty and time intervals.

The fuzzy logic previously described is a standard Zadeh time-independent logic, whereby the membership function is **time invariant** (i.e., it does not change with time). Here, we introduce a more generalized formalization of a temporal fuzzy logic whereby fuzzy variables and membership functions are functions of time. This includes the notion of fuzzy intervals and delays. The TFL is intended for real-time control of processes where traditional sequential fuzzy logic is not adequate. In TFL, the *if...then, else* statement is applicable.

We shall demonstrate that, in many problems, assuming a time-independent, or static, membership function may not be correct, that the membership function should be described in the time domain, and that its evolution in time should be considered in the defuzzification process.

The notion of membership function as a function of time is illustrated as follows: Consider a membership function that describes highway traffic. Based on traffic and other parameters, a determination must be made as to the best route to direct traffic. The traffic pattern changes during the day, from day to day, and from season to season; in other words, it is time variant. Moreover, it changes dramatically during certain prescheduled occasions, such as football games, and unscheduled events, such as natural disasters and accidents. If we neglect for now the unscheduled events, it is clear that the membership function that describes a traffic pattern should be described in the time domain.

In general, the membership function changes with time. However, if the rate of change is slow, then, for all practical purposes, it may be considered static or time invariant. If, on the other hand, the rate of change is fast, then it is considered time dependent or time variant. In the traffic routing example, in which metropolitan traffic was calculated at 7:30 A.M. and at 7:35 A.M., one may consider time invariant membership functions with very little error. However, between 7:30 A.M. and 9:00 A.M. the membership function has changed dramatically. Moreover, considering time-variant membership functions, an ambiguity as to the correct outcome, during the defuzzification process, may be removed. To demonstrate this, with reference to Figure 4-1, consider that a runner's speed is $x = 2.5$ km/h. This value of x produces two grades of membership that may lead to ambiguity with different results; the certainty for Slow at $x = 2.5$ is 0.25 and that for Moderate is 0.5. Hence, the question: "Is that speed slow or moderate?" Assume, however, that $x = 2.5$ is a runner's speed measured at time instant t_i, and that a second measurement is made at time instant t_{i+1}, and this yields $x = 2.2$. From Figure 4-1, the certainty now is $\mu_{\tilde{A}}(2.2) = 0.4$ and $\mu_{\tilde{B}}(2.2) = 0.2$. Now, the answer to the original question becomes clearer and with more certainty since the difference in speed tends toward Slow, and if this *trend* continues, then surely it will be slow.

4.7.1 Time-Invariant Membership Function

Consider real-time control problems, where the grade of membership is either not changing with time or is slowly varying with time, compared with other processes in the system. What may change with time is the value of x and, hence, the grade of membership. The time-dependent grade of membership (i.e., the evaluation of the membership function at some time) is expressed by

$$\mu_{\tilde{F}}(x_i), \tag{4.4}$$

where x_i is the value of x at time instant t_i.

In our discussion, the ambiguity of an outcome and the grade of the membership function at different time intervals led us to identifying a trend. Here, the confidence rate, $\mathcal{R}$, is defined as a function of the difference of the grade of membership over a time interval. It indicates the rate of confidence about the true value of a fuzzy variable:

$$\mathcal{R}_{\tilde{F}} = -\eta f \left(\frac{\delta \mu_{\tilde{F}}}{\delta t} \right) \Bigg|_{\text{at} \mu_t(x_i)}, \tag{4.5}$$

where $\eta \in R \geq 1$ is a positive multiplicative factor, a scalar, called the *confidence index*, and $\mu_{\tilde{F}}(x_i)$ is the grade of membership at point time t_i. More explicitly, the confidence rate is expressed by

$$\mathcal{R}_{\tilde{F}} = -\eta \frac{\mu_{\tilde{F}}(x_i) - \mu_{\tilde{F}}(x_{i+1})}{\delta t} \Bigg|_{\text{at} \mu_{\tilde{F}}(x_i)}, \tag{4.6}$$

where x_i and x_{i+1} are the values of x measured at subsequent time points t_i and t_{i+1}. For example, for $\delta t = 1$ time units, $\eta = 10$, and $\mu_{\tilde{A}}$ and $\mu_{\tilde{B}} = 0.2$, as before, then $\mathcal{R}_{\text{slow}} = +1.5$ and $\mathcal{R}_{\text{moder.}} = -3$. The sign of the confidence rate indicates the direction of confidence; the -3, compared with $+1.5$, indicates that the confidence that x belongs to Slow becomes stronger than the confidence that x belongs to Moderate; hence, the moderate possible solution may be ignored.

One of the applications of the rate of membership is in adaptive fuzzy systems whereby the initial fuzzy system is ambiguous as to the most accurate solution. Calculating the confidence rate, however, decreases the ambiguity.

4.7.2 Time-Variant Membership Function

Assume that the membership function for "slow," "moderate," and "fast" in our example has changed within a specific amount of time, as in Figure 4-8. Consider that membership functions are time variant. One may say that most membership functions are time variant. However, if the change is very slow compared with the change of a real-time process, they then may be viewed as time-invariant functions. If, conversely, they change at a comparable speed, then time-variant functions should be treated as such. Time-variant membership functions are expressed as

$$\mu_{\tilde{F}}(x, t), \tag{4.7}$$

and the grade of membership is expressed by

$$\mu_{\tilde{F}}(x_i, t_i), \tag{4.8}$$

where x_i is the value of x at time instant t_i.

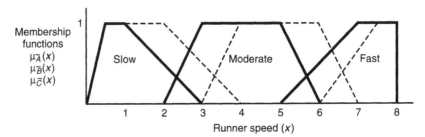

Figure 4-8 Membership functions at $t = T$ (solid line) and $t = T + 1$ (dashed line).

The confidence rate now is expressed by

$$\mathcal{R}_{\tilde{F}_{t_i}} = -\eta \frac{\mu_{\tilde{F}}(x_i, t_i) - \mu_{\tilde{F}}(x_{i+1}, t_{t+1})}{\delta t}\bigg|_{\text{at}\mu_{\tilde{F}}(x_i, t_i)}, \tag{4.9}$$

where x_i and x_{i+1} are the values of x measured at time points t_i and t_{i+1}. With reference to Figure 4-8 (dashed line), the rate of confidence at $x = 2.5$ and $\eta = 10$ yields $R_{\text{slow}} = +5$ and $R_{\text{moder.}} = -5$. Hence, the initial ambiguity (see Figure 4-1) is lifted, and the value $x = 2.5$ is declared to belong to the membership function μ_{slow}.

4.7.3 Intervals

Time intervals play a pivotal role in real-time systems, real-time control, and other areas. In the next two sections the definitions of interval and theoretical operators on intervals are given and their applicability is illustrated.

A *singleton* interval τ_i is a quantum of time starting from time point i and ending at, but not on, time point $i + 1$ such that the end of interval τ_i and the beginning of interval τ_{i+1} are continuous but not overlapping. An extensive reasoning of time points versus time intervals is found in [13]. Here we focus on control applications and refrain from philosophical definitions of time. Hence, an interval of time τ_0^n is defined by a nonempty sequence of singleton intervals, or time steps, such as $\tau_0, \ldots, \tau_{n-1}$, where $\tau_i \in N$. The length of an interval is the sum of consecutive time steps, not the number of time points; however, time points define the beginning of an interval:

$$|\tau_0^n| = |\langle t_0, \ldots, t_n \rangle| = n \times \tau_{\text{time units}}. \tag{4.10}$$

For example, the interval between time points t_2 and t_9 (t_9 not included) is

$$|\tau_2^9| = |\langle t_2, \ldots, t_9 \rangle| = \sum_{i=2}^{9-1} \tau_i = |9 - 2| = 7\tau_{\text{time units}},$$

or, diagrammatically,

4.7.4 Semilarge Intervals

Two cases of semilarge intervals are now defined, the *prefix interval* and the *postfix interval* [20]:

$$\text{postfix}(\tau_j) = |\tau_j^\alpha| = |\langle t_j, \ldots, t_\alpha \rangle|, \tag{4.11}$$

or, diagrammatically;

and

$$\text{prefix}(\tau_i) = |\tau_0^i| = |\langle t_0, \ldots, t_i \rangle|, \tag{4.12}$$

or, diagrammatically,

We assume no negative times and that the symbol $\propto$ is a very large number. In a strict mathematical sense it may mean infinity.

A consequence of postfix and prefix is

$$|\tau_0^\propto| - \text{prefix}(\tau_i) = \text{postfix}(\tau_{i+1}) \qquad (4.13)$$

and

$$|\tau_0^\propto| - \text{postfix}(\tau_i) = \text{postfix}(\tau_{i-1}), \qquad (4.14)$$

and for $i > j$,

$$\text{prefix}(\tau_i) \wedge \text{postfix}(\tau_j) = |\tau_0^i \wedge \tau_j^\propto| = |\tau_j^i| \qquad (4.15)$$

with time interval length

$$\|\tau_j^i\| = (i - j) \times \tau_{\text{time units}}$$

or, diagrammatically,

4.7.5   Interval Operators

In some real-time applications, the length of time interval between two events needs to be scaled up or down. For example, real-time multiplexers (such as in time-division multiple-access (TDMA) systems) receive real-time events from various sources at a specified rate, compress the time interval of events, and multiplex them. The output provides all multiplexed events within the same time interval. The description of such operations necessitates an operator that scales time intervals up or down. Herein, two operators are distinguished: expansion and compression operators. Interval operators are useful in certain real-time applications where time compression and time expansion are routinely done by changing the bit rate of the digital information.

The Time Expansion Operator D_λ

If a time interval is τ time units, the expanded interval is

$$\underset{\lambda}{\tau} = D^\lambda \tau = (\lambda \tau)_{\text{time units}}, \qquad (4.16)$$

where $1 \leq \lambda \in R$ is a coefficient, $\underset{\lambda}{\tau}$ is the expanded by λ interval τ, and D^λ is the expansion operator. The effect of the D^λ on a sequence of time intervals is

$$D^\lambda\{\tau_0, \ldots, \tau_n\} = \{\tau_0^\lambda, \ldots, \tau_n^\lambda\} \tag{4.17}$$

and

$$D^\lambda|\tau_0^n| = |\overset{\lambda}{\tau_0^n}| = D^\lambda \sum_{i=0}^{n-1} |\tau_i| = (\lambda n \tau)_{\text{time units}}. \tag{4.18}$$

The Time Compression Operator D_λ

Similarly, the compressed interval is

$$\underset{\lambda}{\tau} = D_\lambda \tau = \left(\frac{\tau}{\lambda}\right)_{\text{time units}}, \tag{4.19}$$

where, again, $1 \le \lambda \in R$ is a coefficient, $\underset{\lambda}{\tau}$ is the compressed by λ interval τ, and D_λ is the compression operator.

The effect of the D_λ operator on a sequence of time intervals is

$$D_\lambda\{\tau_0, \ldots, \tau_n\} = \{\underset{\lambda}{\tau_0}, \ldots, \underset{\lambda}{\tau_n}\} \tag{4.20}$$

and

$$D_\lambda|\tau_0^n| = |\underset{\lambda}{\tau_0^n}| = D_\lambda \sum_{i=0}^{n-1} |\tau_i| = \left(\frac{n\tau}{\lambda}\right)_{\text{time units}}. \tag{4.21}$$

Time Discretization

In the previous section two time interval operators were introduced. In analog systems, variables are changing continuously, and the passage of time is viewed as a continuous variable. Hence, the notion of interval between two time points is mathematically elaborate since a time point has no dimensions. Here, no effort is made to elaborate this point; mathematicians and philosophers may answer what the time interval is between two "successive time points." This issue becomes simpler and less argumentative, however, if we consider events that, for all practical purposes, are sampled at equal discrete time intervals T; the notion of a system clock that "ticks" every period T is common in discrete time systems. Discrete time is a mathematical convenience that allows for the algorithmic description of time-dependent events. Even though events evolve continuously, they are "sampled" at every period T. The time interval between two successive clock ticks provides a measurement of the period of the system clock, and the value of a variable at the tick of the clock is the instantaneous value of the variable. For all practical purposes, the time interval operators and the operators listed in the next section are with reference to this clock.

4.7.6 Temporal Fuzzy Logic Syntax

In mathematics, there is often a need to introduce special symbols to describe operations. For example, the symbols $+$, $-$, $\times$, and $/$, although trivial, are special. Similar to other logics, temporal fuzzy logic also uses a syntax with *constant symbols* (such as 0, 1, 2, ...), *variable symbols* (such as letters, underscores, and dashes), *function letters* (such as $+$), *predicate letters* (such as $=$ and $<$), and *propositional connectives* (such as $\bar{x}$ (for inversion), $\vee$, $\wedge$, $\rightarrow$, and $\leftrightarrow$).

Moreover, temporal fuzzy operators are used to transfer linguistic statements to a *notational description*. These operators are defined herein, and examples demonstrate the translation from the linguistic expressions to symbolic expressions. The first five operators adapt the notation of temporal logic after Manna-Pnueli, and the sixth after [21]; the definitions of the remaining operators are introduced for the first time. For brevity, the term *fuzzily true/false* has been shortened to "true/false."

1. The $\bigcirc$ for *next*; $\bigcirc\mu_A(x, t_i)$, paraphrased as $\mu_A(x, t_i)$, becomes true at the next instance or at the next tick of a clock. The next tick of a clock should not be confused with the *next state* unless states change at the tick of a clock. In general, it is not known when the next state will occur. Then $\bigcirc\mu_A(x, t_i) = \mu_A(x, t_{i+1})$.

2. The $\square$ for *henceforth*; $\square\mu_A(x, t_i)$ means $\mu_A(x, t_i)$ will be true henceforth, or from this clock period and all subsequent periods.

3. The $\Diamond$ for *eventually*; $\Diamond\mu_A(x, t)$ means $\mu_A(x, t)$ eventually will be true.

4. The U for *until*; $\mu_A(x, t)$ U $\mu_B(x, t)$ means $\mu_A(x, t)$ will be true until $\mu_B(x, t)$ is.

5. The $\wp$ for *precedes*; $\mu_A(x, t_i)$ $\wp$ $\mu_B(x, t_j)$, $i \leq j$, means $\mu_A(x, t_i)$ will be true prior to $\mu_B(x, t_j)$.

6. The Δ for *event* [21]; $\Delta\mu_A(x, t)$ means the event $\mu_A(x, t)$ is about to occur. This operator is similar to but not the same as the operator $\bigcirc$. The Δ operator implies that if a variable becomes true, then the event $\mu_A(x, t)$ will occur next; it is used in conjuction with complex expressions.

7. The ∂ for *while*; $\mu_A(x, t) \, \partial \, \mu_B(x, t)$ means $\mu_A(x, t)$ will become true *if* $\mu_B(x, t)$ is true, and it stays true for as long as $\mu_B(x, t)$ is true.*

8. The $\cent$ for *concurrence*; $\mu_A(x, t) \, \cent \, \mu_B(x, t)$ means that when $\mu_A(x, t)$ becomes true, then (synchronously) $\mu_B(x, t)$ becomes true; the reverse is also true. This operator is used in symbolic expressions of synchronous operations where events occur simultaneously.

9. The **W** for *wait*; $\mathbf{W}\mu_A(x_i, t_i)$ means calculate the grade of membership $\mu_A(x_i, t_i)$ and wait until another operator terminates the validity of this operator.

10. The W^n for *wait for n*; $W^n \mu_A(x_i, t_i)$ means wait for n consecutive intervals and then calculate the grade of membership $\mu_A(x, t_i)$.

11. The $\overset{n}{\rightarrow}$ for *shift-in n times*; $[\mu_A(x_i, t_i)] \overset{n}{\rightarrow} X$ means shift the grades of membership $\mu_A(x_i, t_i)$ n consecutive times in X, where $X = \{x_1, \ldots, x_m\}, n \le m$, and $i = 1, \ldots, n$.

12. The $\alpha\{ \quad \}$ for *contents* of location α; $\alpha\{\mu_A(x_i, t_i)\}$ means the contents of α are the grade of membership $\mu_A(x_i, t_i)$ at time t_i.

13. The M^α for *store in address*; $M^\alpha \mu_A(x_i, t_i) = \alpha\{\mu_A(x_i, t_i)\}$ means store the grade of membership $\mu_A(x_i, \tau_i)$ in location α. Here, a model of a memory is assumed such that it has several nodes (the classical locations), where each node is accessible for updates and reads. The memory model may or may not be a matrix model.

14. The M_α for *recall from address*; M_α means get the contents from location α. If $\alpha\{\mu_A(x_i, t_i)\}$, then $M_\alpha = \mu_A(x_i, t_i)$.

15. The $\emptyset$ for *null* or *empty set*.

16. The L^n for *loop*; $L^n[F_{op}]$ means do $[F_{op}]$ recursively n times, where $[F_{op}]$ is a predefined fuzzy operation.

17. The Φ^n for *while do*; $\Phi_A^n[F_{op}]$ means that while A is true, do F_{op} n times recursively, where F_{op} is a predefined fuzzy operation.

In addition, the equality, the containment, the complement, the union, and the intersection are defined (here we adapt the Zadeh fuzzy logic language) as follows:

---

* This definition of "while" differs from that of Bochmann [22].

1. Equality of A^i with B^j:

$$A^i = B^j \leftrightarrow \mu_A(x, t_i) = \mu_B(x, t_j),$$

where A^i means the value of A at time i (if analog processes are considered) or sample i of A (if discrete processes are considered).

2. Containment of A^i in B^j:

$$A^i \subset B^j \leftrightarrow \mu_A(x, t_i) \le \mu_B(x, t_j).$$

3. Complement of A:

$$\bar{A} = (\text{compl.})A \leftrightarrow \mu_{\bar{A}}(x, t_i) = 1 - \mu_A(x, t_i).$$

4. Union of A^i and B^j:

$$A^i \cup B^j \leftrightarrow \mu_{A^i \cup B^j}(x, t) = \max\{\mu_A(x, t_i), \mu_B(x, t_j)\}.$$

5. Intersection of A^i and B^j:

$$A^i \cap B^j \leftrightarrow \mu_{A^i \cap B^j}(x, t) = \min\{\mu_A(x, t_i), \mu_B(x, t_j)\}.$$

4.8   Applying Temporal Fuzzy Operators

In general, a temporal fuzzy logic problem follows the heuristic approach. This is best explained with examples.

Example 4.7: Delayed Action

Do not evaluate the state A for the next five intervals:
    Linguistically:

if $\mu_A(x, t)$ is true at $t = t$,

then evaluate $\mu_A(x, t)$ at $t = t + 5$.

    Using operators:

$$\bigcirc[W^5 \mu_A(x, t_5)],$$

where $W^5 \mu_A(x, t)$ waits for five clock periods and then it evaluates $\mu_A(x, t)$ at the next period.

Example 4.8: Sample and Store

Get n time-consecutive grades of a membership function at point x_k and store the sampled values in locations $\alpha + 1$ to $\alpha + n$.

$$\bigcirc[L^n[M^{\alpha+i}\mu_{\tilde{F}}(x_k, t_i)]], \qquad i = 1, \dots, n,$$

or, by definition of the loop operator,

$$\bigcirc[L^n[M^{\alpha+n}\mu_{\tilde{F}}(x_k, t_n)]],$$

where n starts with $n = 1$ and ends at $n = n$, by definition.

Example 4.9: Sample at Different Times and Store

Evaluate a membership function at $t = 1$ and $t = 5$ and store the two grades of membership in locations α and $\alpha + 1$.

$$\bigcirc[M^{\alpha}\mu_F(x, t_1)W^4M^{\alpha+1}\mu_F(x, t_5)].$$

Example 4.10: Reset Memory

Reset memory location α at the next time point.

$$\bigcirc[M^{\alpha}\emptyset].$$

Example 4.11: Reset Register

Reset the shift register $SR(n)$ in the next n time points.

$$\bigcirc[\emptyset \overset{n}{\to} SR(n)].$$

Example 4.12: Move a Block

Move a block of p locations (starting from k) to another block in a memory (starting from m) as soon as possible (at the next instance).

$$\bigcirc[L^p[M_{k+i-1}M^{m+i-1}]] \qquad \text{for } i = 1, \dots, p,$$

or, by definition of the loop operator,

$$\bigcirc[L^p[M_{k+p-1}M^{m+p-1}]],$$

where p starts with $p = 1$ and ends at $p = p$, by definition. The inner brackets recall the contents of memory location $k + p - 1$ and store in memory location $m + p - 1$. The loop operator L repeats this recall-store process p times, advancing the value of p each time. Moreover, this operation may also be expressed with the "event" operator:

$$\Delta[i = 0 \wedge L^p(M^{m+1}M_{k+1} \wedge (\bigcirc i = i + 1))].$$

Example 4.13: Set Initial Conditions

Set the initial conditions of fuzzy functions $\mu_{F_i}(x, t)$ to the initial conditions given by the set $IC = (Ic_1, \dots, Ic_n)$ stored in memory locations $p + 1$ to $p + n$ if only a condition B

is true and for as long as it remains true. Initializing memberships is typically encountered in adaptive fuzzy systems.

$$\bigcirc[L^n[M_{p+i}[IC]\,\partial\,\mu_{\tilde{B}}(x,t)] \rightarrow \mu_{F_i}(x_i,t)], \qquad i = 1,\ldots,n.$$

Example 4.14: Queue Control

Consider that vehicles arrive and depart from a terminal. The congestion in the terminal needs to be controlled. Fuzzy variables are defined as vehicles arriving (A), vehicles in the queue (Q), vehicles departing (D), and action of the controller (C). The fuzzy values are "few," "some," and "many" for A and D, "almost empty," "almost half," and "almost full" for Q, and "release few," "release some," and "release many" for C (where the full and empty conditions are included in the membership functions almost full and almost empty).

Consider that the problem is defined by the following set of linguistic expressions:

if presently A = few
    and   Q = almost half
    and   D = some
    and $\mathcal{R}_Q < 2$,
    then   C = release few,
else
    if presently A = many
    and   Q = almost full
    and   D = some
    and $\mathcal{R}_Q > 4$,
    then   C = release many,
else, ...

The initial conditions (at $t = 0$) are Q = empty (empty is also a fuzzy number) and $1 < \eta_1 < 10$.

With temporal fuzzy logic notation, the above is expressed as

$$\Phi^2_{\mu_{Q_H}}[M^{\alpha+i}\mu_{Q_H}(x_k,t_i)] \vee \Phi^2_{\mu_{Q_F}}[M^{\alpha+i}\mu_{Q_F}(x_k,t_i)], i = 1,2,$$

and

$$\Delta[\mu_{A_F} \wedge \mu_{Q_H} \wedge \mu_{D_S} \wedge (\mathcal{R}_Q < 2) \rightarrow C_F]$$
$$\vee \Delta[\mu_{A_M} \wedge \mu_{Q_F} \wedge \mu_{D_S} \wedge (\mathcal{R}_Q > 4) \rightarrow C_M] \vee \Delta[\cdots].$$

The first expression stores two samples of μ_{Q_L} or μ_{Q_F} for the calculation of $\mathcal{R}_{Q_H}$ or $\mathcal{R}_{Q_F}$, and the second and third express the linguistic statements. The subscripts are F = full, H =

half full, S = some, and M = many, and $\mathcal{R}_Q$ is the confidence rate for Q.

Example 4.15: Real-Time Control

A real-time controller is governed by a digital clock. Here, A, B, and C are time-variant membership functions. Define the real-time controller expressed linguistically as

> if   A (at $t = 1$) AND B (at $t = 3$),
> and A (at $t = 2$) WHILE C (at $t = 2$),
> and A (at $t = 3$),
> then
> if $\mathcal{R}_C$ (at $t = 3$) ≤ 5,
> then
> do F

where F is a specified activity using operators.
Then

$$\bigcirc[M^\alpha \mu_A(x, t_1), M^\beta \mu_C(x, t_1)]$$

$$\wedge W^1 \vee \wedge[\mu_A(x, t_2) \, \partial \, \mu_C(x, t_2)]$$

$$\wedge W^1 \, \emptyset \wedge [M_\alpha \wedge \mu_B(x, t_3) \wedge \mu_A(x, t_3)]$$

$$\wedge [\mathcal{R}_{C(3)} \geq 5] \to F,$$

where the left bracket of the first-line expression starts with storing the value of μ_A in location α and the value of μ_C in β at time $t = 1$. Then it waits for one clock period and tests if μ_A is true while μ_C is valid. The second-line expression waits for another clock period and tests the validity of expression A ($t = 1$) AND B ($t = 3$) AND A ($t = 3$). The third-line expression calculates the confidence rate and tests if it is at least 5; notice that in the first line the value of μ_C at $t = 1$ was stored for later usage.

Example 4.16: Real-Time Multiplexer

The grades of membership of two fuzzy variables A and B arrive synchronously within a time interval τ at a real-time two-input multiplexer. The multiplexer compresses the two grades of membership in the time domain and outputs both over the same interval τ on a single output with A first.
The multiplexer is described with operators as follows:

$$D_2[\mu_A(x, t)] W^{\tau/2} D_2[\mu_B(x, t)].$$

> The time period τ is divided in two by the interval operators. The duration of the value of μ_A is compressed by 2, waits for a half-period, and the duration of the value of μ_B is then compressed by 2 follows. Hence, within a full period τ both values have been multiplexed.

From the foregoing definitions, certain relations between operators are identified. For example, by combining the "loop" (L) and the "for while" (∂) operators we may have an equivalent "for while do" operator (Φ), as follows:

$$L^n[F_{\text{op}}] \, \partial \, A \approx \Phi_A^n[F_{\text{op}}].$$

The left side is expressed as: execute the predefined fuzzy operator F_{op} n times while condition A is true. The right side is expressed as: for as long as condition A is true, execute the operator F_{op} n times. It is assumed that condition A remains true for at least the duration of n iterations. If A ceases to be true before that, then the validity of this expression, and hence its execution, is terminated.

Similarly, in the expression

$$L^n[\varnothing] \approx W^n \, \varnothing$$

the left side means "do nothing" for n iterations, which is equivalent to the right side "wait for n" iterations on an empty set.

Also, in the following expression the right side is equivalent to the left side:

$$[\mu_A(x,t) \, \partial \, \mu_B(x,t)] \wedge [\mu_B(x,t) \, \partial \, \mu_A(x,t)] \approx \mu_A(x,t) \, \not\subset \, \mu_B(x,t).$$

These examples demonstrate the interrelationships of the fuzzy operators and the flexibility they provide in symbolically expressing linguistic expressions. Although the shortest notation is preferred, this flexibility becomes desirable for a long string of operations.

4.9   Defuzzification of Temporal Fuzzy Logic

The defuzzification process in temporal fuzzy logic is similar to the defuzzification process of fuzzy logic. As demonstrated, based on the linguistic definition or rules of a fuzzy problem, it is possible to have two or more answers to a question; see Figure 4-1 where $\mu_{\text{slow}}(2.5) = 0.25$ and $\mu_{\text{moder.}}(2.5) = 0.5$. These two results yield two outcomes. In certain applications, with more than one outcome, either additional judgment is applied to select one of the outcomes or the outcomes are further tested to select the one best representing the solution to the problem.

Techniques have been developed to produce an output that may be viewed as a "balancing act" in removing this uncertainty of the result. The three most used are the **maximizer**, by which the maximum output is selected, the **weighed average**, which averages weighed possible outputs, and the **centroid** and its variations, which find the center of mass to yield the output. In temporal fuzzy logic, defuzzification follows any of the processes developed for fuzzy logic. However, the certainty of the output is greatly enhanced if the confidence rate, $\mathcal{R}$, is used. This becomes clearer when membership functions overlap and the value lies in the overlapping range. Values in the overlapping range with regular logic often yield at least two solutions, as shown above. However, when the confidence rate is used, then, as explained earlier, it provides an indication of the trend of the grade of membership that may be used to select one of the many potential solutions and to reject the others.

The confidence rate also becomes particularly important in real-time fuzzy logic problems where membership functions are overlapping. This overlapping may yield ambiguity of the outcome, as explained. Using the confidence rate, this ambiguity is lifted (or at least is greatly reduced) and the selection of the most likely solution is simplified. Consequently, using the confidence rate produces outputs such that a simple defuzzification method, such as the maximizer, may be sufficient; refer to Section 4.7.1 and to Examples 4.14 and 4.15.

4.10   Example: Applicability of TFL in Communications Systems

The real-life example given here attempts to identify where time becomes critical and where fuzzy logic and/or TFL may be applied in a communications system. No prerequisite knowledge of communications systems is required.

Macroscopically, communications systems are synchronous, real-time deterministic systems that reliably transport voice/data from point A to a remote point B. Microscopically, however, they are distributed operating systems that consist of many concurrent (micro) programmed sequential processors (or ASICs) to control the many operations that describe their internal structure and protocol specification.

When a signal departs from point A for point B, an adventurous travel begins that affects the integrity of the signal and yields a corrupted or distorted, or a *fuzzy*, signal. For example, the integrity of the signal is subject to algorithmic manipulations (equalization, digital processing, analog-to-digital conversion), to transformations (sound to electronic, photonic, on electromagnetic waves), and to external influences (electromagnetic, environmental). Moreover, the integrity of the signal depends on the technology used in the system—its architecture, implementation, networking, and interface specifications. Numerous network communications transactions, if not successfully completed, corrupt the signal. Consequently, several factors that affect the integrity of the signal are time dependent.

Consider a communications system that consists of the following major functions (Figure 4-9):

- **Channel units:** Each terminates an analog voice or digital data signal. Here, equalization and other signal defuzzification processes, which may use neural networks and/or fuzzy neural networks, take place. The restored received analog signal is then pulse-code-modulated (PCM) at 64 kb/s. Many variables that affect the quality of the signal change with time; thus, membership functions could be considered time variant.

- **The on-hook/off-hook detector:** This circuitry detects the state of the external apparatus (i.e., telephone, modem) and provides an off-hook/on-hook indication, even if erroneously detected. This case is more extensively elaborated.

- **A time compressor/multiplexer:** A number of 64-kb/s PCM signals are time compressed and multiplexed into a higher bit rate; this is known as *time division multiplexing* (TDM). Although the signal has been defuzzified, the time compression operator is used to describe the TDM operation. Moreover, the time compression/decompression operators can be readily used to describe this operation.

- **The high-speed interface unit:** This unit synchronizes to the received bitstream from a remote system (neural and/or fuzzy neural networks may be used here) and transmits/receives high-speed bipolar signals. Jitter in received clock may also be considered as fuzzified clock phase or clock period. Then the membership function may also be time variant.

- **A time-slot interchanger (TSI)**: This constitutes a space-time crosspoint, or a *cross-connect fabric*, of multiplexed channels.

- **The controller:** This controls the flow through the cross-connect dynamically, monitors the system performance, provisions the various units of the system, provides maintenance and telemetry, monitors system operation, removes uncertainty (defuzzifies) from the on-hook/off-hook state transitions, initiates and terminates call processing, removes uncertainty from channel assignment, and establishes the connectivity path through the cross-connect fabric. This part has to deal with many temporally uncertain processes, where neural and/or fuzzy logic concepts may be extensively used.

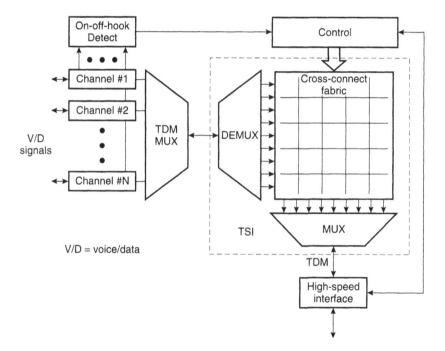

Figure 4-9 TDM system functional architecture.

When an on-hook to off-hook transition is detected by the TDM system, there is a degree of uncertainty as to the change of state in the time domain. The system must recognize that change and defuzzify it. When the state is defuzzified and the system is certain of the transition, it requests from the network an end-to-end communication path. Figure 4-10 illustrates the fuzzy change of state in three sequential confidence levels, or membership functions: low (L), medium (M), and high (H).

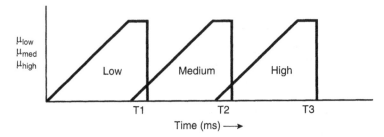

Figure 4-10 Membership functions for on-to-off-hook state.

In our example the system, before requesting a communication path, constructs a time dependency (or history) of the state for a predetermined period of time. Then, depending on the membership grades within that time period, it decides whether a path should be requested. This process is also repeated when a voice/data channel becomes inactive, or "on-hook"; in this case the path is disconnected.

4.10.1   Temporal Fuzzification

When a telephone goes off-hook it represents a change in state from a logic 1 to a logic 0. Now, for many reasons that are beyond the purpose of this example, the change of state becomes temporarily fuzzy—the state may change temporarily, or it may oscillate for a very short period (Figure 4-11), such that it is not perceived as a definite 1 or a definite 0, and then reach a steady state. Hence the question: To what degree is the telephone off-hook?

The function of the temporal fuzzy signal is described by $F(t) = \sum_{ij} r_H^i(t) + r_L^j(t)$, where $r_H^i(t)$ is a random number that indicates the ith length (in time units) at state 1, and $r_L^j(t)$ is the jth length at state 0. In our case, t takes discrete values (in increments of 10 ms). For example, $r_H^2(t) = 50$ indicates that the second high-level segment is 50 ms.

Notice in this example that the behavior of mechanisms that cause fuzzification is difficult to know in detail in the time domain. However, an empirical possibilistic behavior is composed, as is the case with most "fuzzy" problems, and rules to defuzzify the problem are developed, where

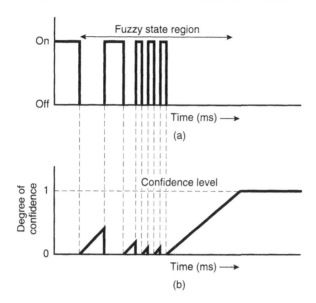

Figure 4-11 (a) Temporal fuzzy signal and (b) certainty level.

time is explicitly included and the rate of confidence is extensively used in the defuzzification process.

4.10.2   Rules and Temporal Defuzzification

In our communication system, for robustness we have set simple defuzzification rules. The rules of the temporal fuzzy problem in linguistic statements are as follows:

1. If L & $\bar{M}$, then
     if r_H & $\bar{r}_L$,
   then next
       if $\mathcal{R} > 0$, then
   repeat 1 until $\mathcal{R} = 0$ (or $L = 1$),
   else $t = 0$.

2. If M & previous L, then
     if r_H & $\bar{r}_L$,
   then next
       if $\mathcal{R} > 0$, then
   repeat 2 until $\mathcal{R} = 0$ (or $M = 1$),
   else $t = 0$, go to 1.

3. If H & (previous) M & (previous) L, then
  if r_H & $\bar{r}_L$,
  then next
    if $\mathcal{R} > 0$, then
    repeat 3 until $\mathcal{R} = 0$ (or $H = 1$),
    then next
    declare off-hook steady state and request a communication path
  else $t = 0$, go to 1.

Where L = low, M = medium, H = high, & = and operator, and $\mathcal{R}$ = rate of confidence (with $\eta = 1$).

These linguistic statements are expressed in temporal fuzzy notation as

$$\Phi_{\mu_L(x,t_i) \wedge \mu_{\bar{M}}(x,t_i)}[\bigcirc(r_H \wedge \bar{r}_L \wedge (\mathcal{R} > 0)U(\mathcal{R} = 0)], \rightarrow$$

$$\bigcirc[\Phi_{\mu_M(x,t_{i+A}) \wedge \mu_L(x_A,t_A)}[\bigcirc(r_H \wedge \bar{r}_L \wedge (\mathcal{R} > 0)U(\mathcal{R} = 0))]], \rightarrow$$

$$\bigcirc[\Phi_{\mu_H(x,t_{i+B}) \wedge \mu_L(x_B,t_B)}[\bigcirc(r_H \wedge \bar{r}_L \wedge (\mathcal{R} > 0)U(\mathcal{R} = 0))]] \rightarrow \bigcirc F_{\text{off-hook}}$$

where $F_{\text{off-hook}}$ is the final activity **declare off-hook state valid**. This activity invokes a request for a communication path.

Moreover, the request for a communications path is another process subject to time-dependent uncertainties. Another similar process takes place here that is beyond the scope of this example. However, when all is done successfully and the communications path is granted, the controller makes the association of granted path to channel number across the time slot interchanger and establishes connectivity.

4.11 Review Questions

4.1. Plot the distribution: {50,0), (45,1), (40,2), (35,3), (30,4), (25,5), (20,6), (15,7), (10,8), (5,9), (0,10), where the first number in the parentheses denotes amplitude and the second denotes length (e.g., in cm). Plot the normalized distribution.

4.2. Let Close be defined by the normalized distribution: 1 at 1 cm, 0.9 at 2 cm, 0.8 at 3 cm, and so on. Let Far be defined by the distribution: 0 at 6 cm, 0.1 at 7 cm, 0.2 at 8 cm, 0.3 at 9 cm, 0.4 at 10 cm, and so on. Let Medium Distance be defined with a distribution 0 at 4 cm, 1 at 8 cm, and 0 at 12 cm. Plot the three distributions. What do you observe? In fuzzy logic, what are these distributions called?

4.3. Consider question 4.1. What is the membership value for a distance of 6 cm?

4.4. Let the distribution of two membership functions A and B be: $A = \{(1,0), (0.9,1), (0.8,2), (0.7,3), (0.6,4), (0.5,5), (0.4,6), (0.3,7) (0.2,8), (0.1,9), (0,10)\}$ and $B = \{(0,2), (1,6), (0,10)\}$, where the second number in each pair of parentheses denotes distance in cm. Find the value of C at $x = 3$ cm, based on the relationships $C = \{A$ and $B\}$ and $F = \{A$ or $B\}$.

4.5. Let the distribution of membership A be $A = \{(1,0), (0,10)\}$, and of B be $B = \{(0,4), (1,14)\}$ at time $t = 1$; the second number in each pair of parentheses denotes a variable x. What is the membership value for $x = 5$ at time $t = 1$? What is the membership value at time $t = 2$ if the memberships have changed to $A = \{(1,0), (0,5)\}$ and $B = \{(0,4), (1,8)\}$. What conclusion may be drawn from this?

4.6. Find the center of gravity for:
   a. A rectangle with height of 1 and width of 6.
   b. An equilateral triangle with base 1.2.

For answers, see page 189.

REFERENCES

[1] L. A. Zadeh, "Fuzzy Sets," *Inform. and Control*, vol. 8, pp. 338–353, 1965.

[2] L. A. Zadeh, "A Theory of Approximate Reasoning," in *Machine Intelligence*, vol. 9, J. Hayes, D. Michie, and L. I. Mikulich, eds., pp. 149–194, Halstead Press, New York, 1979.

[3] P. A. Laplante, *Real-Time Systems Design and Analysis, an Engineer's Handbook*, IEEE Press, Piscataway, N.J., 1993.

[4] Z. Manna and P. Wolper, *Synthesis of Communicating Processes from Temporal Logic Specifications*, Report No. STAN-CS-81-872, Department of Computer Science, Stanford University, 1981.

[5] Z. Manna and A. Pnueli, *The Temporal Logic of Reactive and Concurrent Systems-Specification*, Springer-Verlag, New York, 1992.

[6] N. Rescher and A. Urquhart, *Temporal Logic*, Library of Exact Philosophy, Springer-Verlag, New York, 1971.

[7] J. S. Ostroff, *Temporal Logic for Real-Time Systems*, Research Studies Press, Ltd., London; and John Wiley & Sons, New York, 1989.

[8] V. Cingel and N. Fristacky, "A Temporal Logic-Based Model for Event-Driven Nets," *Jour. Real-Time Systems*, vol. 3, pp. 407–428, 1991.

[9] J. F. Knight and K. M. Passino, "Decidability for a Temporal Logic Used in Discrete System Analysis," *Int. Jour. Control*, vol. 52, no. 6, pp. 1489–1506, 1990.

[10] K. M. Passino and P. J. Antsaklis, "Branching Time Temporal Logic for Discrete Event System Analysis," in Proceedings of 26th Annual Allerton Conf. on Communication, Control and Computing, Urbana-Champaign, p. 10, 1988.

[11] F. Kroeger, *Temporal Logic of Programs*, Springer-Verlag, Berlin, 1987.

[12] L. A. Zadeh, "The Calculus of Fuzzy If/Then Rules," *AI Expert*, pp. 23–27, March 1992.

[13] M. Sugeno, "An Introductory Survey of Fuzzy Control," *Inform. Sci.*, vol. 36, pp. 59–83, 1985.

[14] D. Dubois and H. Prade, *Fuzzy Sets and Systems—Theory and Applications*, Academic Press, New York, 1980.

[15] L. M. Zia and X. D. Zhang, "On Fuzzy Multiobjective Optimal Control," *Eng. Appl. Artificial Intelligence*, vol. 6, no. 2, pp. 153–164, 1993.

[16] S. V. Kartalopoulos, "Temporal Fuzzy Logic," submitted for publication.

[17] S. V. Kartalopoulos, "Temporal Fuzziness in Communications Systems," *ICNN Proc.*, vol. VII, pp. 4786–4791, 1994.

[18] J. F. Allen, "Maintaining Knowledge about Temporal Intervals," *Commun. ACM*, vol. 26, no. 11, pp. 832–843, 1983.

[19] L. Console, A. J. Rivolin, and P. Torasso, "Fuzzy Temporal Reasoning on Causal Models," *Int. Jour. Intelligent Systems*, vol. 6, no. 2, pp. 107–133, 1991.

[20] R. Hale, "Using Temporal Logic for Prototyping: The Design of Lift Controller," *Proc. of Temporal Logic in Specification*, B. Banieqbal, H. Barringer, and A. Pnueli, eds., pp. 375–408, Springer-Verlag, New York, 1987.

[21] J. G. Thistle and W. M. Wonham, "Control Problems in a Temporal Logic Framework," *Int. Jour. Control*, vol. 44, pp. 943–976, 1986.

[22] G. V. Bochmann," Hardware Specification with Temporal Logic: An Example," *IEEE Trans. Comp.*, vol. C-31, no. 3, pp. 223–231, 1982.

5

FUZZY NEURAL
NETWORKS

We have seen that one of the characteristics of artificial neural nets is that they can classify inputs. This is useful if plasticity is maintained; that is, the ANN can continuously classify and also update classifications. We have also seen from past learning that it can retrieve crisp information from incomplete (or fuzzy) input. We have studied the stability of ANNs and how robust ANNs are when inputs become less defined (i.e., fuzzy inputs) or when some of the neurons do not function properly (i.e., fuzzy network parameters). In addition, we have seen that fuzzy systems deal with current fuzzy information and are capable of providing crisp outputs. However, in fuzzy systems there is no learning and, even vaguely, the input-output relationships—the fuzzy rules—must be known a priori.

Neural networks and fuzzy systems each have their own shortcomings. When one designs with neural networks alone, the network is a black box that needs to be defined. This is a highly compute-intensive process. One must develop a good sense, after extensive experimentation and practice, of the complexity of the network and the learning algorithm to be used and of the degree of accuracy acceptable by the application. Fuzzy systems, on the other hand, require a thorough understanding of the fuzzy variables and membership functions, of the input-output relationships as well as the good judgment to select the fuzzy rules that contribute the most to the solution of the application. For example, if one considers a fuzzy system with three inputs and one output and with five membership functions at each input, then the total number of rules is $5^3 = 125$, and for four inputs it becomes 3125. This is a large number of rules, and many may not contribute significantly to the problem. Hence, good judgment is needed to eliminate unnecessary rules.

Neural nets and fuzzy systems, although very different, have a close
relationship: they both can work with imprecision in a space that is not
defined by crisp, deterministic boundaries. The shortcomings of neural
networks and of fuzzy systems may be overcome if we incorporate fuzzy
logic operations into neural networks and learning and classification of
neural networks into fuzzy systems. The result is called a **fuzzy artificial
neural network** (FANN).

5.1   Fuzzy Artificial Neural Network (FANN)

In the fuzzy artificial neural network [1, 2], the neural network part is
primarily used for its learning and classification capabilities and for pattern
association and retrieval. The neural network part automatically generates
fuzzy logic rules and membership functions during the training period.
In addition, even after training, the neural network keeps updating the
membership functions and fuzzy logic rules as it learns more and more
from its input signals. Fuzzy logic, on the other hand, is used to infer and
provide a crisp or defuzzified output when fuzzy parameters exist. The
interested reader may learn more about combining fuzzy logic and neural
networks in the *IEEE Communications Magazine* special issue, "Fuzzy
and Neural Networks," September 1992, in the articles by J. C. Bezdek
and by G. A. Carpenter and S. Grossberg. The latter article provides an
excellent review of the ART systems and of the fuzzy ARTMAP. Also see
the Proceedings of the International Conference on Fuzzy Logic Neural
Networks, IIZUKA 90 and IIZUKA 92 (Iizuka, Japan).

The **fuzzy neuron** approximates the McCulloch-Pitts neuron. There
are some fundamental differences, however: in place of scalar weights w_{ij},
the fuzzy neuron uses fuzzy sets, and in place of the activation function,
a fuzzy set may also be used. A fuzzy neuron works as follows. When
the signal S_i is received, the fuzzy neuron sums the elicited measure of
the fuzzy weights w_i and inputs $F_z w_i$, arbitrated by an attenuation factor
Ω. The sum $\sum_{i=1}^{N} F_z w_i \Omega$ represents the cumulative input strength. This
signal is then mapped to a fuzzy set region corresponding to the possible
activation levels associated with the number of active signals or the attenuated strength of the cumulative signal. Then, using a defuzzification
method such as the centroid (see Chapter 4), the fuzzy region is collapsed
to a scalar value representing the expected value of the fuzzy region under
the signal conditions (Figure 5-1). If the signal strength lies above a min-

imal threshold, then the neuron fires; otherwise it does not. However, if the activation function is also a fuzzy set, then the output obtained is not a classical firing signal but a signal with varying degrees of strength. In this case, the threshold is also fuzzy.

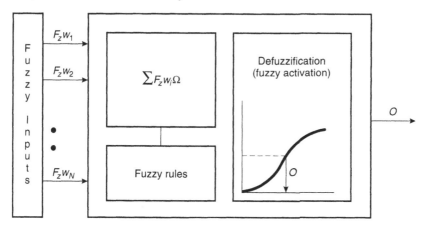

Figure 5-1 General fuzzy neuron model.

Integrating fuzzy logic with neural networks has become more and more popular [3]. Many researchers follow the outline described, but there is no standard model that can be followed, as evidenced by the variability of the proposed fuzzy neural networks [4–12]. Nevertheless, this variability should not be viewed as a deficiency of the method. Rather, it should be viewed as the versatility of a powerful method to bring the best of both methods into one and to solve the problem for which the FANN is designed in the most efficient way.

5.2 Fuzzy Neural Example

Consider that we have a situation where (a) an output must be generated based on the weighted sum of a number of inputs and (b) that each input is the possibilistic outcome from a set of fuzzy external inputs, as defined in Chapter 4, that conform to the *if. . .then* category. That is, if the external inputs are $x_1, x_2, \ldots, x_n$ and if a set of rules is defined as

$$\text{Rule } k : \textit{ If } x_i \textit{ AND } x_j, \textit{ then } F_k,$$

then a fuzzy neural network of the type illustrated in Figure 5-2 represents the problem at hand. Here, the neural network may be one of the paradigms described in Chapter 3. For example, consider the perceptrons shown in Figure 3-5, particularly the plurality perceptron; its function may be expressed in the form of *if. . .then* statements as part of the rules of the problem. To determine the weights of Figure 5-2, start from all possible values of external inputs and determine all possible outputs, based on the fuzzy rules; the rules drastically reduce the number of data points. Then these outputs are used as inputs to the neural network.

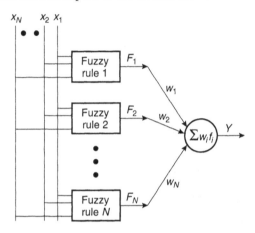

Figure 5-2 Fuzzy artificial neural network.

5.3 Neuro-Fuzzy Control

In this section a basic description of control with neural, fuzzy, and fuzzy-neural networks is given. The interested reader may read more advanced sources on the subject such as *Neuro-Control Systems*, edited by M. M. Gupta and D. H. Rao, IEEE Press, 1994; *Fuzzy Logic Technology and Applications*, edited by R. J. Marks II, IEEE TAB, 1994; *Industrial Applications of Fuzzy Logic and Intelligent Systems*, J. Yen, R. Langari, and L. A. Zadeh, IEEE Press, 1995; and other publications.

5.3.1 Traditional Control

Here, the term *traditional control* means the continuous or discrete control systems that have no learning capabilities. In general, traditional controllers are classified into *open-loop* and *closed-loop* systems. The task of a control system is to make adjustments, indicated by arrows in

Figure 5-3, on the output of a plant such that its actual output is very close to the desired one, based on the reading of sensors that constitute the input of the controller. The open-loop system controls the output of a plant (Figure 5-4); the output, however, is expected to be deterministic and stable. If the plant output deviates from the predetermined path to an unpredictable one, then the system loses its controlling capability and becomes unstable. This system instability was soon recognized and was addressed with the closed-loop, or feedback, system (Figure 5-5). The closed-loop control system feeds back its output, which is conditioned by a function, and the conditioned output along with the input are used to control the actual output. Hence, if the actual output tends to deviate from its desired one, it is detected and a correction is made on the actual output.

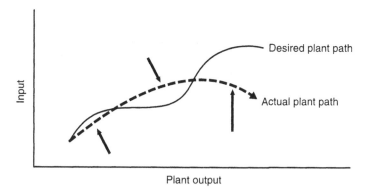

Figure 5-3 Desired and actual plant path.

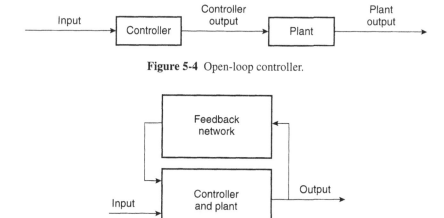

Figure 5-4 Open-loop controller.

Figure 5-5 Closed-loop controller.

5.3.2 Neural Control

Neural networks have found many applications in control. In general, a neural network may be trained to respond to variations of the input such that the output is maintained as closely as possible to the desired one. As in traditional control, we may also consider an open-loop and a closed-loop control system. In the first case, consider a neural net trained to respond to input values with a desired output (Figure 5-6). If an input value is not contained in the training data set, however, then it is not always clear what the output of the neural network will be and whether the output will cause instability of the plant. As in traditional control, a feedback neural network may be included (Figure 5-7). In this control network, the forward network is trained to the initial input-output relationships; that is, it is trained to respond to inputs known a priori with outputs known a priori. The feedback network continuously learns, classifies, and generates new input-output associations and updates the forward network. Thus, this feedback network, within certain boundaries of knowledge, has the intelligence to learn and adapt continuously.

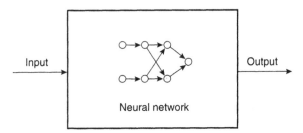

Figure 5-6 Open-loop ANN controller.

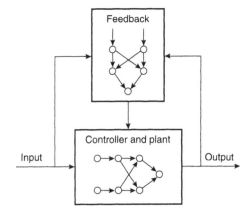

Figure 5-7 Closed-loop ANN controller.

5.3.3 Fuzzy Control

Fuzzy systems are also used in control, as already described in Chapter 4. Here, consider an open-loop system where the network consists of inputs and outputs, as shown in Figure 5-8. The input-output relationships here are known in a "fuzzy way." The rules of the control plant, the variables, and their membership functions are known. Here, no learning takes place, as in the neural networks. Based on this, the sensors of the plant provide inputs to the fuzzy system and, based on the rules, the fuzzy system generates an output that controls the plant. In this case, the behavior of the plant should be known very well so that a complete set of rules is used. If the set is not complete, then the plant may become unstable.

Figure 5-8 Open-loop fuzzy controller.

5.3.4 Fuzzy-Neural Control

Fuzzy-neural networks combine the best of both worlds. They consider fuzzy inputs and, at the same time, they are capable of learning (see Figure 5-9). Here the forward network is fuzzy and the feedback is a neural network. The neural network receives the inputs and the actual outputs, it creates new classifications and input-output associations, and it generates new rules. It also updates the forward network with the new rules. A variation to the network in Figure 5-9 is to have a microprocessor-based network in place of the neural network. The microprocessor then behaves algorithmically like a neural network.

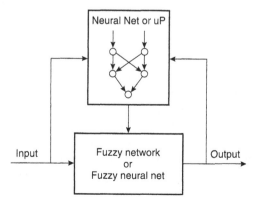

Figure 5-9 Closed-loop FANN controller.

5.4 Fuzzy Neural Nets—A Reality?

Many articles describing the integration of fuzzy logic with neural networks have been published, and a substantial amount of research is under way in many labs around the globe. In addition, state-of-the-art products have already found their way from the lab into the market. However, most of these products are in "soft" form; that is, they are software products that algorithmically emulate FANNs. We briefly describe two tools, the NeuFuz4 (National Semiconductor Corp.) and the NeuroFuzzy module (Inform Software). These examples were selected at random and not on the merits of performance or preference.

NeuFuz4 is a Windows-based software tool that uses neural network learning to create fuzzy logic rules and membership functions, based on desired input-output relationships, automatically. The input-output data may be obtained from measurements of a running system or written as specifications to be learned. The accuracy of data and the inaccuracy of each given data point are specified. However, since inaccuracy of data may impact the learning time and the solution accuracy, some judgment should be made on the degree of inaccuracy. NeuFuz4 then verifies the solution and creates machine code for running on one 8-bit embedded microcontroller.

NeuFuz4 supports four inputs and one output at five membership functions each, for a total of 3125 possible fuzzy rules. Fortunately, in most applications not all rules equally contribute to the desired solution. To eliminate noncontributing rules, NeuFuz4 has an optimizer and verifier module that supports a fuzzy rule deletion mechanism—the deletion factor, which is a threshold that indicates the minimum contribution a fuzzy rule should make to the solution in order to be retained. The user defines a value between 0 and 1 for the deletion factor. For example, a deletion factor of 0.15 would eliminate all fuzzy rules that contribute less than 15% to the solution.

The NeuroFuzzy module is an add-on to the *fuzzy*TECH development environment. It works with the same data representation as the *fuzzy*TECH tool and uses a neural network with back-propagation learning or other learning techniques to generate fuzzy logic rules automatically. The files produced by the NeuroFuzzy module are descriptions of a fuzzy logic system that can be accessed by all other parts of the design system. The NeuroFuzzy module includes the linguistic variable editor, the rules editor, the graphic analyzer, and the interactive debugger. The rules editor displays a graphic representation of the rules matrix, also known as fuzzy associative memory (FAM). The user, by examining the rules matrix, may select sets of rules and evaluate their performance by using the simulator or the graphic analyzer.

From the two examples given, we see that there are no stereotype fuzzy artificial neural networks. The designer selects the type of neural network and the learning algorithm and, from the known input/output data, defines or derives the input-output relationships and the membership functions. The designer then defines the architecture of the FANN that best suits the particular architecture, selects the development tool, and then begins.

5.5   Review Questions

5.1. A neural network detects the level of a liquid in a cylindrical container 10 cm high. The main function of the neural network is to maintain the level of the liquid in a cylinder by opening and closing two valves, one at the top that supplies liquid and the other at the bottom that removes liquid from the container. The neural network detects the liquid levels at high points 0, 2, 4, 6, 8, and 10 cm. Obviously, for intermediate levels (e.g., between 2 and 4 cm), the controlling action is not accurate. It has been decided to incorporate fuzzy logic concepts to better control the level at the intermediate levels. Discuss how this can be done.

5.2. Consider that the cylindrical container in question 5.1 is plastic and that its diameter changes at different heights as a function of time. How can better control be achieved?

For answers, see page 189.

REFERENCES

[1] S. C. Lee and E. T. Lee, "Fuzzy Sets and Neural Networks," *Jour. Cybernetics*, vol. 4, pp. 83–103, 1974.

[2] S. C. Lee and E.T. Lee, "Fuzzy Neural Networks," *Math. Biosci.*, vol. 23, pp. 151–177, 1975.

[3] S. V. Kartalopoulos, "A Plateau of Performance?" Guest Editorial, *IEEE Communications Magazine* special issue on fuzzy logic and neural networks, Sept. 1992.

[4] E. Cox, "Integrating Fuzzy Logic into Neural Nets," *AI Expert*, pp. 43–47, June 1992.

[5] A. Bulsari and H. Saxen, "Fuzzy Simulation by an Artificial Neural Network," *Eng. Appl. Artificial Intelligence*, vol. 5, no. 2, pp. 401–406, 1992.

[6] B. Kosko, *Neural Networks and Fuzzy Systems*, Prentice Hall, Englewood Cliffs, N.J., 1992.

[7] G. A. Carpenter, S. Grossberg, and D. B. Rosen, "Fuzzy ART: Fast Stable Learning and Categorization of Analog Patterns by an Adaptive Resonance System," *Neural Networks*, vol. 1, pp. 759–771, 1991.

[8] N. Hataoka, "Large Vocabulary Speech Recognition Using Neural-Fuzzy and Concept Networks," in *Neural Networks*, L. B. Wellekens and C. J. Wellekens, eds., Proceedings of EURASIP Workshop 1990, Portugal, pp. 186–196, Springer-Verlag, New York, 1990.

[9] R. C. Johnson, "Fuzzy-Neural Hybrid Born," *Electr. Eng. Times*, pp. 29–33, Aug. 27, 1990.

[10] R. C. Johnson, "Making the Neural-Fuzzy Connection," *Electr. Eng. Times*, pp. 33–36, Sept. 27, 1993.

[11] R. C. Johnson, "When Neural and Fuzzy Wed," *Electr. Eng. Times*, p. 41, October 4, 1993.

[12] T. Williams, "New Tools Make Fuzzy/Neural More Than an Academic Amusement," *Computer Design*, pp. 69–84, July 1994.

6

APPLICATIONS

Artificial neural networks and fuzzy logic are not scientific curiosities anymore. They have been applied in various products; examples are many. In metro trains fuzzy logic is used to determine the proper start, stop, and cruising speed of the train; in washing machines, it determines the amount of water and the number of rinses; in cameras and camcorders, it adjusts the color, contrast, brightness, focus, and so on; in vacuums, it determines the suction power based on the amount and size of particles; in automobiles with automatic transmission, it determines the proper gear; in intelligent vehicular systems, it finds the best route and automatically guides an automobile; and in communication systems, it processes signals, schedules and routes channels, and controls the system. Other examples include a variety of systems. In financial engineering, the performance of stocks may be predicted; in pattern recognition it recognizes speech and optical patterns; in security systems, fingerprint and/or voice are identified to validate and confirm the owner; and in robotics, it guides and controls movement, recognizes optical patterns, and manipulates objects.

In this chapter we describe the applicability of neural networks, fuzzy logic, and fuzzy neural networks in a number of fields. It is almost impossible to give a complete account of all the applications, since new applications are announced daily. Our purpose is simply to outline the applicability in various areas. Particular attention is given to signal processing (equalization, echo cancellation), data processing (voice, image), communications systems (traffic flow control, switching), and control (controllers, robotics).

Neural networks may be designed with digital circuitry, analog circuitry, or a combination of both. Designing with digital circuitry [1] is easiest. Digital circuits are better known and used more often than other methods; the inputs and outputs are binary and this makes calculations much easier. However, digital neural networks address only a limited set of applications.

Designing with analog circuitry [2] is more involved. Operational amplifiers are used, so the theory of operational amplifiers, including compensating and scaling techniques, must be mastered. Moreover, understanding analog computers will be helpful to serious technologists. The interested reader may find an abundance of textbooks and "cookbooks" on operational amplifiers [3], as well as introductory textbooks in neural network circuitry [4, 5].

In addition to digital and analog implementation of neural networks, there is the algorithmic implementation. A microprocessor (typically a high-performance CPU) is integrated with a digital-to-analog converter (DAC) and an analog-to-digital converter (ADC), as well as RAM and ROM and, optionally, a digital signal processor (DSP) or a math unit to perform fast mathematical operations. Such an approach is useful in speech recognition and synthesis when a microphone with an input amplifier is used at the analog input and an output amplifier and a loudspeaker are used at the output (Figure 6-1). This network is a virtual neural network with weight values stored in RAM, the algorithm in ROM, and multiplications and summations executed per microprocessor instructions; that is, the microprocessor processes/calculates an output based on the input and weight values and on an algorithm that represents the connection machine. The optional DSP or math unit performs intensive mathematical calculations to accelerate the pattern recognition and synthesis process. In short, the microprocessor algorithm emulates the actual neural network. Such a network is trained by a supervised learning algorithm, whereby the input data are words (sound) applied at the microphone and the actual response is obtained at the loudspeaker. The input sound is sampled in the time domain and digitized by the ADC, the algorithm performs signal processing of the digitized time samples, and the algorithmic neural network sets its weights, which are stored in the RAM. The processed speech samples are postprocessed and converted into an analog signal by the DAC and they are heard from the loudspeaker. If the output is not what is desired, the processor adjusts the network weights until the desired output is obtained. Using this approach, a low-cost microprocessor for speech recognition and synthesis solutions has been developed, based on a reduced instruction set computer (RISC).

An issue in designing neural networks is the implementation of the connection weights. Plasticity of the network implies that the weight values may change; however, a resistor implementation does not foster plasticity

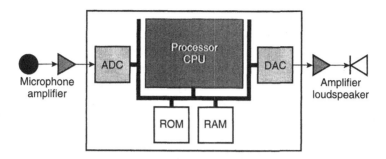

Figure 6-1 Algorithmic implementation of ANNs in speech applications.

but rigidity. This has been recognized by the neural network community, and a serious effort has been made to overcome this difficulty by using memory or complementary MOS (CMOS) solutions [6–13] for weights.

Integrating neural networks in one chip has been the goal of many scientists in universities and corporations. With integration, small size, low-power circuitry makes it possible to incorporate neural networks in real-world applications. Very large–scale integration (VLSI) neural networks, however, vary in architecture from design to design; each institution designs its own architecture in an attempt to make its design better than its predecessor. Although general-purpose VLSI neural networks have been developed [14–18], there is a substantial development in more specialized VLSIs, such as visual information processing [19], handwritten character recognition [20, 21], and other applications [22].

6.1   Signal Processing

In digital communications systems, distorted signals cause intersymbol interference. This problem has been studied extensively, and automatic techniques have been developed since the pioneering work of R.W. Lucky [23]. Lucky's solution to equalization employed a tapped-delay line having adjustable tap gain settings (transversal filter). Since the evolution of neural networks, neural network approaches have been proposed [24], employing multilayer perceptrons [25–28], whereby the inputs are the outputs from a delay line, time-delay neural network (i.e., a TDNN). Figure 6-2 illustrates a neural network application in equalization. An analog tapped-delay line and an 8-12-12-1 perceptron [29] (i.e., a TDNN) have been integrated in a VLSI and applied to equalization of digital communication channels.

Adaptive filtering (i.e., separation of signal from varying noise) based on multilayer neural networks with delay lines [30] and on fuzzy rules [31, 32] have been proposed to filter out noise from image. Besides noise filtering, image reconstruction due to information loss in a block-based image-coded system is an area where neural and fuzzy logic have been used [33]. Similar techniques using a TDNN are employed in compact discs to equalize the optical signal, which is believed to increase the storage capacity 4.7 times [34]. Additionally, applications that use TDNNs have been reported in the area of error correction [35–38]. Because image signals are corrupted with additive noise, techniques have been developed to remove that noise. Many of these techniques, however, affect the edges of the image signal. A nonlinear filter to overcome this problem using fuzzy control techniques has been proposed [39].

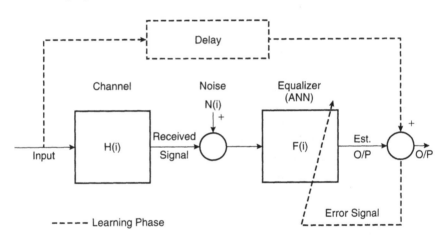

Figure 6-2 Baseband channel with equalization.

Speech recognition has received enormous attention. Its significance in the information arena cannot be adequately described. Speech processing typically involves three modules: the **front end**, which samples the speech and extracts its features; the **word processor**, which finds the probabilities of words in the vocabulary that match the features of the spoken words; and the **sentence processor**, which determines if the recognized word makes sense in the sentence. In general, because of the real-time nature of speech, real time in speech recognition systems is crucial. However, systems with a large vocabulary database require large RAMs. Consequently, the large bottleneck in a speech recognition system with a large vocabulary is the memory access time. To overcome this, special techniques are used, such as memory partitioning and replication, concurrency, extensive pipelining, and scalable architectures. See Figure 6-1 for a speech processing application.

Experiments with neural networks to recognize speech automatically [40] have been conducted, and many methods involving phoneme or syllable recognition have been proposed [41–44]. One method, based on neural networks with radial basis functions [45], approximates speech spectrograms and extracts their features.

An early application in speech recognition was Kohonen's "phonetic typewriter," which could automatically recognize a vocabulary, convert it into text, and type it [46].

A problem in speech recognition is that the sound of speech is corrupted with other unwanted noise sources. To overcome this problem, an alternative approach has been proposed that uses neural networks to decode speech from both the acoustic source and the talker's image [47] (a speaker's moving mouth and speech). Thus, by recognizing facial movement and correlating with speech, the noise is removed. A technique with a different twist, using associative string processors, has also been reported [48].

Analog-to-digital conversion is done with several techniques, one of which is a Hopfield-type neural network [49].

6.2   Image Data Processing

6.2.1   Handwritten Character Recognition

One of the most published applications by many companies is handwritten character recognition. One of the most recent and also most impressive is an optical character reader (OCR) that uses 10 million weight connections and 36,000 nodes and can recognize 7000 Kanji (Japanese) characters in 50 different fonts and in different sizes and orientations with an accuracy of 90%. To train the network, the hardware has to execute approximately 10 trillion operations using a variation of the LVQ algorithm—the shift-tolerant learning vector quantization (STLVQ)—to increase accuracy to 98%, as compared with the LVQ2 at 95.7% and back propagation at 94.1%. However, the STLVQ requires 10 times the number of calculations compared with other state-of-the-art conventional techniques.

6.2.2   Visual Image Recognition

Visual image recognition has many applications, particularly in object recognition for automatic handling and machining and in image processing, such as image enhancement, image compression, image transformation, and special effects in cinematography and other real-time graphics applications. It is also used in identification [50] and security, palm recognition, fingerprint recognition, iris recognition, and face recognition.

Generally, the methods for pattern recognition may be classified as follows:

- *statistical pattern recognition*, where features are algorithmically extracted and template matching techniques are used,

- *structural pattern recognition*, where primary components of patterns are extracted and the relations between them are defined with decision trees or graphs, and

- *neural networks*.

Consider an application of object identification. Assume that a feeder delivers parts that land on a table with random orientation (see Figure 6-3). A camera (the eye of the robot) forms an image of the parts, and the robot must analyze the picture and determine the position and orientation of each part on the table and the type of part. The robot proceeds as follows. The camera brings one part in the field of view and focuses on it. This can be done automatically in two steps: the part is located by training a neural network to output the location of the center of the object, and the camera focuses on it by using fuzzy logic, as in commercial cameras. Thus, the coordinates of the part on the table are provided. Once the part has been centered in the field of view, the orientation is determined by using neural networks. Picture processing takes place by the *tiling technique*. The camera image consists of 1024×1024 pixels; processing all these pixels algorithmically requires a tremendous amount of time and power. By tiling, the picture is subdivided in squares or tiles, say 64×64 pixels. For each tile consider a neural network that has been trained to recognize features of the part. The edges of the image cross a number of tiles. Now assume that the part has certain distinguishable features. The neural network that recognizes a feature will provide an output that also indicates the orientation of the part. Hence, the part, the position of the part on the table, and its orientation can be identified.

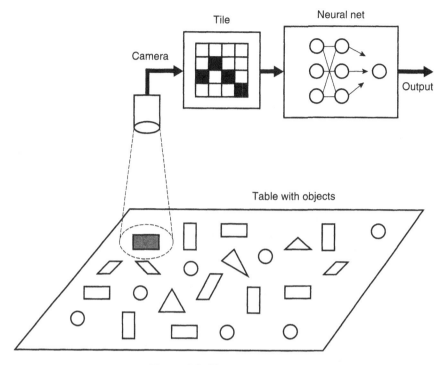

Figure 6-3 Object recognition.

6.3 Communications Systems

6.3.1 Call Processing

Call processing takes place from the time the handset of a telephone, for example, is off-hook until the dial tone is heard. The communication path of a signal in the communications network is quite complex. Figure 6-4 attempts to illustrate the various paths in a network that influence the signal integrity and the neural network and/or fuzzy logic applicability. During that time (milliseconds), a communications protocol has been executed between the communication system that links the telephone with the switching system. Subsequent to this, when the destination telephone number is dialed, the switch establishes a path between the originating and destination apparatus. During call processing, uncertainties should be resolved by the communications system to establish that the originating

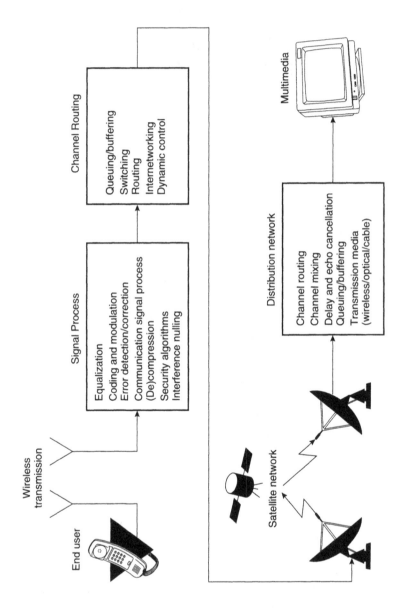

Figure 6-4 Communication paths causing signal distortions and network functionality.

telephone is, first, off-hook, and, second, to ensure that protocol issues are resolved. These uncertainties represent fuzzy states that are resolved by applying fuzzy logic concepts [51]. Section 4.10 provides a more in-depth description of this application.

6.3.2 Switching

A *switch* in a communications network is a system that determines the path of a channel. During call processing, a path is requested. The switch, based on the availability of free paths, grants a path to the orig-inating telephone. The switch, in general, may be viewed as an $n \times m$ matrix where a packet at one of the n inputs should be connected with one of the m outputs (see Figures 6-5 and 6-6). The connectivity path is established based on the destination number, the availability of physical links at the switch, and many other parameters. Neural networks have been proposed [52] that solve this switching problem (see Figure 6-7) [53–56].

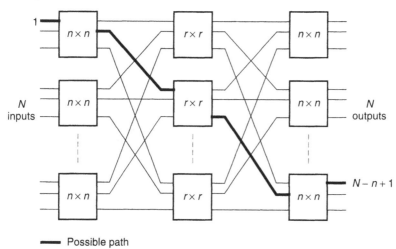

— Possible path

Figure 6-5 A three-stage $N \times N$ cross-bar switch.

6.3.3 Traffic Control

In broadband communications networks it is necessary to evaluate the per-formance of the general traffic of the system. Generally, this is a queue

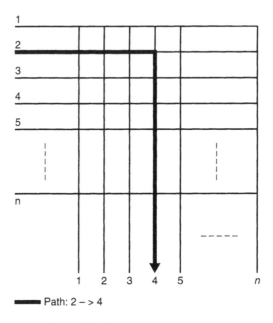

Figure 6-6 An $n \times n$ cross-bar switch.

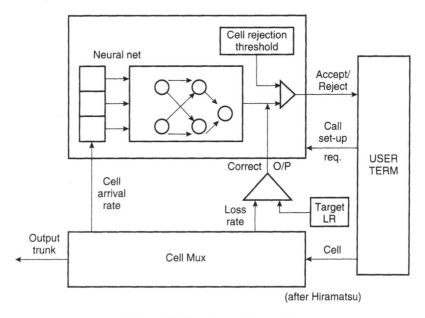

(after Hiramatsu)

Figure 6-7 Sample neural network.

problem. To date, this has been addressed with approximation methods, such as diffusion approximation and interpolation approximation. The first method performs well when the traffic load is heavy; when the traffic is not heavy, accuracy is not practical. The second method becomes less accurate as the variability of the interarrival times and the service times becomes large. A method has been proposed [57] that uses a simple three-layer feedforward neural network trained with the back-propagation training algorithm.

In addition, the characterization of packetized voice traffic in asynchronous transfer mode (ATM) networks has been exploited with back-propagation neural networks [58, 59]. Moreover, traffic prediction using a three-layer back-propagation neural network has been used [60]. Work with neural networks on traffic control continues and other applications are reported [61].

6.3.4   Packet Radio Network Routing and Scheduling

Multihop packet radio networks—networks that hop, or dynamically change, the transmitting/receiving carrier frequency—assume noninterfering nodes, with periodically-recurring time-slots in which they transmit their packets. Contention-free channel access, otherwise known as *link activation* or *scheduling*, is of primary importance since this results in the minimum number of time slots in which packets are transmitted. In spread-spectrum code-division multiple-access (CDMA) systems it is possible for several nodes of the network to transmit simultaneously as long as they use different frequency-hopping sequences or patterns. Determining the schedules that satisfy the traffic demand in the minimum number of time slots is a difficult combinatorial-optimization problem.

An alternative approach to link-activation schedules is to use a Hopfield neural network to generate the communication schedules [62, 63, 64]. Hence, the Hopfield neural network in this application performs a relatively simple optimization task.

Additionally, in communications networks a winner-take-all neural network has been applied to routing under normal and abnormal conditions [65]. Further work on routing with neural networks is continually reported [66, 67], and it is expected that it will continue due to its importance in telecommunications.

6.3.5   Communication Channels over Power Lines

When power lines are used as a communications medium, channel characteristics change as the power load changes. A neural network with unsupervised learning may be used here because of its ability to track the changing parameters. A neural network with selectively unsupervised learning [68] has been reported to have been applied to an electric power line spread-spectrum communication application.

6.4 Intelligent Control

Adaptive control [69] using computers [70] has progressed dramatically since the 1970s. Significant research in intelligent control continues and many applications have found their way in the marketplace using fuzzy logic [71, 72] and neural networks [73, 74, 75].

One concern in industrial motor control is the ability to predict system failures. Motor failure depends on specific motor parameters, such as transient currents, aging characteristics, motor positioning, and others that make failure prediction a very difficult task. Neural networks are employed to learn the motor-current invariants as well as installation characteristics [76]. An 80–90% accurate prediction rate has been achieved, compared with 30% with other state-of-the-art techniques.

Many different neural network applications merge in robotics. Typically, the simplest robot is stationary with a moving arm and a set of sensors (e.g., a video camera) to sense objects. Robots are taught to execute various tasks. The simplest tasks are arm movement [77], object recognition, and object manipulation [78, 79]. More intelligent robots are nonstationary, recognize objects, and execute multiple tasks such as motion and balance control, guidance control, collision avoidance, multiple-arm control, object identification, handling and manipulation, speech recognition, voice generation, elementary reasoning, and data communications.

Neural networks and fuzzy logic have been used in many vehicular applications, including trains, automatic transmission shifting, and smart automobiles. The ALVINN (autonomous land vehicle in a neural network) [80] is a project for vehicle autonomous navigation [81]. More work in this area with fuzzy logic control systems is proposed to control the idle speed of an automotive engine [82].

In steel rolling machines the strip thickness is controlled within very tight tolerances. The controller has to account for several variables, many of them nonlinear. Some are the thicknesses at entry and output, rolling force, locations of thickness sensors, and speed of the strip as it moves between the rollers. A proposed application uses a radial basis function neural network with a Gaussian function [83].

6.5   Optimization Techniques

Optimization techniques are used in many disciplines. A neural network training algorithm is an optimization algorithm (see Section 2.4). However, certain optimization problems are used to evaluate the performance of neural networks, two of which are the traveling salesman problem (TSP) [84, 85, 86] and the knight's tour dilemma (KTD) [87]. The traveling salesman problem states that given n cities with an intercity distance d_{ij} between cities i and j, find the shortest tour visiting every city only once and returning to the first city (Figure 6-8). The knight's tour dilemma is to move a knight, in L-shape moves only, on an $n \times n$ chessboard such that it traverses all squares on the board, visiting each square only once, and finally returning to the origin square (Figure 6-9).

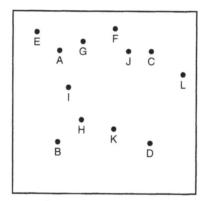

Figure 6-8 Determine the TSP for cities A to L.

In a neural network approach to the knight's tour dilemma a move represents a state [88]. Each state consists of two neurons: one for coming into the square and one for going out from the square. The network uses McCulloch-Pitts neurons with some hysteresis for stability purposes. A total of $p(p - 1)/2$ neurons is required, where p is the number of squares in the chessboard matrix.

The Towers of Hanoi is another mathematical puzzle that has attracted neural network designers [89]. This puzzle, known since 1883, starts with three pegs mounted on a board and a set of rings graded in size; all the rings are initially stacked on one peg in order of size, with the largest at the bottom (Figure 6-10). The puzzle requests that the rings should be moved

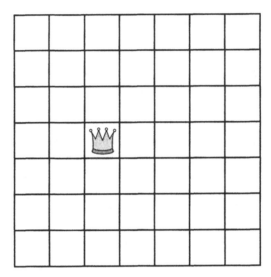

Figure 6-9 Determine the KTD for a 7 × 7 board.

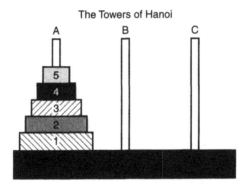

Figure 6-10 Move the five rings from the left
peg to another.

from the original peg to one of the other pegs stacked in the same initial
order by using two simple rules: move only one ring at a time, and never
stack a larger ring on top of a smaller one.

6.6   Other Applications

A potpourri of neural networks and/or fuzzy logic applications is recognized; as mentioned, the applicability of neural networks and fuzzy logic
increases daily. They are used for recognition of faces, speech reproduc-

tion from text, onboard satellite navigation systems, validation of written signatures and checks, classification of aircraft radar signals, automatic target recognition, real-time process visualization, automatic guidance systems, servo control, forecasting solar flair activity, classification of blood cell reactions and blood analysis, cancer detection, spectroscopic analysis, gasoline analysis, chemical engineering, fatigue life of mechanical components, prediction of lightning strikes, loan eligibility prediction, credit-card fraud detection, stock market prediction, problem solving, magnetic levitation vehicles, and domestic appliances, among many others.

6.7   Tools and Companies

Fuzzy logic and neural network development are supported by an abundance of tools offered by many companies. This list is incomplete, but the goal is to indicate the companies that provide software simulation tools, hardware, prototype boards, digital integrated circuits (ICs), analog ICs, and/or services in neural networks and/or fuzzy logic only.

Adaptive Solutions	Nestor
AI Ware	Neural Computer Sciences
American NeuralLogix	Neural Semiconductor
AND America	Neural Systems
Applied Cognetics	NeuralWare
Aptronix	Neurix
California Scientific Software	NeuroDynamX
Epic Systems Group	NeuroSym
Fuzzy Systems Engineering	Olmstead & Watkins
Hecht-Nielsen Neurocomputers	Omron Electronics
Hitachi	Peak Software
Hyperlogic	Promised Land Technology
ImagSoft	Ricoh
Inductive Solutions	SAIC Artificial Neural Systems
Inform Software	Science Applications International
Intel	Sensory Circuits
Martingale Research	Sharp
Micro Devices	SGS-Thompson Microelectronics
Modico	Software Bytes
Motorola	Software Frontiers

Synaptics   Togai InfraLogic
Syntonic Systems   VeriFone
Talon Development   VLSI Technology
Texas Instruments   Ward Systems Group
The Mathworks

6.8 Review Questions

6.1. Name possible design implementations of neural networks.

6.2. a. What is an algorthmic implementation of neural networks?
b. What are the advantages and the disadvantages of this approach?

6.3. Assume that we want to recognize 8-bit patterns in real time using a trained neural network. Which paradigm would you recommend if the pattern is a. serial, b. parallel?

6.4. Assume that you need to design a neural network that controls the eye of a robot such that when an object is detected on the surface of a table, the eye brings in its field of view that object only and focuses on it. Consider a 2 by 2 ft white surface and two black circular objects with diameters of 2 in and 6 in. Describe a conceptual process to identify the two different objects.

For answers, see page 190.

REFERENCES

[1] Y. Hirai, K. Kamada, M. Yamada, and M. Ooyama, "A Digital Neuro-Chip with Unlimited Connectability for Large Scale Neural Networks," in Proceedings of IEEE IJCNN'89, pp. II-163–II-169, Washington, D.C., June 18–23, 1989.

[2] P. Mueller, J. Van der Spiegel, D. Blackman, T. Chiu, T. Clare, J. Dao, C. Donham, T. P. Hsieh, and M. Loinaz, "A General Purpose Analog Neural Computer," in Proceedings of IEEE IJCNN'89, pp. II-177–II-182, Washington, D.C., June 18–23, 1989.

[3] J. Dostal, *Operational Amplifiers*, 2d ed., Butterworth-Heinemann, Stoneham, Mass., 1993.

[4] E. Rietman, *Experiments in Artificial Neural Networks*, TAB Books, Blue Ridge Summit, Pa., 1988.

[5] K. W. Przytula and V. K. Prasanna, *Parallel Digital Implementation of Neural Networks*, Prentice Hall, Englewood Cliffs, N.J., 1993.

[6] R. Ramesham, S. Thakoor. T. Daud, and A. P. Thakoor, "Programmable Analog Memory Resistors for Electronic Neural Networks," *NASA Tech. Briefs*, pp. 18–22, Feb. 1990.

[7] H. P. Graf, L. D. Jackel, R. E. Howard, B. Straughn, J. S. Denker, W. Hubbard, D. M. Tennant, and D. Schwartz, "VLSI Implementation of a Neural Network Memory with Several Hundreds of Neurons," *Proc. of AIP Neural Networks for Computing*, pp. 182–187, New York, Amer. Inst. of Physics, 1986.

[8] L. D. Jackel, H. P. Graf, and R. E. Howard, "Electronic Neural Network Chips," *Appl. Optics*, vol. 26, no. 23, pp. 5077–5080, 1987.

[9] F. M. A. Salam, N. Khachab, M. Ismail, and Y. Wang, "An Analog MOS Implementation of the Synaptic Weights for Feedback Neural Nets," in Proceedings of IEEE ISCAS'89, pp. 1223–1226, 1989.

[10] T. Borgstrom and S. Bibyk, "A Neural Integrated Circuit Utilizing Programmable Threshold Voltage Devices," in Proceedings of IEEE ISCAS'89, pp. 1227–1230, 1989.

[11] M. Holler, S. Tam, H. Castro, and R. Benson, "An Electrically Trainable Artificial Neural Network (ETANN) with 10240 'Floating Gate' Synapses," in Proceedings of IEEE IJCNN'89, pp. II-191–II-196, Washington, D.C., June 18–23, 1989.

[12] M. White and C.-Y. Chen, "Electrically Modifiable Nonvolatile Synapses for Neural Networks," in Proceedings of IEEE ISCAS'89, pp. 1213–1216, 1989.

[13] G. Moon, M. E. Zaghloul, and R. W. Newcomb, "VLSI Implementation of Synaptic Weighting and Summing in Pulse Coded Neural-Type Cells," *Trans. Neural Networks*, vol. 3, no. 3, pp. 394–403, May 1992.

[14] "SU3232 Neural Synaptic Unit, and NU32 Neural Nodal Unit," data sheet, Neural Semiconductor, Inc.

[15] pRAM-256, Data Sheet, Dept. Electronics and Electrical Engineering, King's College, London, U.K.

[16] A. P. Thakoor, A. Moopenn, J. Lambe, and S. K. Khanna, "Electronic Hardware Implementations of Neural Networks," *Appl. Optics*, vol. 26, no. 23, pp. 5085–5092, Dec. 1987.

[17] S. Eberhardt, T. Duong, and A. Thakoor, "A VLSI Analog Synapse 'Building-Block' Chip for Hardware Neural Network Implementations," *Proc. of 3d Annual Parallel Processing Symposium*, Fullerton, Calif., pp. 257–267, March 29–31, 1989.

[18] A. J. Agranat, C. F. Neugebauer, and R. D. Nelson, "The CCD Neural Processor: A Neural Network Integrated Circuit with 65536 Programmable Analog

Synapses," *IEEE Trans. Circuit and Systems*, vol. 37, no. 8, pp. 1073–1075, 1990.

[19] C. A. Mead and M. A. Mahowald, "A Silicon Model of Early Visual Processing," *Neural Networks*, vol. 1, no. 1, pp. 91–97, 1988.

[20] E. Sackinger, B. E. Boser, J. Bromley, Y. LeCun, and L. D. Jackel, "Application of the ANNA Neural Network Chip to High-Speed Character Recognition," *IEEE Trans. Neural Networks*, vol. 3, no. 3, pp. 498–505, 1992.

[21] P. Aubry and F. El Guibaly, "A VLSI Design of a Character Recognition Algorithm," in Proceedings of IEEE Pacific Rim Conference on Communications, Computers, and Signal Processing, pp. 521–523, June 4–5, 1987.

[22] B. Linares-Barranco, E. Sanchez-Sinencio, R. W. Neucomb, A. Rodriguez-Vasques, and J. L. Huertas, "A Novel CMOS Analog Neural Oscillator Cell," in ISCAS'89, pp. 794–795, 1989.

[23] R. W. Lucky, "Automatic Equalization for Digital Communication," *BSTJ*, vol. 44, no. 4, pp. 547–588, 1965.

[24] A. Cichocki and R. Unbehauen, *Neural Networks for Optimization and Signal Processing*, John Wiley & Sons, New York, 1993.

[25] S. K. Jha, J. J. Soraghan, and T. S. Durrani, "Equalization Using Neural Networks," *Proc. of the First IEE International Conference on Artificial Neural Networks*, pp. 356–360, Oct. 1989.

[26] J. Cid-Sueiro and A. R. Figueiras-Vidal, "Improving Conventional Equalizers with Neural Networks," *Proc. of the International Workshop on Applications of Neural Networks to Telecommunications*, pp. 20–26, Lawrence Erlbaum Associates, Publishers, Hillside, N.J., 1993.

[27] T. X. Brown, "Neural Networks for Adaptive Equalization," *Proc. of the International Workshop on Applications of Neural Networks to Telecommunications*, pp. 27–33, Lawrence Erlbaum Associates, Publishers, Hillside, N.J., 1993.

[28] N. Benvenuto, F. Piazza, and A. Uncini, "A Neural Network Approach to Data Predistortion with Memory in Digital Radio Systems," in Proceedings of IEEE ICC'93, pp. 232–236, May 23–26, 1993,

[29] S. H. Bang, B. J. Sheu, and J. Choi, "Programmable VLSI Neural Network Processors for Equalization of Digital Communication Channels," *Proc. of the International Workshop on Applications of Neural Networks to Telecommunications*, pp. 1–12, Lawrence Erlbaum Associates, Publishers, Hillside, N.J., 1993.

[30] B. Widrow and R. Winter, "Neural Networks for Adaptive Filtering and Adaptive Pattern Recognition," *Computer*, vol. 21, pp. 25–39, March 1988.

[31] K. Arakawa, "Intelligent Signal Processing Based on Fuzzy Rules," in Proceedings of IEEE ISPACS'93, pp. 66–70, Sendai, Japan, Oct. 27–29, 1993.

[32] H. Takashima, A. Tagushi, and Y. Murata, "Nonlinear Filtering Using Fuzzy Control Laws," in Proceedings of IEEE ISPACS'93, pp. 71–76, Sendai, Japan, Oct. 27–29, 1993.

[33] X. Lee, Y.-Q. Zhang, and A. Leon-Garcia, "Image and Video Reconstruction Using Fuzzy Logic," in Proceedings of IEEE Globecom'93, pp. 975–979, Houston, 1993.

[34] "JVC Ups for CD Capacity Fourfold," *Electr. Eng. Times*, p. 22, Aug. 10, 1992.

[35] J. Bruck and M. Blaum, "Neural Networks, Error-Correcting Codes, and Polynomials over the Binary n-Cube," *IEEE Trans. Inf. Theory*, vol. IT-35, no. 5, pp. 976–987, 1989.

[36] W. R. Caid and R. W. Means, "Neural Network Error Correcting Decoders for Block and Convolutional Codes," in Proceedings of IEEE Globecom'90, pp. 1028–1031, 1990.

[37] S. K. Mak and A. H. Aghvami, "Soft-Decision Decoding of Block Codes Using Neural Networks," in Proceedings of IEEE Globecom'93, pp. 971–974, Houston, 1993.

[38] Y. Takefuji, P. Holis, Y. P. Foo, and Y. B. Cho, "Error Correcting System Based on Neural Circuits," *Proc. of IEEE 1st International Conference on Neural Networks*, vol. 3, pp. 293–300, 1987.

[39] H. Takashima, A. Taguchi, and Y. Murata, "Nonlinear Filtering Using Fuzzy Control Laws," in Proceedings of IEEE ISSPACS'93, pp. 71–76, Sendai, Japan, Oct. 27–29, 1993.

[40] Y. Bengio, R. DeMori, and M. Gori, "Experiments on Automatic Speech Recognition Using BPs," in *Second Italian Workshop on Parallel Architectures and Neural Networks*, pp. 223–232, World Scientific Publishing Co., 1990.

[41] T. Matsuoka, H. Hamada, and R. Nakatsu, "Syllable Recognition Using Integrated Neural Networks," in Proceedings of IEEE IJCNN, pp. I-251–I-258, Washington, D.C., June 18–23, 1989.

[42] M. L. Rosen and J. A. Anderson, "Representation Issues in a Neural Network Model of Syllable Recognition," in Proceedings of IEEE IJCNN, pp. I-19–I-25, Washington, D.C., June 18–23, 1989.

[43] J. B. Hampshire and A. H. Webel, "A Novel Objective Function for Improved Phoneme Recognition Using Time Delay Neural Networks," in Proceedings of IJCNN, pp. I-235–I-241, Washington, D.C., June 18–23, 1989.

[44] N. Hataoka, "Large Vocabulary Speech Recognition Using Neural-Fuzzy and Concept Networks," in *Neural Networks*, L. B. Almeida and

C. J. Wellekens, eds., Proceedings of EURASIP Workshop 1990, Kluwer, pp. 186–196, February 1990.

[45] M. Niranjan and F. Fallside, "Speech Feature Extraction Using Neural Networks," in *Neural Networks*, L. B. Almeida and C. J. Wellekens, eds., Proceedings of EURASIP Workshop 1990, Kluwer, pp. 197–204, February 1990.

[46] T. Kohonen, "The 'Neural' Phonetic Typewriter," *Computer*, vol. 21, pp. 11–22, March 1988.

[47] T. J. Sejnowski and M. Goldstein, *Massively Parallel Network Architecture for Automatic Recognition of Visual Speech Signals*, Technical Report AFOSR-TR-90-0949, 1986, The Johns Hopkins University, Baltimore.

[48] A. Krikelis, "Continuous Speech Recognition Using Associative String Processor," *Proc. IEEE ISCAS*, pp. 183–186, 1989.

[49] D. W. Tank and J. J. Hopfield, "Simple 'Neural' Optimization Networks: An A/D Converter, Signal Decision Circuit, and a Linear Programming Circuit," *IEEE Trans. Circuits and Systems*, vol. 33, no. 5, pp. 533–541, May 1986.

[50] B. Miller, "Vital Signs of Identity," *IEEE Spectrum*, pp. 22–30, Feb. 1994.

[51] S. V. Kartalopoulos, "Temporal Fuzziness in Communications Systems," in Proceedings of the IEEE ICNN 1994, Orlando, Fla., June 26–30, 1994, vol. VII, pp. 4786–4791.

[52] T. X. Brown, "Neural Networks for Switching," *IEEE Commun. Mag.*, pp. 72–81, Nov. 1989.

[53] A. Marrakchi and T. Troudet, "A Neural Net Arbitrator for Large Crossbar Packet Switches," *IEEE Trans. Circuits and Systems*, vol. 36, no. 7, pp. 1039–1041, 1989.

[54] A. Hiramatsu, "ATM Communications Network Control by Neural Networks," *IEEE Trans. Neural Networks*, pp. 122–130, March 1990.

[55] A. Amin and M. Gell, "Constrained Optimization for Switching Using Neural Networks," *Proc. of the International Workshop on Applications of Neural Networks to Telecommunications*, pp. 107–111, Lawrence Erlbaum Associates, Publishers, Hillside, N.J., 1993.

[56] Y.-K. Park, V. Cherkasky, and G. Lee, "ATM Cell Scheduling for Broadband Switching Systems by Neural Network," *Proc. of the International Workshop on Applications of Neural Networks to Telecommunications*, pp. 112–118, Lawrence Erlbaum Associates, Publishers, Hillside, N.J., 1993.

[57] T. Okuda, M. Anthony, and Y. Tadokoro, "A Neural Approach to Performance Evaluation for General Traffic System," *Proc. of the ISPACS'93*, pp. 239–244, Sendai, Japan, Oct. 27–29, 1993.

[58] A. A. Tarraf, I. W. Habib, and T. N. Saadawi, "Characterization of Packetized Voice Traffic in ATM Networks Using Neural Networks," in Globecom'93, pp. 996–1000, Houston, 1993.

[59] A. A. Tarraf, I. W. Habib, and T. N. Saadawi, "Neural Networks for ATM Traffic Prediction," *Proc. of the International Workshop on Applications of Neural Networks to Telecommunications*, pp. 85–92, Lawrence Erlbaum Associates, Publishers, Hillside, N.J., 1993.

[60] E. S. Yu and C. Y. R. Chen, "Traffic Prediction Using Neural Networks," in Proceedings of IEEE Globecom'93, pp. 991–995, Houston, 1993.

[61] E. Nordstrom, "A Hybrid Admission Control Scheme for Broadband ATM Traffic," *Proc. of the International Workshop on Applications of Neural Networks to Telecommunications*, pp. 77–84, Lawrence Erlbaum Associates, Publishers, Hillside, N.J., 1993.

[62] J. J. Hopfield and D. W. Tank, "Neural Computation of Decisions in Optimization Problems," *Biol. Cybernetics*, vol. 52, pp. 141–152, 1985.

[63] J. E. Wieselthier, C. M. Barnhart, and A. Ephremides, *The Application of Hopfield Neural Network Technique to Problems of Routing and Scheduling in Packet Radio Networks*, NRL Memorandum Report 6730, Naval Research Laboratory, Nov. 9, 1990.

[64] A. Jagota, "Scheduling Problems in Radio Networks Using Hopfield Networks," *Proc. of the International Workshop on Applications of Neural Networks to Telecommunications*, pp. 67–75, Lawrence Erlbaum Associates, Publishers, Hillside, N.J., 1993.

[65] M. Collett and W. Pedrycz, "Application of Neural Networks for Routing in Telecommunications Networks," in Proceedings of IEEE Globecom'93, pp. 1001–1006, Houston, 1993.

[66] M. Littman and J. Boyan, "A Distributed Reinforcement Learning Scheme for Network Routing," *Proc. of the International Workshop on Applications of Neural Networks to Telecommunications*, pp. 45–51, Lawrence Erlbaum Associates, Publishers, Hillside, N.J., 1993.

[67] M. W. Goudreau and C. Lee Giles, "Discovering the Structure of a Self-Routing Interconnection Network with a Recurrent Neural Network," *Proc. of the International Workshop on Applications of Neural Networks to Telecommunications*, pp. 52–59, Lawrence Erlbaum Associates, Publishers, Hillside, N.J., 1993.

[68] T. Hasegawa and Y. Ogihara, "On the Detection System with the Selectively Unsupervised Learning Neural Network Using a Fast Learning Algorithm in Electric Power Line Spread-Spectrum Communications," in ISPACS'93, pp. 233–238, Sendai, Japan, Oct. 27–29, 1993.

[69] E. Mishkin and L. Brawn, eds., *Adaptive Control Systems*, McGraw-Hill, New York, 1961.

[70] C. J. Haris and S. A. Billings, eds., *Self-Tuning and Adaptive Control*, rev. 2d ed., Peter Peregrinus, London, 1985.

[71] C. G. Moore and C. J. Harris, "Indirect Adaptive Fuzzy Control," *Int. Jour. Control*, vol. 56, no. 2, pp. 441–468, 1992.

[72] S. Daley and K. F. Gill, "A Design Study of a Self-Organizing Fuzzy Logic Controller," *Proc. Inst. Mech. Eng.*, vol. 200, pp. 59–69, 1986.

[73] K. S. Narendra and S. Mukhopadhyay, "Intelligent Control Using Neural Networks," *IEEE Control Systems*, pp. 11–18, 1992.

[74] M. A. Santori and P. T. Antsaklis, "Implementation of Learning Control Systems Using Neural Networks," *IEEE Control Systems*, pp. 49–57, 1992.

[75] W. T. Milles III, R. S. Sutton, and P. I. Werbos, eds., *Neural Networks for Control*, MIT Press, Cambridge, Mass., 1990.

[76] J. Shandle, "Neural Networks Are Ready for Prime Time," *ED*, pp. 51–57, Feb. 18, 1993.

[77] C. G. Atkeson and D. J. Reinkensmeyer, "Using Associative Content-Addressable Memories to Control Movement," in *Neural Programming*, Masao Ito, ed., Japan Scientific Societies Press, Tokyo, 1989.

[78] A. C. Sanderson, "Applications of Neural Networks in Robotics and Automation for Manufacturing," in *Neural Networks for Control*, pp. 365–385, MIT Press, Cambridge, Mass., 1990.

[79] J. A. Frankling and O. G. Selfridge, "Some New Directions for Adaptive Control Theory in Robotics," in *Neural Networks for Control*, pp. 365–385, MIT Press, Cambridge, Mass., 1990.

[80] M. Caudill, "Driving Solo," *AI Expert*, pp. 26–30, Sept. 1991.

[81] D. A. Pomerleau, "Efficient Training of Artificial Neural Networks for Autonomous Navigation," *Neural Computation*, vol. 3, no. 1, pp. 88–97, 1991.

[82] G. Vachtsevanos, S. S. Farinwata, and D. K. Pirovolou, "Fuzzy Logic Control of an Automotive Engine," *IEEE Control Systems*, pp. 62–68, June 1993.

[83] D. Shabaro-Hofer, D. Neumerkel, and K. Hunt, "Neural Control of a Steel Rolling Mill," *IEEE Control Systems*, pp. 69–75, June 1993.

[84] E. L. Lawler et al., *The Traveling Salesman Problem*, John Wiley & Sons, New York, 1985.

[85] J. L. Bentley, "Fast Algorithms for Geometric Traveling Salesman Problems," *ORSA Jour. Computing*, vol. 4, no. 4, pp. 387–411, 1992.

[86] A. P. Thakoor and A. W. Moopenn, "Neural Network Solves 'Traveling-Salesman' Problem," *NASA Tech. Briefs*, p. 22, Dec. 1990.

[87] R. W. W. Ball and H. S. M. Coxeter, *Mathematical Recreations and Essays*, University of Toronto Press, Toronto, 1st ed., 1892, and 12th ed., 1974.

[88] Y. Takefuji, *Neural Network Parallel Computing*, Kluger Academic Publishers, Boston, 1992.

[89] J. Cardoso, "Revisiting the Towers of Hanoi," *AI Expert*, pp. 49–53, Oct. 1991.

Chapter Review Answers

Chapter 1 Answers

1.1 The neuron.

1.2 The dendritic tree, the soma, the axon, and the axonic ending.

1.3 The phospholipid molecule that consists of the polar head group (hydrophilic) and the hydrocarbon group (hydrophobic). A double array of phospholipid molecules with the polar head groups at the outer side of the array and the hydrocarbon inside the array.

1.4 In general, a synapse is the contact between two neurons. It consists of the presynaptic terminal, the cleft, and the postsynaptic terminal.

1.5 The excitatory and the inhibitory.

1.6 Vesicles containing the neurotransmitter, a chemical messenger, approach the cleft of the synapse; they release their contents, which are absorbed by the postsynaptic terminal.

1.7 When a neuron has been depolarized at several synapses, then all postsynaptic potentials are summed spatio-temporally at the axon hillock. If the sum exceeds the threshold of the neuron, then the action potential is propagated down the axon.

1.8 The pump proteins, the channel proteins, the receptor proteins, and the enzymes.

1.9 It is false. The resting potential is between -65 and -85 mVolts.

1.10 At rest, sodium is at higher concentration in the exoplasm (outside the neuron), whereas potassium is at higher concentration in the endoplasm (inside the neuron).

1.11 It is not true. Neuronal diversity or specialization is found in many parts of the nervous system as well as in many organs (e.g., the eye).

1.12 Cones are responsible for color vision and rods are responsible for gray.

1.13 The optic nerve is a bundle of axons of the ganglion neurons that communicates information from the eye to the brain.

1.14 No, it is not true. The visual information is preprocessed at the retina of the eye where elemental features are extracted and transmitted to the brain for further processing.

1.15 No. The rods are much more sensitive to light than the cones.

1.16 In the fovea area.

1.17 Color pictures would be perceived achromatic, i.e., shades of gray.

1.18 The cones and rods, the amacrine, the horizontal, the bipolar, and the ganglions.

1.19 At the retina the elemental features of the image take place, as well as information about color and spatio-temporal relationships among the elemental features.

1.20 The neural network of the eye has feedback controlling mechanisms that adjust the responsiveness of rods and cones to the amount of light received.

Chapter 2 Answers

2.1 No, and this is one of the basic differences between a digital computer and a neural network.

2.2 The basic model consists of an output signal that is the conditioned sum of the weighted inputs less a threshold value.

2.3 The sigmoid, the hard-limiter, and the ramp.

2.4 Learning is the process by which the neural network continuously adapts itself to a stimulus and eventually (after making the proper adjustments to its synaptic strengths) produces a desired response.

2.5 Supervised learning assumes that for every input the output is known a priori. This is different from unsupervised learning whereby there are no outputs known a priori.

2.6 When an input is applied, the obtained output is compared with the desired or target output. From this comparison, if they do not match, an error signal is generated that is used to make parametric adjustments in the neural network until the desired output becomes equal to the target output.

2.7 During learning the error signal (as explained in question 2.6) is used to make parametric adjustments of the neural network. These adjustments are made based on an optimization algorithm such as the Delta rule or back-propagation.

2.8 The synaptic strength is modified according to the degree of correlated activity between input and output of two cells.

2.9 Collective and synergistic computation, robustness, learning, and asynchronous operation.

2.10 This is a linearly separable network.

2.11 This most likely is a nonlinearly separable or a multilinearly separable network.

2.12 Based on the stability-plasticity dilemma, a highly stable network may result in a very rigid network.

Chapter 3 Answers

3.1 Input, hidden, and output layer.

3.2 The program of a neural network is the final (after learning has been completed) set of values for weights and thresholds of the neurons that are distributed all over the network.

3.3 The McCulloch-Pitts model.

3.4 Yes, it is true.

3.5 The McCulloch-Pitts model.

3.6 $E = T - O$.

3.7 It is an optimization algorithm based on the least square error that is used to minimize the error signal during learning.

3.8 One may find the local minimum but not the global. Different techniques, however, have been developed to avoid such situations.

3.9 The MADALINE consists of many ADALINE paradigms.

3.10 No. It has many inputs and many outputs.

3.11 It uses unsupervised learning.

3.12 No. When the back-propagation algorithm is used, the error calculated at output layer N is used to make changes on the weight values at the inputs of layer N. Then, based on these changes, an error is calculated at the outputs of the previous layer $(N-1)$ that is used to make changes on the weights at the inputs of layer $N-1$. This process is repeated, successively comparing the input values of each layer, until learning is completed.

3.13 To design a controller that stems from the functionality of the brain.

3.14 The ART uses unsupervised learning and solves problems where categories should be autonomously identified and learned.

3.15 It is a single-layer network.

3.16 Whether the input matches a stored pattern (it has been recognized).

3.17 In a RAM, the address input is presented and the contents of the addressed location are retrieved; in a CAM, a pattern is presented at the input and a match or no-match of the input pattern with stored patterns is reported.

3.18 Yes. This is where the name bidirectional associative memory (BAM) comes from.

3.19 It is a cyclic sequential encoder with feedback paths.

3.20 The LVQ, for a certain input, activates the output that corresponds to the best match.

3.21 It assures that the minimization will continue until a global minimum is reached and that it will not stop at a local minimum.

Chapter 4 Answers

4.1 The normalized distribution is obtained by dividing the amplitude by the largest number in the distribution, 50. By doing so, the following results are obtained: {1,0), (0.9,1), (0.8,2), (0.7,3), (0.6,4), (0.5,5), (0.4,6), (0.3,7), (0.2,8), (0.1,9), (0,10)}.

4.2 The three distributions are called membership functions for close, far, and medium distance, respectively, and they overlap each other.

4.3 At 6 cm, the membership value for close is 0.4, for medium distance is 0.5, and for far is 0. The distance 6 cm is definitely not far; more likely it is medium distance with less likelihood to be close.

4.4 A at 3 cm yields a membership value of 0.7 and B of 0.25. Consequently, $C = \min(0.7, 0.25) = 0.25$ and $F = \max(0.7, 0.25) = 0.7$.

4.5 At $t = 1$ and $x = 5$, then $A(5) = 0.5$ and $B(5) = 0.1$. At $t = 2$ and $x = 5$, then $A(5) = 0$ and $B(5) = 0.3$. The conclusion is that at $x = 5$, the membership value of B prevails over the membership value of A; notice that the two memberships of A and B overlap.

4.6 a. (0.5,3), b. ($\frac{1}{3}$,0.6).

Chapter 5 Answers

5.1 Membership functions for the intermediate levels are constructed. The inputs of the neural network assume fuzzy inputs, and a fuzzy neural network is constructed similar to the one in Figure 5-2. It may be necessary to add two sensors, one at each valve to detect flow. Then, the fuzzy statements are of the form "if. . .then, else."

5.2 Better real-time control may be achieved if the fuzzy part of the fuzzy neural network uses temporal fuzzy logic; i.e., if membership distributions in the time domain are considered. The latter is accomplished if the diameter of the cylinder at different heights, and hence the capacity of the liquid, is expressed as a function of height and time.

Chapter 6 Answers

6.1 Digital, analog, digital/analog, and algorithmic.

6.2 a. With algorithmic implementation conventional processors are used. Neural network training is accomplished algorithmically, the neural network representation is also described algorithmically, and the weights of the network are stored in RAM or ROM-type memory.

b. Advantages: Utilization of well-understood and inexpensive technology. Weights may be easily updated. The same circuit may be reprogrammed and used in a variety of different applications. Disadvantages: Not full exploitation of neural network technology. Algorithmic implementation cannot solve certain problems more efficiently than neural networks (which were developed specifically to solve because of the massive parallelism required). Going back to the old (processor) paradigm will not advance neural technology.

6.3 a. The time delay neural network (TDNN) would be very suitable for such applications. It should consist of an 8-bit serial delay network that shifts in the 8-bit serial pattern, which is decoded by a feedforward neural network.

b. A feedforward network with 8 inputs would suffice.

6.4 The table is subdivided into a grid of 2×2 in squares. The initial field of view of the neural network is 2×2 ft. A neural network is trained to detect objects in the grid (i.e., dark squares). When one or two consecutive squares (horizontally or vertically) are dark, then the network knows that there is a 2 in circular object at the location of the dark squares, finds the center of the gravity of the dark squares (via a trained network), and focuses on the center of gravity with a 2×2 in field of view. When three or four consecutive squares (horizontally or vertically) or more are dark, then the network knows that there is a 6 in circular object and focuses on the center of gravity with 6×6 in field of view.

INDEX

NOTE: Bold page numbers indicate figures and tables.

control. *See* specific forms of control
"cost function", 47
crisp logic
  as fuzzy logic, 123
  and time-dependent fuzzy logic, 130
  variable values in, 121
  See also fuzzy logic
Culbertson's model, 110
cytoplasm, enclosure of by membrane, 4

D

decomposition process, of three
  variables, **126**–28
Delta learning algorithm, described,
  70–72
Delta rule, 46, 53, 70
dendrite, **1**, 2, **21**
  in neuron function, **13**, **16**
dendritic tree, **1**, 11, 15
  role of in memory formation, 17
deoxyribonucleic acid (DNA), 6
depolarization
  described, 2, 11–12
  function of, 10, 14
diffusion, 8
digital circuitry, compared to analog
  circuitry, 163–64
discrete-time Hopfield net, **90**
  See also Hopfield model
discrimination ability, 53–58
distribution of truth, in fuzzy logic, 122
dot
  as recognizable feature, 38
  See also feature extraction; pattern
    recognition

E

electrochemical seeking radar (ECSR),
  15–16
11-*cis*-retinal (11-*cis*), 25
Encephalon project, 110–11
energy, cellular conversion of, 4

enzymes
  function of, 4, 8
  role of in vision, 25
  See also proteins
error function, 166
  back-coupled error correction, 65
  use of in learning algorithm, 53
error signal, function of, 43–44
ESCR. *See* electrochemical seeking radar
evolution
  as factor in neural network, 19
  of technology, 22
excitation of neuron, 2, 17, 19
  in vision, 24
excitatory dendritic contact, 15
excitatory potential, 3, 14
  described, 10
Exclusive-OR function, 56, 65
  neural network implementation of, **57**
exocytosis, 13
experience
  acquisition of, 21
  See also learning
extracellular fluid, 1
eye
  cross section of, **23**
  vision processing in, 10, 15, **29**
eye's neural network, 22–31, 64
  photochemical reactions, 24–25
  retina image processing, 27–29
  retina neural network, 25–27
  retina structure, 22–**23**
  rods and cones, 23–24
  visual pathways, **29**–31

F

failure prediction, 174
failure sensitivity, as neural network
  parameter, 50
FANN. *See* fuzzy artificial neural network
feature demons, 64